John Blash

John Blashford-Snell, a Royal Engineer, is the veteran of many success-ful expeditions. He and his colleagues formed the Scientific Exploration Society, and went on to launch Operations Drake and Raleigh. He is the author of several bestselling books including *In the Steps of Stanley*, his autobiography *Something Lost Behind the Ranges* and *Mammoth Hunt*.

Richard Snailham

Richard Snailham has taken part in expeditions to places as far apart as Mongolia, Honduras, Chile and Zaire. He was a Senior Lecturer at the Royal Military Academy, Sandhurst, and now leads tour groups to Bolivia, Peru and Ethiopia. He was Honorary Foreign Secretary of the Royal Geographical Society for six years and is currently the chairman of the Anglo-Ethiopian Society.

Also by John Blashford-Snell

Weapons and Tactics (with Tom Wintringham)
Expeditions, the Experts' Way (with Alistair Ballantine)
Where the Trails Run Out
In the Steps of Stanley
A Taste for Adventure
In the Wake of Drake (with Mike Cable)
Operation Drake (with Mike Cable)
Mysteries: Encounters with the Unexplained
Operation Raleigh: The Start of an Adventure
Operation Raleigh: Adventure Challenge (with Ann Tweedy)
Operation Raleigh: Adventure Unlimited (with Ann Tweedy)
Something Lost Behind the Ranges (autobiography)
Mammoth Hunt (with Rula Lenska)
Kota Mama (with Richard Snailham)

Also by Richard Snailham

The Blue Nile Revealed
A Giant among Rivers: The Story of the Zaire River Expedition
Sangay Survived: The Ecuador Volcano Disaster
Normandy and Brittany
Kota Mama (with John Blashford-Snell)

East to the Amazon

*In Search of Great Paititi and
the Trade Routes of the Ancients*

JOHN BLASHFORD-SNELL
and
RICHARD SNAILHAM

JOHN MURRAY

This book is dedicated to Yolima Cipagauta and our many friends in South America, without whose help the Kota Mama expeditions would never have taken place

© The Scientific Exploration Society 2002

First published in 2002 by John Murray (Publishers)
A division of Hodder Headline

Paperback edition 2003

The moral right of the author has been asserted

A CIP catalogue record for this title is available from the British Library

ISBN 0-7195-6504 9

Typeset in 11.5/13pt Bembo by Servis Filmsetting Ltd, Manchester

Printed and bound in Great Britain by
Clays Ltd, St Ives plc

John Murray (Publishers)
338 Euston Road
London
NW1 3BH

Contents

Illustrations

The authors and publishers would like to thank the following for permission to reproduce illustrations: Plate 7, Popperfoto; 11 and 13, Andrew Holt; 15, 16, 17, 18, 19 and 20, Graham Catchpole. All other photographs by John Blashford-Snell.

Acknowledgements

We are most grateful for the help received from the library staff at Canning House and the Royal Military Academy Sandhurst.

This book was not easy to write, as ill health meant that Richard was unable to join the expedition until the second half. Before Richard arrived John kept a detailed log, and during the first six weeks Alasdair Crosby of the *Jersey Evening Post* made detailed notes from which he was able to do much to help with the opening chapters.

When the fleet had reached the Bolivia–Brazil border and Richard had arrived, he and John wrote during every spare hour and were greatly assisted in typing the text by Jenny Campbell, Yolima Cipagauta and Bill Holmes. Peter Kannangara kept the computers running, and even had to buy an electric fan to keep them cool in temperatures touching 90 °F.

Back at the Scientific Exploration Society base the bulk of the typing fell on Anne Gilby's shoulders, and her efficiency and tolerance in handling this burden deserves the highest praise. Gerard Clarke, Richard's Windsor neighbour, did much valuable printing, and Darren Ward was as prompt and accurate as usual in typing a reworked text.

Emma Harris-Curtis earns our gratitude for translation of Hans Ertl's *Paititi*, and Jim Masters, Melissa Dice and Anne-Marie Wilkinson for assistance of varied kinds. Bill Holmes carried out some careful research in Oxford. Thanks are also due to Shirley Critchley and Judith Blashford-Snell for reading the text, Sarah-Jane Lewis for help with publicity, and Brenda Wynn, executive secretary of the SES, for all her encouragement. We are also grateful to Ian Lauder, in whose beautiful garden in Mallorca the epilogue was completed.

The support of Simon Trewin of PFD in finding us a publisher, of

Acknowledgements

Caroline Knox and Gail Pirkis of John Murray, and of our copy-editor, Bob Davenport, were much appreciated.

John Blashford-Snell, Richard Snailham

Maps

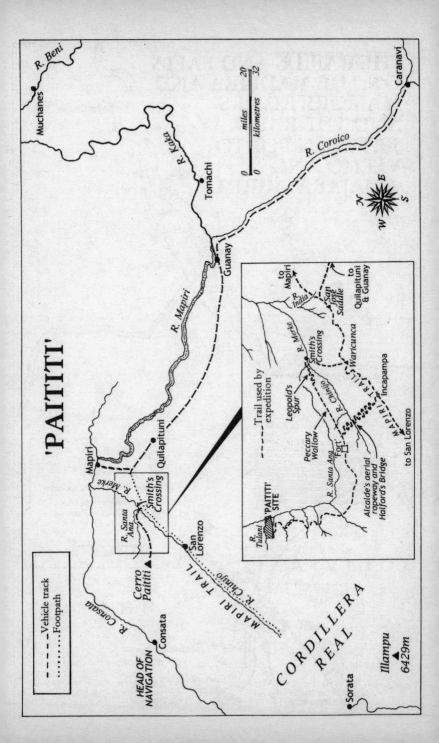

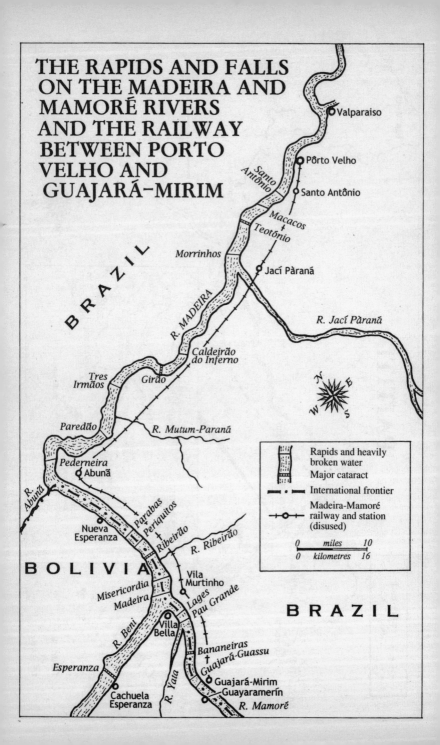

THE RAPIDS AND FALLS
ON THE MADEIRA AND
MAMORÉ RIVERS
AND THE RAILWAY
BETWEEN PORTO
VELHO AND
GUAJARÁ-MIRIM

Valparaiso

BRAZIL

Santo Antônio

Pôrto Velho

Santo Antônio

Macacos

Teotônio

Morrinhos

Jací Pàraná

R. MADEIRA

R. Jací Pàraná

Caldeirão
do Inferno

Tres
Irmãos

Girão

N

W E

S

Paredão

R. Mutum-Paraná

Pederneira

Abunã

Rapids and heavily
broken water

Major cataract

International frontier

Madeira-Mamoré
railway and station
(disused)

R. Abunã

Parabas
Periquitos

Nueva
Esperanza

Ribeirão

R. Ribeirão

0   miles   10
0   kilometres   16

BOLIVIA

Vila
Murtinho

Misericordia

Madeira

Lages

Pau Grande

BRAZIL

R. Beni

Villa
Bella

Bananeiras

Guajará-Guassu

Esperanza

R. Yata

Guajará-Mirim

Guayaramerín

Cachuela
Esperanza

R. Mamoré

THE RIVER MADEIRA

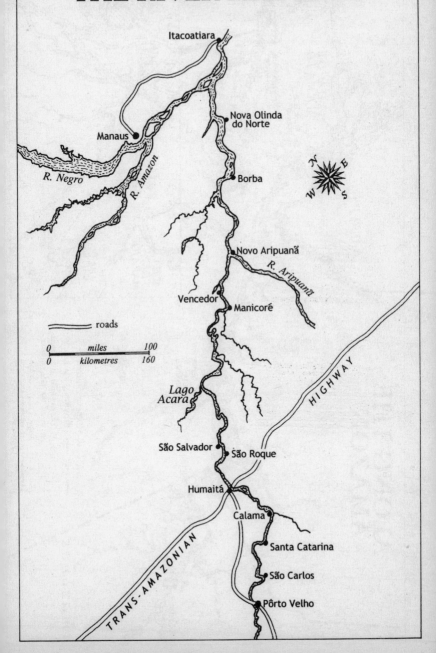

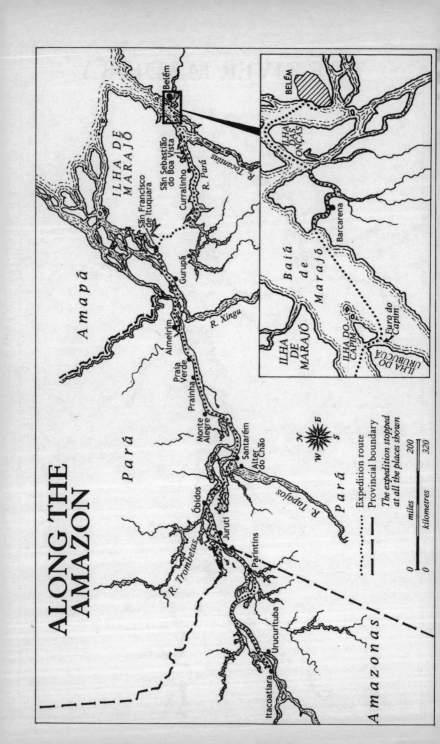

ALONG THE AMAZON

Amapá

ILHA DE MARAJÓ

Belém

Almeirim

San Francisco de Ituquara

San Sebastião do Boa Vista

Curralinho

Gurupá

R. Pará

R. Tocantins

R. Xingu

Praia Verde

Prainha

Monte Alegre

Óbidos

Santarém

Alter do Chão

R. Tapajós

Juruti

Parintins

R. Trombetas

Urucurituba

Itacoatiara

Pará

Amazonas

N E S W

Expedition route

Provincial boundary

The expedition stopped
at all the places shown

miles   200

kilometres   320

0

0

BELÉM

ILHA DAS ONÇAS

Baiã de Marajó

Barcarena

ILHA DE MARAJÓ

ILHA DO CAPIM

ILHA DO URUBUCUA

Furo do Capim

Prologue

The only true failure would be not to explore at all.

Sir Ernest Shackleton

IN 1998 AND 1999 I led two expeditions in South America. They were called *Kota Mama 1* and *Kota Mama 2*, *Kota Mama* means Mother of the Lake in the language of the Aymara Indians, who occupy parts of the high Andes in Bolivia, where both expeditions started.

These two ventures had aimed to show that ancient peoples might have sailed boats made of *totora*, a special kind of reed from Lake Titicaca in the Andes, southward and eastward to the Atlantic Ocean. Boats of this kind are still made on the shores of the lake. Our first fleet had navigated from the lake along the Desaguadero river south across the Bolivian Altiplano towards Lake Poopó. The second, more ambitious, had run the Paraguay and Paraná rivers from Bolivia's most easterly point to the Rio de la Plata and the Atlantic. Both expeditions had also made significant archaeological discoveries and carried out community-aid projects and wildlife-conservation tasks.

They were part of an ongoing programme organized by the British-based Scientific Exploration Society. This had been started by a small group of friends in 1969. In the previous year I had been asked by the British Army to follow up an invitation by Emperor Haile Selassie to lead a sixty-five-strong team to explore the Ethiopian stretches of the Blue Nile. This was the first expedition to navigate these perilous waters, and many useful scientific discoveries had been made – Dr Derek Yalden, a zoologist from Manchester University, had, among others, worked on our findings for the ensuing twenty years, and over thirty monographs had flowed from the expedition. Others had learned how to navigate boats – both inflatable and rigid – down wild white water, and how to survive in remote, bandit-ridden country. The team had pioneered the use of special Avon inflatables for river running, and received widespread publicity and support. It seemed a pity to let all this experience and expertise dissipate. Why not invite expedition members and other like-minded people to join a society dedicated to undertaking and encouraging similar enterprises?

It all began modestly enough – round my kitchen table in Camberley, Surrey. My friends Richard Snailham and Alastair Newman, both colleagues on the lecturing staff of the Royal Military Academy Sandhurst, became secretary and treasurer. We set an annual subscription of ten shillings, and life membership could be had for £10.

Today the Scientific Exploration Society (SES) has 700 members, individual and corporate, produces an illustrated newsletter, holds meetings at which distinguished explorers and travellers give talks in central-London hotels, and organizes expeditions for its members on a regular basis worldwide.

In the last five years, at the request of Bolivia's National Institute of Anthropology and Archaeology (DINAAR), there have been three major expeditions in that country, which is rich in largely untapped archaeological treasures and with a fascinating history of reed-boat manufacture carried out over many centuries on Titicaca's shores.

Our archaeological work in Bolivia has been guided by Oswaldo Rivera Sundt, whom I have known since the mid-1990s. Nut-brown, mercurial and energetic, he is now Bolivia's foremost archaeologist. I met him in La Paz, Bolivia's administrative capital, after the 1999 expedition.

'How did it go?' he asked.

'Well,' I told him, 'it took us three months, but *Kota Mama 2* reached Buenos Aires in good order. Mind you, she set off weighing eight tons and ended up at about twenty-one.' Reed boats absorb water steadily, and at the same time develop an abominable smell.

'How much longer before she sank?' Oswaldo enquired.

'Erik reckoned she could have gone on another six months.'

Erik Catari, a twenty-seven-year-old engineering student, and his father, Máximo, live at the village of Huatajata on Lake Titicaca. Short, sturdy and with the thick neck and swarthy features typical of the Aymara, they had collaborated to make *Kota Mama 2* and all our previous boats. They are two of the last remaining practitioners of the craft of *totora*-reed boat-building.

'Was there much damage to the boat?' Oswaldo continued.

'We had some severe southerly winds against us and hit some big waves on the Paraná. They gouged a layer of reeds from the bows about five inches deep on the waterline.'

Nevertheless, we had reached the Atlantic. It was true that, in the face of almost constant strong southerly winds, we had for much of the time used an outboard engine to push the big reed boat along. Early men might have taken many more months to complete the journey, but we had jobs to return to in most cases, and could not afford to spend an indefinite time waiting for the wind to relent and floating down the Paraguay and the Paraná on their currents alone. We were, however, able to show that reed boats (we had two) could stand up to a long immersion and a considerable buffeting from wind and wave. Materials with which to build a new boat for the return journey could have been found by the Atlantic shore, and we reckoned that the same winds that had impeded our journey southward would have driven early traders back upstream against the current with little difficulty, for we had seen many sailing craft hugging the banks and successfully making ground northward in this way. Early river voyages over these big distances were not proved to have occurred, but were shown to have been possible.

What evidence was there that early Andean peoples had undertaken such journeys? There were cogent reasons for believing that there had been trade links between the Old World and the New long before Iberian caravels or even Viking longships struck the Americas. Dr Svetla Balabanova, carrying out tests on authentic twenty-first-century BC Egyptian mummies from a Munich museum in 1992, had found traces of cocaine and nicotine in two of them. She was astonished: these substances come from the coca and tobacco plants, which in the mummies' era were found exclusively in the Americas. She reran the tests with doubly sterilized equipment and the results were incontrovertible: cocaine and nicotine were present in the bodies of two ancient Egyptian priestesses.

How had these substances come to them? Dr Balabanova agonized over every possibility, and could only conclude that they had been imported. Early Mediterranean peoples – Egyptians or Phoenicians, both considerable seafarers – had perhaps, even four millennia ago, reached the mouths of the Amazon or the Plate, preceding Pedro Álvares Cabral, the Portuguese who discovered Brazil by accident in 1500. Or it was equally possible that inhabitants of South America could have taken their trade goods on favourable currents and winds across to Africa. Dr Thor Heyerdahl was convinced that an advanced maritime culture had existed on the coasts of South America. His remarkable sea voyages in craft built of traditional materials had shown that early trans-oceanic traffic was quite possible.

Furthermore, in 1996 the respected American explorer Gene Savoy, a legend for his studies of the early civilizations of Peru, had made a fascinating discovery. High in the Andes he had found symbols carved on the wall of an ancient tomb. The most striking of these bore a close resemblance to a symbol also found in the Middle East. Savoy believes that it could be translated to mean 'Ophir', the biblical name of an unidentified land where, he said, '[The King of Tyre's] Phoenician sailors loaded their ships with gold and precious stones from King Solomon's mines to adorn, in Jerusalem, the walls of Solomon's Temple.' Descriptions began to appear of other inscriptions almost identical to Savoy's find in the Andes. One glyph from a site near Tel Aviv had marked a clay pot of gold carried in an ancient Phoenician ship. Gene Savoy believes that this is strong evidence of early trans-oceanic trading voyages. Could the Andes have been the 'Ophir' from where Solomon obtained his gold?

I

Setting the Goals

Viejas tradiciones cuentan que en . . . camino antiguo que baja de Sorata a Mapiri los Incas . . . escondieron una fabulosa cantidad de oro en algun valle cercano al cerro Paititi.

[Tradition has it that . . . along an old road which comes down from Sorata to Mapiri the Incas . . . carried away a fabulous quantity of gold into some valley in the vicinity of Mount Paititi.]

Sigfried Trippolt, *Revista Semana* (La Paz), 12 November 2000

LA PAZ IS the highest capital city in the world. At 12,000 feet or so it fills an immense hemispherical depression in the eastern flank of the Andes. Guidebooks differ over its exact height above sea level: it depends, I suppose, where you measure to. Its affluent suburbs lie comfortably lower down at its bottom end, while the brick cabins of the poorer classes sit in terraces below the rim of the hemisphere.

In October 1999 our plane circled the airport at El Alto – which, as its name implies, is even higher, on the flat plain known as the Altiplano into which the depression sinks – and Yolima Cipagauta and I could see the lights of the high-rise buildings in downtown La Paz where our next scientific expedition would begin. El Alto now has a resuscitation room for incoming tourists, but we had no qualms about landing at such a height. I had done it countless times before, as had Yolima, the Scientific Exploration Society's representative in South America and my assistant and interpreter on many expeditions in that continent. Yoli, a petite and smiley lecturer in economics, is from Colombia, which has its own bit of the Andes, and she is part Inca anyhow. I knew that a few cups of *mate de coca*, the local herbal tea, in our hotel in La Paz, would help us to overcome the altitude malaise.

'Who do we see first: the Admiral or Oswaldo?' I asked.

Bolivia, though now landlocked, still has a considerable navy. It lost its Pacific-coast ports in 1884 after a disastrous war with Chile, but it shares Lake Titicaca with Peru and has a great many enormous rivers which still need patrolling.

'Oswaldo, I think,' she said. 'I'll look up his number when we're in the taxi.'

As a former director of the National Institute of Anthropology and Archaeology, Oswaldo's views on the possibility of other ancient trading routes from the Bolivian coca fields to the Atlantic, in addition to those we had already explored, were of special interest to us.

'I've been thinking,' he said when we met him.

This was ominous. Oswaldo, often inscrutable and enigmatic, has a penchant for dramatic throwaway observations.

'Ancient traders may well have reached the Atlantic from Mapiri by going down north-eastern-flowing rivers and not south-eastern ones.'

'Where's Mapiri?' asked Yoli.

'It's on the east side of the Cordillera Oriental, the great ridge of the high Andes on the eastern side of the Altiplano, and on a navigable river which could have taken them to the Amazon. And it's only six to eight days' walk from Titicaca. They could have carried reeds over and made their boats there. It's in the area where many people have hoped to find a legendary city called Paititi. If you could find some significant ruins it would be enormously beneficial to the local inhabitants. They're very poor, and need some tourist money.'

Now my interest was roused. Scientific work and community aid, digging up the past in a way that might help an impoverished region: it's a good mixture.

'It could be another Machu Picchu,' said Oswaldo, with an excited gleam in his eye. Machu Picchu, a genuinely lost Inca city, not even discovered by the Spanish conquistadors, has attracted hundreds of thousands of visitors and much prosperity to a hitherto virtually inaccessible part of Peru since its discovery by Hiram Bingham in 1911.

Back at the Sucre Palace Hotel after this conversation, my thoughts turned to those rivers that flow north-east from the high Andes down through a foothill region known as the Yungas towards the Rio Madeira, one of Amazon's longest tributaries. These rivers of the Yungas, and of the area to the north around Mapiri, quickly become more or less navigable, the rapids with which they are sewn being merely sporting rather than outright dangerous. They run through the region known as Paititi, where stone remains of the last refuges of the Inca proliferate.

Next day, in the Instituto Geografica Militar, Yoli and I sought maps of the area. Sergeant de Silva thumbed through the massive reference books and shook his head.

'*Mi coronel*, there are no maps of that part; we have not made them yet.'

I felt a frisson of excitement: an unmapped area, little known and barely explored. The curiosity that has led me into so many quests was stimulated.

'Maybe there are some air photographs,' said the helpful sergeant. 'Where is the place you wish to see?'

'We don't know exactly,' explained Yoli, rather less helpfully, 'but can we see some photos of the area immediately south of Mapiri?'

The sheets showed not a single road, not a single house – only mountains covered in unrelieved jungle, with the occasional steep-sided valley through which torrents flowed north.

'This will be a needle-in-haystack problem,' I said. 'We'll need the help of the local quinine-hunters, a very fit team and a thorough recce.'

Oswaldo's reference to a lost city called Paititi lingered in my mind. I knew of early attempts to find it – by Berg in 1950 and, in the 1950s and '60s, by Manuel Posnansky, son of Arthur, the great historian of Tiwanaku, Bolivia's greatest ancient site, and by Sebastian Snow in Peru. I had heard about it again when Oswaldo, on one of my earlier visits, spoke of Hans Ertl, an elderly German expatriate living in a remote corner of Bolivia. In 1954–5 Ertl had allegedly discovered a city in the eastern foothills of the Andes to which he claimed the remnants of the defeated Inca had fled with their treasure after the Spanish conquest of 1532. According to Oswaldo, Ertl had failed to persuade people in La Paz to invest in a continuation of his exploration. Few really believed him. However, in 1998 Oswaldo had been working in the area and had met gatherers of the bark of quinine trees. They seemed to confirm the German's story, and talked of extensive ruins in the shadow of a local mountain, Cerro Paititi.

Some years earlier I had read a fascinating book by a former BBC man, Ross Salmon, who had looked for Paititi in the 1960s and '70s. He reasoned that thousands of the 13 million Inca peoples must have escaped from death or oppression under the Spanish. But where did they go? 'Bolivia was the only area of South America that fitted almost all the right conditions. If indeed there was a lost Inca empire it must be here,' he had written.

He looked for and found Incallajta, south-east of La Paz, a fort built to protect food-supply routes from the predations of the Guaraní in the east. This magnificent, well-preserved site had been built by the Inca Huayna Capac just before the Spanish arrived. Salmon went on searching westward to Puca Puca, Pumparacay, Incaracay – all small military forts with fine masonry walls. It became bewildering: '[We] were hopeful that we would now be able to persuade even the most sceptical of academics that this indeed was the lost city of the Incas,' he said of one. 'We did not know at this time, as I was to find out later, that it was merely another lost city of the Incas, one of several in Bolivia.'

Salmon recorded an interview with Dr Carlos Ponce Sanginés, the then doyen of Bolivian archaeologists. It began in chilly fashion. 'Which lost city of the Incas is it?' the Doctor asked. 'There are at least ten such lost cities that we have discovered in Bolivia in the last decade, and there are probably many more left to be discovered,' he added.

With remarkable determination, Salmon went on to find more – Iscanwaya, with ninety-eight houses and two large buildings; Karrie, in its 20-acre site; Pucanwaya, a small fort. In others he found gold objects, pyramidal altar stones, an aqueduct. Chuamaya, 'a great city' north of Cochabamba, had 13-foot-high walls 190 yards long, a large temple and fourteen stone houses on terraces up the hillside on the way to a lookout tower. It was heady stuff.

Dr Carlos Ponce, now co-operative, sent him hither and thither, accompanied by young archaeologists from DINAAR, the regulating body for their discipline. One of these was Oswaldo Rivera, who was then working on his Ph.D. thesis and was considered 'one of the bright young university graduates'. He was tasked to take Salmon on a tour of Tiwanaku, Lake Titicaca and Copacabana.

After all his wanderings over many years, Salmon concluded that 'there is an area east of Santa Ana [on the upper Rio Beni], about the size of Britain, which is totally unknown and unexplored. This whole region I believed to be the location of the lost empire of the Incas.'

The lure of lost empires and cities is a potent and abiding one. Every habited continent's history bristles with examples of man's search for them. The hunt for the Seven Cities of Cibola, where the Spaniards hoped to find temples covered in emeralds and gold, led Hernando de Soto in 1539 and Francisco Vázquez de Coronado in 1540 to discover the seemingly limitless plains of the southern USA from the Mississippi to Arizona. They found no cities of gold, but Coronado's party were the first Europeans to stare down into the Grand Canyon.

South America has a good tally of such lost cities. Paititi is just one of the more recent ones. Sir Walter Ralegh, fired by a lust for the gold of El Dorado, the gilded monarch of Guyana, looked for 'the great city of Manoa . . . Whatever prince shall possess it shall be lord of more gold . . . and of more cities and people, than either the King of Spain or the Grand Turk.' Of course it was not there. Nor was there evidence of the exiled Inca court which Ralegh had predicted he would find there.

It is generally believed that the British explorer Colonel Percy Fawcett was murdered by Indians in 1925 while searching for a non-existent 'lost' city west of the Rio São Francisco in Brazil. The supposed dispersal of the Inca peoples after 1532 has led to the search for many more lost cities: Vilcabamba was found in 1966, but the lost treasures of the Inca – thought to have been taken to Paititi – await discovery.

My own enthusiasm for lost cities is thus only a part of a long tradition. Indeed in 1979 our SES team had discovered Acla, the city built by Vasco Núñez de Balboa, discoverer of the Pacific, on the Caribbean shores of Panama.

In July 1984 Gregory Deyermenjian, a psychologist from Boston, Massachusetts, took up the challenge from Ross Salmon. His conclusions were very different. He agreed that Paititi was the name of a place to which, after the fall of Vilcabamba to the Spanish in 1572, the Inca took the remains of their treasure. But where was it?

He believed it might have been in the territory of the Machiguenga Indians in Peru. Led by an Indian who had married into the Machiguenga, his party of six went down the Rio Mamería in south-eastern Peru and found terraces, walls in late Imperial Inca style, pottery, bronze and alloy tools: 'Undisturbed for centuries . . . under the enveloping mat of vegetation . . . the remains exist further into the eastern jungles than Inca habitation is generally thought to have occurred.' We now believe that the Inca people pushed far further east than this. But was it Paititi?

A book by Father Juan Carlos Polentini in 1999 led Deyermenjian to investigate claims that Paititi had been found on a range to the west of the Rio Nistron in south-eastern Peru. Deyermenjian's 2000 Paititi expedition reached Atalaya on the Madre de Dios river, which the Incas called Amaru Mayu, or the Great Serpent river. He took a *peke-peke* (a noisy little motorized canoe with a long propeller shaft) up the Rio Pinipini, the Nistron and the Choritiari until he reached the latitude and longitude (12° 37′S, 71° 42′W) given by Polentini. Nothing was found there. Paititi, 'the ultimate refuge city' remained elusive.

Yoli and I wondered if Paititi could perhaps be far further east, in the northern flatlands of Bolivia, where earlier civilizations had been reported. Recent Bolivian writers César Augusto Machicao Gámez and Said Zeitum López have retold the story of Inca armies of between 10,000 and 15,000 men descending in three waves from the eastern cordillera of the Andes and reaching the confluence of the Beni and the Madre de Dios. One notable leader was the Inca Yupanqui (or Yawar Huacaj), whose men were orderly and disciplined and brought not violence to the people of the plains but gifts. They disappeared like the lost legion of the Romans, but some may have settled in the region of Riberalta among the indigenous Mojos people.

Later the Spanish conquistadors were attracted by the idea of another El Dorado, perhaps as rich as the Cerro Potosí in the Andes, which was then fuelling their homeland and empire with unimaginably rich quantities of gold and silver. This might be the mythical land of Great Paititi to the east of the Andes in the savannah of the Mojos. No doubt encouraged to press on by Indians in the foothills, who wanted rid of them, men like Juan Alvarez Maldonado, Francisco Paz and Juan Nieto struggled eastward into the hot plains, but found nothing. A Jesuit historian, Father José Guevara, wrote of this Paititi in terms reminiscent of Plato's description of the legendary drowned island Atlantis, but it was a chimera. Paititi was not there, and the Spanish withdrew to the high Andes and Asunción.

'Is Hans Ertl still alive?' I asked Oswaldo.

'I think so, but he must be very old now,' he replied.

'We really ought to get someone to interview him and pick his brains about Paititi while we can.'

I could think of no one more fitted for this task than our friend the wife of the British ambassador to Bolivia. A determined raven-haired lady, Peter (*sic*) Minter had been with us on our 1999 expedition. Resident in La Paz, she could track down the old German and get more of his story. And indeed, after I had returned to England, she found him living a hermit-like existence in a rambling house in the bush near Santa Cruz.

Germany has had many connections with South America, and on the 1999 *Kota Mama* expedition we had visited Nueva Germánia. In 1886, near the banks of the Rio Aguaray Guazú in the remote Paraguayan hinterland, this town had been founded by Elisabeth, the sister of the German philosopher Friedrich Nietzsche, her husband, Bernhard Förster, and fourteen German families – all united by a hatred of Jews. More families had joined them, but the colony had not really taken off: some settlers had returned, others married into Paraguayan families, others just dispersed to more easily cultivable farms. Nietzsche's complex philosophies were later to be hijacked by the Nazis, even though they were mostly at variance with National Socialist thinking, and Elisabeth, who returned to Germany in 1893, found herself lionized in later life by Hitler, Goebbels and the rest of the pack.

In 1932 Germany had supported Bolivia with military advisers and equipment for its war with Paraguay over the disputed Chaco territory. For some of the time the Bolivian Army was commanded by the German general Hans Kundt. The indecisive conflict had cost the lives of 60,000 Bolivians and 30,000 Paraguayans, and German military links remained.

A great number of Germans fled to South America after the Second World War, and many of them settled in Bolivia, Chile and Paraguay, finding that the authorities there were accommodating and didn't ask any difficult questions. The most notorious of the *Altekameraden* in Bolivia was Klaus Barbie, the 'Butcher of Lyons' – responsible for the deaths of some 26,000 people, mostly Jews – who was extradited to France in 1983.

Of course, with their homeland in ruins, many decent, honourable Germans also moved to South America, and because Ertl had been among the first to do so didn't necessarily make him a Nazi with a past to hide.

'How did it go?' I asked Peter Minter when we returned to Bolivia in July 2000.

'It was an uphill task,' she said. 'I'm afraid he was too old to recall much. After all, he's ninety-three now.'

Ertl had been in the *Wehrmacht* during the Second World War, but he always denied having been a Nazi. Before the war he had been a professional photographer, and was one of the inner circle of cameramen who provided the myriad pictures of Hitler needed for publicity purposes. Soon he was referred to as 'Hitler's photographer'. He had close contact with the Führer while working with the internationally renowned director Leni Riefenstahl on her film of the 1936 Berlin Olympics – remembered as one of the great examples of Nazi propaganda. In a break during filming, Riefenstahl tried to show Hitler in a more human light by embracing him while Ertl took a photograph. When this attractive woman kissed the astonished Führer on the cheek, he wiped off the lipstick with the help of a small pocket mirror proffered by Hermann Goering. Meanwhile a member of the SS stepped forward, but was prevented from confiscating Ertl's film by Riefenstahl herself.

'Anyway he did give me a Spanish translation of his book,' said Peter, handing me a copy. I was grateful to Peter for her efforts. It cannot have been easy raking up the past with this elderly expatriate.

Ertl's book – *Paititi: Ein Spähtrupp in die Vergangenheit der Inkas* (Paititi: An Investigation into the Inca Past) – had come out in 1963. Yoli, now with us in La Paz, began to read the Spanish translation immediately. 'The text is really very confusing, and the lack of maps doesn't help!' she reported.

Ertl claimed that he had found marvellous ruins and great treasures in the depths of the jungle. He was, however, none too explicit about where these ruins were situated, and the book's illustrations of carvings and artefacts that he had found were not photographed with any identifiable background or context for the finds.

This obscurity was doubtless intentional: it is possible that, as he was trying to raise funds for another expedition back to 'Paititi', he did not want to reveal precisely where this ruined city could be found. Nevertheless, there were enough details to show roughly in what part of the country Ertl had been travelling. No serious explorers had since tried to find this lost-city site. Was Ertl just spinning a yarn in the hope of getting some money, or was there something out in the jungle that could really have been the 'lost city' of his description?

In early 2001 we had news of Ertl's death, and with it a fascinating account of his past began to emerge. Before the Second World War he was involved in the mysterious work of an arm of the SS known as the *Ahnenerbe*, the Ancestral Heritage Society. Its task was to find anthropological and archaeological evidence to support the bizarre creed of the Thule Society, an extreme nationalist group which believed in the earlier greatness of the *Herrenvolk*. Heinrich Himmler, head of the SS and the Gestapo, was an enthusiastic member and strongly supported the Nazi belief in the racial superiority of the ancient northern Europeans, the Aryans, seeing the SS as modern-day Teutonic knights whose goal was the conquest of eastern Europe.

From my research I had learned that the *Ahnenerbe* mounted expeditions worldwide, to study, for example, traditional medicine in South America and examine Tibetan skulls in a secret and possibly mythical Himalayan city called Shambhala. In the late 1930s Ertl had travelled to the Himalayas on one such trip. An attempt was also made to discover Atlantis, to show that those who survived when it was submerged by the sea had reached Europe and become the Aryan master race.

After the outbreak of war, Ertl joined the army and served in the North African campaign, working for Field Marshal Erwin Rommel, whom he worshipped. 'He is like a God to me,' he is reported to have said. There was no doubt that Ertl was clever and industrious, and during the war he invented submersible and airborne cameras for which he was awarded the Iron Cross. He also wrote no fewer than twelve books on his military experiences. After the end of the war he moved to Chile, and in 1950 he appeared in Bolivia carrying out tests on photographic plates at high altitude for the German company Siemens. Within a few months he had bought a farm he named La Dolorida – The Heart-Sick One – 530 miles south-east of La Paz.

A picture of an aged, heavily bearded Hans Ertl clutching a photograph of himself in his wartime uniform had been published by Reuters. He seemed very fond of his uniform, and a journalist who visited him shortly before his death found him still wearing his old *Wehrmacht* jacket.

'So what had induced this talented photographer, film-maker, inventor and author to spend so much time and money searching for Paititi?' Richard asked as we leafed through the documents in the Scientific Exploration Society's office at Motcombe, Dorset.

'It may have been his old links with the *Ahnenerbe* that got him interested in the hunt for lost Inca cities in Bolivia,' I replied. 'Or he may have thought Paititi was part of the empire of Atlantis.'

'It all sounds like *Raiders of the Lost Ark* to me.'

'Yes, it does,' I replied, 'And there's another long shot: Bolivia welcomed Jewish refugees from Austria and Germany in 1938. Perhaps some of them wrote back to relatives in Germany about the fabled lost cities and it got to the ears of the SS.'

'What about Klaus Barbie?' Richard asked.

'Barbie seems to have escaped to South America with other Nazi war criminals thanks to a deal set up by the CIA. He became a Bolivian citizen in 1957, and began helping the security forces and neo-fascist elements in Argentina and Bolivia. Ertl's daughter Monika came to know Barbie as "Uncle" because he was such a friend of her father. Ertl helped Barbie to get a job in Bolivia.'

Barbie is still remembered in La Paz for an incident at a reception in the German Club in 1966. As the West German ambassador proposed a toast to the Federal Republic, he was interrupted by a shout of 'Heil Hitler!' from Barbie, who stood giving the Nazi salute and was bundled out of the club yelling abuse at the ambassador. Barbie was allowed to return a few years later. In those days it seems there were many in sympathy with the Nazi cause.

Monika, who had grown up in Bolivia, was a member of the 1954–5 Ertl expedition to Paititi. Later she became a disciple of Che Guevara, and after his death she joined a Bolivian urban-terrorist organization, the Ejército de Liberación Nacional, headed by Inti Perado, a very close friend of hers. In 1969 Perado was killed by the Bolivian Secret Service under Colonel Roberto Quintanilla Pereira, the chief of the anti-guerrilla police and reportedly involved in Che Guevara's death. Two years later Monika took her revenge.

Quintanilla, now forty-three, had been rewarded for his services to the regime by being appointed Bolivia's consul-general in West Germany, with an office in Hamburg. On 1 April 1971 a blonde woman who had given her name as Imilla saw him by appointment. Entering Quintanilla's office, she pulled out a Colt Cobra revolver and, shooting quickly and accurately, killed him. The dying man's wife rushed in and grappled with the assassin, who fled, leaving a blonde wig and her gun behind. The revolver was traced to Giangiacomo Feltrinelli, a wealthy left-wing Italian publisher. As the manhunt spread throughout Europe, the Austrian police recognized Feltrinelli with Monika Ertl at a hunting lodge. There was little doubt that Imilla was Monika, but nevertheless she escaped to La Paz – leaving Feltrinelli to blow himself up a year later with his own bomb while attacking an electricity pylon.

Back home, Monika married a Bolivian of German origin and continued her activities as an urban terrorist. However, money was short and in 1973, it was understood, she hit on the idea of kidnapping Klaus Barbie and selling him to the French government, who were eager to get their hands on the notorious war criminal. Sadly for Monika, Barbie got wind of her plan and she was gunned down – either by the Butcher's followers or possibly by the Bolivian Secret Service, eager to be rid of a troublesome urban guerrilla.

By the end of 1999 I had determined on a dual aim for an expedition. On to the original plan of taking a reed boat from the high Andes to the Atlantic by a north-eastern river route had been grafted an attempt to find and survey the supposed site of Paititi that Hans Ertl had visited in 1954–5.

The expedition was timed to start in May 2001, and with these enlarged aims it was scheduled to last for over four months – throughout the summer of 2001. Plans to build a new reed boat have to begin early. The reeds (*Scirpus totora*) must be cut at the right time of year; there has to be suitable weather over Lake Titicaca for the reeds to dry out; and the Catari family must then marshal their friends and begin to bind the reeds together.

Dr Thor Heyerdahl was the first to show us what balsa rafts and reed boats can do. At a time when astonishing trans-oceanic voyages were attempted less often than they are today, he took the balsa raft *Kon-Tiki* from Peru to the Polynesian islands, and, on his second attempt, in 1970 he sailed *Ra II* – made in Africa, but by Aymara Indians and with reed from Lake Titicaca – from Morocco to Barbados. I met the venerable Dr Heyerdahl, discussed our project with him, and found him most encouraging.

Thor Heyerdahl was one of the first to see that, even if the art of building big boats of great strength from bundles of reeds had mostly died out elsewhere, it was alive and reasonably well on the shores of Lake Titicaca. In fact it is largely through the efforts of the Catari family that the ancient reed-boat-building skills have been maintained, and, as we knew from the *Kota Mama* expeditions in 1998 and 1999, they build extremely robust craft. Máximo Catari Cahuaya not only had inherited these skills but had studied boat-building in – of all places – New York, Chicago and Philadelphia. Erik Catari Gutierrez had also researched the traditional methods of construction back to pre-Christian times. 'The people who lived on the lake', he told us, 'and who met the Spanish conquistadors had explained to them how their ancestors had been taught to build these reed boats by bearded, white-skinned strangers like the Spanish themselves. These early newcomers had put up massive step pyramids near the shore, where the ruins of Tiwanaku now stand. They were later forced out,' he concluded, 'and went down to the Pacific coast and sailed away.' The Spanish had recorded all this – including the name of the leader of these people: Kon-Tiki, or Viracocha in the language of the Quechua, the most prominent people of the Peruvian Andes. He was said to be a divine ruler, descended from the sun, yet still human.

The Cataris knew their stuff. They had recently built a 70-foot sea-going reed boat that had crossed from Arica in Chile to Easter Island in forty-four days. In 1998 they had built three smaller boats for me for 9,000 bolivianos – some $1,400 – each. I now ordered another – but it was to cost $28,000.

Time constraints meant that we would have to cut some corners, and I did not plan to ask the Cataris to transport reed to Mapiri, where north-east-flowing rivers become navigable, and construct the boat there, as their forefathers might have done. We would commission a boat to be built at their home in Huatajata, on the shores of the lake, and then move it to the Mapiri river by army lorry.

The design of the boat was important. In consultation with Jim Masters, the veteran white-water expert from Somerset who had been our 'Admiral of the Fleet' in 1999, we decided to try to make the journey not in a single-hulled craft as before, but in a multi-hulled vessel. It was the knowledge that we would have to run down some formidable rapids at the point where we would join the Madeira river that persuaded Jim and Erik that a broad multi-hull might provide greater stability. In the end they came up with a plan for a trimaran with three hulls loosely linked by strong cordage. This, it was hoped, would give both strength and flexibility in the nineteen or twenty cataracts that awaited us.

Among the few sources of information that could be used to help design a craft as similar as possible to an early one were drawings of a boat captured by the Spanish during their first forays south from Panama. In 1525 Bartolomé Ruiz, a pilot with Francisco Pizarro's first expedition to Peru, made an early contact with the Incas when he met a large ocean-going craft made of balsa wood and set with cotton sails off the coast of today's Ecuador. Its twenty-strong crew carried merchandise and were clearly on a regular trading run. Earlier than the Spanish, seagoing reed boats with masts and sails appear on Moche ceramics originating from north-west Peru in about AD 600.

The design that Jim came up with, in collaboration with the Cataris, would give us a larger central hull with two smaller outriggers attached, the whole ensemble being some 40 feet long and 18 feet wide and weighing about 3 ½ tons. We believed that the separate reed hulls would move up and down independently in the rapids, so absorbing the impact of the waves. The central hull would have two A-frame masts, each with a lateen sail like the ones seen by Bartolomé Ruiz. Each hull would have wooden rubbing-strakes, to prevent it from chafing against its neighbour. Dagger boards, lowered through slots in the middle hull, would be fitted to increase stability and steerage. The three impressive bows each would sport a reed jaguar's head – mouths agape, teeth asnarl, but nevertheless with popping eyes suggestive more of a surprised domestic tabby than of its wild cousin.

It was to be a very basic craft, with only some simple planking in the middle of the central hull. There would be no cabin, no cover – the crews would need their sunblock. We planned to fix a Mariner 25 out-board motor on to a transom between the central and port hulls, to give a bit of drive when to sail would be too laborious and time-consuming. The Brazilian Navy had insisted on this alternative propulsion, so that we could avoid the commercial shipping on its rivers.

The Cataris began gathering the *totora* reed in September 2000, and we were deeply gratified to learn that our good friends J. P. Knight Ltd, tug operators of Rochester on the Medway, were once again to sponsor our flagship.

2

Reconnaissance

In my view, to sign on to an expedition bound for the interior of Brazil is neither laudable or extraordinary but rather the reverse. Most people of my age [twenty-four] would do it like a shot, if they had the chance . . . it is unpleasant to be regarded as a lunatic or a hero when you know perfectly well that you are merely going to take an exceptionally long holiday.

Peter Fleming, *Brazilian Adventure*, 1933

PREPARATION FOR AN expedition lasts many times longer than the expedition itself. A reconnaissance has to be carried out and a team selected; stores and equipment have to be procured, and funds raised. It took just over a year to get things together for our four months in Bolivia and Brazil. The council of the Scientific Exploration Society approved plans for a reconnaissance expedition to fly to La Paz in July 2000. One group would head for Mapiri and investigate the route to 'Paititi' as far as time permitted. A second group was to visit the rapids on the Mamoré and Madeira rivers on the Bolivia–Brazil border and assess their degree of difficulty.

Yolima Cipagauta, our tireless representative, made several visits to Britain and kept us informed about what was going on in South America, while at Motcombe the SES base was a hive of activity.

A central figure in both the reconnaissance and the expedition itself was seventy-two-year-old Jim Masters, who had already been involved with the design of our boat. I have known Jim for almost forty years. We were both Royal Engineers, and had served together in Cyprus. Commissioned later, he had handled the difficult river-running aspects of the 1968 Blue Nile Expedition and the Zaire River Expedition of 1974–5. A gentle, caring man, it was typical of him that he returned to Zaire to co-ordinate the distribution of medical supplies over that vast country. Now Jim's cheerful, craggy features were much in evidence at Motcombe as he planned for the river phases of the expedition.

Jim led the reconnaissance group which investigated the rapids on the Mamoré and the Madeira, and took with him his younger brother Gerry, a mere sixty-five, who might normally have been restoring a Somerset church. Also in his group were a stocky Pittsburgh schoolteacher, Eric Niemi – of Finnish descent, and an experienced diving instructor and wildlife enthusiast – and Drew Craig, a Scots Territorial Army lieutenant, who went along to produce a useful report on the cataracts.

At the top north-eastern corner of Bolivia there is a border crossing to Brazil much used by backpackers and smugglers. Each country has its frontier town – Guayaramerín in Bolivia and Guajará-Mirim in Brazil – and these are separated by the half-mile-wide Mamoré river, which can be crossed in a succession of launches. The rapids begin here, and for two weeks in July 2000 Jim, Gerry, Eric and Drew studied as many of the nineteen or twenty cataracts as possible, ending up downstream at the Brazilian city of Pôrto Velho, where the Madeira river begins its uninterruptedly navigable stretch – 672 miles to its junction with the Amazon.

Meanwhile I went from La Paz to Guanay, a Wild West sort of town in the foothills of the Andes, north-east of La Paz. This was near Mapiri, and looked to be the best place for us to base ourselves.

With Yoli and me were a number of old friends and acquaintances: Tania John, a quiet, conscientious young doctor from Bath; Major Clive Smith of the Royal Monmouthshire Royal Engineers; American archaeologist Maria Mason (who had in 1978–80 been a key member of the team for our Operation Drake project, in which young people circumnavigated the world in a chartered brigantine) and her daughter Brittain, for whom the expedition was a sixteenth-birthday present; and, from Switzerland, Prince Leopold d'Arenberg, a prince of the Holy Roman Empire and an extremely fit mountaineer as well as being resolute and Spanish-speaking – a very useful man to have on this quest. Oswaldo Rivera joined us, and also Pablo Rendon, a former Boy Scout and one of the DINAAR archaeologists.

Oswaldo had persuaded the prefectura of La Paz to provide three Toyota pickups to convey us to Guanay. Each swallowing a large cup of *mate de coca* to warm us, we piled our kit on the cars and set off through the squalid suburbs. The road rose through stark, barren mountains where snow and ice still packed the gullies. The highest point, at 15,500 feet, was La Cumbre, and shortly afterwards we were stopped at a military checkpoint where travellers are examined for drugs. However, a wave of the official letter from the office of the Bolivian president, General Hugo Banzer Suárez, and Yoli's cry of '¡*Misión oficial!*' got us through.

The road then dropped away into the clammy, jungle-clad valleys of the Yungas, and became frighteningly narrow – with a 2,500-foot sheer drop on one side and a cliff on the other. There was no protecting guard rail, just an ominous succession of crosses and other memorials to those who had plunged over the edge. At every bend I felt we were likely to meet a 10-ton Volvo truck, overloaded with bananas, cows, people or timber. My fears were compounded by the sight of a memorial with the Star of David, indicating a recent tragedy in which a minibus full of Israelis had gone over. No wonder the Inter-American Development Bank had designated this 'the most dangerous road in the world'. I noted with interest that descending vehicles always drove on the inside, irrespective of whether it was the right or left of the road. Happily, this convention seemed to be understood by all. Passing, quite literally, under waterfalls and through tunnels that I thought might obstruct the movement of a large reed boat, we crept down this terrifying track.

The temperature and humidity rose, and it was late afternoon when we drew up at the Hotel Panamericano in the sprawling river town of Guanay. 'How cool!' said Brittain, spying a recumbent figure asleep under an enormous sombrero. 'Just as I imagined it.'

Oswaldo went in and emerged with the tubby, genial host, Don Lucho, who rubbed his hands in glee at so many guests. The tiny cells around the courtyard each provided a bed, table and chair, and there was a communal shower, which delivered a dribble of water.

Within minutes, Guanay's alcalde (or mayor) had been made aware that a prince, a colonel, a major, a senior archaeologist and a Colombian economist, plus other important foreigners, were in town. Meetings were hastily arranged, and all was made ready in a remarkably short time for our departure next day on our quest for Paititi.

When we set off again, the dirt road zigzagged up from the Guanay valley into lush green hills that rolled away until they grew into mountains swathed in fluffy clouds. Several shallow rivers were easily forded, and after some hours, we reached a sign of civilization – a squarely built tea factory, silent now, as it was Saturday.

At the barbed-wire gate the manager eyed us with suspicion. 'Gringos in this remote spot must be up to no good,' he seemed to be thinking. Not daring to step outside his protective fence, he gave us little information. 'Yes – there is no phone, but I have a radio and in an emergency will pass a message to Guanay.' Perhaps it was the presence among us of the striking figure of a tall, muscular, curly-haired unemployed miner whose swarthy features betokened African ancestry that worried him. Indeed, Juan Blanco's gold teeth, cast eye, and extensive neck and chest burn scars made him an intimidating sight. Perhaps the manager already knew of his reputation. Some said he had magical powers and, as we were soon to discover, he was something of a shaman or witch doctor. On Don Lucho's advice, we had hired this forceful, deep-voiced figure as our guide. He was a strange, complex character, quite prepared to muddy the waters by providing misleading information, but also of immense help to us by virtue of his considerable physical strength. He proved invaluable when a truck sank deep in mud. It was child's play for Juan Blanco to set it free, stripping down to his underpants and scrabbling in the mire underneath the wheels. Afterwards his body was so heavily caked in mud that he looked like the protagonist of *The Thing That Came in from the Swamp*. On another day, after a long trek through thick jungle, he wandered off to cut down a few young palm trees and bring back their edible hearts to add to the evening meal. But most importantly he claimed to have seen the ruins of Paititi.

At dusk we reached the village of Vilaque Grande, where the tiny shop sold us eggs, bread and biscuits. Here we started our search for pack animals to carry our equipment and rations up to a place Juan Blanco called Incapampa. A mile or two further, as darkness fell, we stopped at Quilapituni. A couple of dozen mud-walled houses and a single-classroom school strung out along the red-earth road, Quilapituni is where you walk off the map: the region immediately west of the village has yet to be surveyed. 'Can we camp here?' I asked Oswaldo. 'Of course. Let's ask if we can sleep in the school.'

That night the spartan classroom was illuminated with showers of sparks as we sharpened our machetes on a portable grindstone produced by Celso, the village chief. By the light of our guttering candles, he told us all he knew of 'Paititi'. Many of his people had seen the ruins, but the route to get to them was overgrown, very long, and difficult. It would take a week to march there, and along the way there were snakes – many, many poisonous vipers – as well as the dreaded tucandera or giant fire-ants and all the other nasties about which Ertl had written.

Pulling on extra clothes against the chill night air, we listened to Yoli's summary of a few passages of Ertl's book. 'He was convinced', she said, 'that a great city existed in the jungle south-east of Cerro Paititi. He took a party of ten with Indian guides to set up a base at Incapampa. They then had to drop into the steep-sided gorge of the Rio Chinijo. He spent three days cutting his way down 600 yards with machetes, and two more building a rope bridge over it. He then goes on about all those fireflies and snakes. He says he was bitten by a snake. The fireflies can drive a man mad. They are found on the *Palo santo* (*lignum vitae*) tree and the *Cecropia*. He tells of how Indians would tie an enemy to a *Palo santo* and let him be eaten to death. After 1½ miles climbing up they find the walls of a fort on the ridge. He discovers slingshot and axe-heads under all the bamboo and other vegetation. In all, he sets up five camps on his way to the mountain – the third one on the Rio Tulani, where he finds ruins. He mentions two hills, rock stairs, a deep pool, and a waterfall with water channels running from it. He thinks they had a ceremonial purpose – perhaps ablution. There are some beehive-shaped buildings. He writes of a supposed Indian pilgrimage each December on which they brought jewels. Frederick Buck, one of his party, says he believes it's pre-Inca Chavin culture. No pottery, but he says he finds some gold objects and tools, now in La Paz. It's difficult to trace his movements on the site itself, even with the marked photograph in the book. It's all a bit confusing. Finally they find a cave blocked by boulders, which they heat and crack. Gold and bronze objects are behind them. He plants fruit trees and rice for future expeditions. There's also a strange carved stone head, like one you see at Potosí, but it's impossible to work out where it was. That's it!'

'Not a lot to go on,' remarked Clive Smith, and most of us agreed. But Juan Blanco and Celso were in no doubt. 'It is there,' they insisted. 'We have seen it with our own eyes.'

If they were correct, this 'Paititi' was lost only to the outside world: to a few locals it was reasonably well known, and from time to time they would make the tiresome march there to scratch around for artefacts that might be sold on the black market. The arrival of an international expedition, with the declared aim of opening up the site for scientific research, was therefore not at all what some of them wanted. Only much later, during the expedition proper, was I to find that the team of cutters sent ahead by the alcalde of Guanay had been prevailed upon to cut the path through the most difficult route.

The night on the cold concrete floor passed surprisingly quickly, and the next morning dawned bright and clear, with beautiful views over the jungle to the cloud-capped summit of Cerro Paititi on the horizon. Having arrived when it was already getting dark, I now had my first opportunity to look around.

Quilapituni, population about 400, was a small village composed almost entirely of thatched cottages. It had been established, we were told later, about 150 years ago, drawing together into one community Indians who had previously lived in small, isolated family groups in the jungle.

To the question 'What has happened to the Incas?', quite a reasonable answer would be 'They live in places like this.' The villagers looked far more Indian than European: much smaller and more lightly boned, with solemn, rather mournful faces that could suddenly open up into a sparkling smile. Their language was Aymara, and their distant ancestors had doubtless lived at the place they now called Paititi.

From outside, their cottages looked almost Iron Age, and inside they were almost as primitive, with beaten-earth floors and cheap furniture. Pigs foraged for food in the street, and chicken and geese wandered up and down, while children played with their dogs. Money was there none, though it sounds trite, they seemed rich in the qualities of friendship, hospitality, and a directness and openness long lost in more affluent parts of the world.

The prefectura's drivers departed early, promising to return a week later. Meanwhile a motley collection of mules and packhorses began to assemble. It was clear that in the time available we could not reach the ruins, but I would be satisfied if we could substantiate at least part of Ertl's report and find a practical route forward. From the start, however, the lack of water worried me. The trail to Incapampa led along a ridge, and for much of the way the only water supply was at a narrow saddle named San José four hours up the mountain. I decided to make for that.

When at last the animals were loaded we set out, tramping along a muddy jungle trail while electric-blue butterflies danced ahead in the shafts of sunlight filtering through the tree canopy. Ferns and crimson flowers aptly named 'Black Women's Lips' lined the way. Juan Blanco, his senses finely tuned, led us forward, pointing out plants, birds and insects. The unmistakable sound of a rattlesnake in the undergrowth brought his razor-sharp machete to hand in an instant, but the reptile was gone in a flash.

The slippery path alternated between dense tropical forest and patches of open grassland, in one of which we came to the point known as San José. A spring produced clean, clear water, and we filled our containers while making camp. 'The next water is at Waricunca,' said Juan Blanco, pointing ahead with his chin. That was about 2½ miles away. 'We'll check it out before moving from here,' I cautioned, knowing that eleven pack animals and eighteen people need a great deal to drink.

'We must hold a *pachamama*,' insisted Juan Blanco. This ceremony, of pagan origin, was to seek protection from evil, snakes and other dangers in the forest. Somewhat reluctantly I agreed, if only to keep the muleteers happy. Thus, after supper, Juan Blanco called us around the fire and, crouching down, produced a newspaper-wrapped packet. He opened this with great reverence, revealing a strange mixture. Coca leaf, boiled sweets, flowers and rice were mixed with llama dung and wool, plus pieces of dried llama foetus. Muttering in a low voice, he sprinkled the concoction with industrial alcohol from a small bottle. The bottle was then passed around, and everyone had to take a sip while offering a prayer to the *pachamama*, or 'Mother Earth'. Blanco, the whites of his eyes gleaming eerily in the firelight, added longer incantations. This went on for an hour or so, during which time everyone was given coca leaf to chew and a cigarette to be puffed but not necessarily inhaled. Finally, the masticated leaf and the cigarette ends were added to the offering in the newspaper. The last of the alcohol was sprinkled on before the packet was wrapped up and placed on the fire. Blanco's prayers and moanings became more intense, and, strangely, his eyes grew bloodshot – though perhaps this was caused by the fumes. Looking intently at the smoke as it curled up into the starlit sky, he whispered, 'The *pachamama* is with us now. It will protect us, for many have gone up to Paititi and not come out alive.' We crept off to our hammocks and tents, feeling a little cold.

The next morning Leopold, who had gone on ahead, reported on his Motorola walkie-talkie that he had found a small stream near Waricunca, and so we advanced again. However, our advance was flawed by the first group of muleteers having made off for Incapampa with the lightest loads. After their departure, we discovered that the heaviest packs had been left for the weakest and slowest animals. Also, the trail was heavily eroded, and we had to use pick and spade to widen the path for the animals and their loads. This, plus the effects of the industrial alcohol on the men, slowed us down considerably. We reached Waricunca with one horse too lame to carry, and at that point it began to rain. Instantly the path became a skidpan, impassable for our beasts. They slipped and stumbled, some falling heavily until they could go no further. We halted in disarray in the middle of a vast patch of burnt grass with no option but to camp. Unfortunately, those who had gone ahead carried the rations and we were left with the tents.

My little group included the ladies of the team – Yoli, Maria, Brittain and Tania. With commendable ingenuity, they rigged up a plastic tarp under which we sat and examined our personal survival kits for food. I had some glucose tablets and Yoli had nuts, but we need not have worried, because Brittain produced a veritable school tuck-box from her pack: cookies, peanut butter and chocolate bars tumbled out in abundance. She seemed to be carrying high-energy food for an army.

Dawn found us enveloped in a mountain mist, but gradually our muleteer Ugarte's head cleared, and the ground dried sufficiently for us to move on.

The route up now ran through narrow, sunken lanes, in dripping-wet forest. It was steep and slippery, but a couple of hours later we reached open grassland again and saw ruined walls of houses, possibly built at the time of the nineteenth-century rubber boom, or by early gold miners. Ahead, on a narrow ridge, was Leopold's camp, which we now made for. Incapampa's water supply was a series of dirty pools in a small hollow. However, Clive Smith had filled all the containers with rainwater, thus averting a serious problem for the time being.

'The city,' said Juan Blanco, pointing to a dark valley nestling at the foot of the dominant mass of Cerro Paititi. There was nothing to identify the site: it was all one massive cabbage patch. 'The path is here,' exclaimed Oswaldo, as he set off down the 50-degree slope towards the Rio Chinijo. Leopold and Clive, having broken out climbing ropes, followed on to reconnoitre the way to the river.

On the ridge we set up simple rain shelters and then scouted forward, seeking other routes that might take us across the Chinijo. Suddenly Oswaldo's excited voice came over the radio: 'We have found walls. It is not far. Come and see.' Treading cautiously down the precipitous path, we soon reached the discovery. Terraced walls, skilfully built of cut stone, lined the valley sides. One section in particular was well-constructed, and here the archaeologists Oswaldo and Pablo Rendon had cleared a length and dug a trench along its base. 'Inca,' said Oswaldo gleefully. 'It fits in with Ertl's description,' remarked Yoli. 'I wonder if there are more on the other side of the valley?'

Leopold and Clive had returned from the river's edge a thousand feet below. 'It's a hell of a descent, and the river is flowing too fast to cross without safety ropes,' reported Clive, who, having had a nasty fall from the path, was looking somewhat battered. 'There is no way we can get mules down to the water,' stated Leopold.

'*Peligroso*,' yelled Celso, slashing with his machete at a small silvery snake that had slithered out of the freshly cleared stonework. Scooping it up on a spade, I popped the little fellow down in the brush, where it wriggled harmlessly away. Celso regarded me as if I had lost my mind. 'Not all snakes are dangerous,' I said in rebuke, but I doubt that my words had much effect. The Indians lived in terror of all snakes, believing that if they failed to kill one it would follow them for ever. Celso was worried that we had no serum.

From Incapampa, we had seen a long ridge running up towards 'Paititi' from the east, and this might provide an easier approach. Leopold and Clive agreed to look at it.

On return to our camp we were surprised to see more tents. The deputy alcalde and council members from Guanay had come to see how we were getting on – or possibly to see what we were up to. Ominously, several carried revolvers and rifles, but these appeared to be only for hunting or defence against snakes. I explained that the route across the Chinijo was dangerous, and we were seeking an alternative approach to the site.

'*We* can cross the river,' said Becky, a voluptuous councillor, her dark eyes flashing with pride and determination. Handing her a walkie-talkie, I wished them well. 'We'll light a fire to show you where we are,' she said, and with that the intrepid council members were off.

Meanwhile, Leopold and Clive had returned to Waricunca and found an old trail that led down the sides of a gorge. At the bottom, the Rio Chinijo and Rio Santa Ana joined to become the Merke. The water, though fast, was only thigh deep, and they had crossed without difficulty at a point we later named Smith's Crossing, in Clive's honour, to reach the foot of the spur separating the two rivers. Leopold had climbed this – it became Leopold's Spur – and over the radio he told me, 'It's very tough, but with improvement by engineers you might get mules up.' I believed that once we had conquered this feature the ridge line to 'Paititi' might be relatively easy. This seemed a more natural route than the extremely steep way via Incapampa. I wondered why Ertl had chosen that approach? By all accounts it had taken him a long time. Had he explored the alternative? His book mentioned a broken bridge on the Chinijo below Incapampa, but we found no evidence of this. How on earth had he got all his equipment and stores up to the Rio Tulani?

Had he used pack animals? I tried to put myself in this Teutonic explorer's mind.

The Motorola crackled. 'It's me, Oswaldo. We're crossing the Rio Chinijo.' He and Pablo Rendon had no safety ropes, and I muttered a prayer. The Good Lord was on our side, for a few minutes later Oswaldo reported that all was well and they were scrambling up the far side of the chasm. For a while there was silence; then, 'We have found more Inca terrace walls.' So Ertl was right. The whole valley of the Chinijo must be terraced, indicating a thriving agricultural community. Juan Blanco and Celso had already pointed out the position on the opposite ridge of what Ertl believed to be a fort. They said they had seen it many times when gathering the bark of quinine trees, and I had no reason to doubt them.

'Look,' cried Yoli – 'smoke!' Sure enough, a thin wisp was filtering out of the trees half way up the slope opposite us. 'Those town councillors must be very fit,' remarked Maria, 'to get that far in so short a time.' This marked the limit of our reconnaissance, but now I was convinced that Ertl's account was largely true. It remained only to locate his 'Paititi', and that would take a major expedition.

Back at our base camp at Incapampa water was running low. Tania had used her socks to filter the muddy water from the pools, but without more rain we could not remain here long. Israel, a muleteer who sported a plastic army helmet from which he fed his beast, came in with a fat *jochi* – a large rodent also called *paca* or *labba* – that he had shot. Brittain eyed the animal thoughtfully. 'Do you know anything about *jochi*?' I asked her. 'Well, I keep guinea pigs back home,' she smiled sweetly. 'That's good,' I replied. 'Will you skin and cook this one for us?' She did, and the meat – not unlike veal – was delicious. It was a welcome change from our dehydrated rations. In my log I noted, 'Future expeditions must bring Millbank bags to filter water, a shotgun for *jochi*, and snake-bite serum – if only to give the locals confidence.'

Thick mist blanketed our ridge as we broke camp next morning and retraced our steps to Quilapituni. Even when the sun rose, the tightly wooded slopes of Cerro Paititi were shrouded in low, clammy clouds. It was as if the area was determined to hide its secrets to the bitter end.

Back in Guanay, the alcalde gave a dinner at which he encouraged us to return and unravel the mystery of 'Paititi'. Doubtless he hoped Oswaldo's flippant suggestion that the site could be another Machu Picchu would bring in hordes of tourists. Indeed, the municipality had long been asking the prefectura to send archaeologists, and proposals had been submitted by a delegation from Guanay. They could hardly believe their luck when we appeared, apparently in prompt response. It was all a coincidence, though the support so readily given to us by the prefectura might have been because of Guanay's request.

Always short of interpreters, I had been pleased to meet a British miner in the town. Tim Williams had spent several years there and, most importantly, knew the rivers. His video of the rapids on the Mapiri and Kaka rivers was especially valuable. If we were to take traditional boats from the Andes to the Atlantic via the Rio Beni, we must first navigate these.

Seated in the Bar Alemán, we ran through it several times. One rapid, known as the *cachuela* (cataract) Retama, could prove an obstacle. Indeed, the redoubtable Colonel Fawcett had almost been wrecked nearby in 1906. A rock the size of a small house stood in the centre of a narrow canyon, dividing the tumbling water. Local boats had capsized here, and lives had been lost. At certain water levels the rock was a real hazard, but from the video I reckoned it was about grade 3 (on a scale up to 6) – moderately difficult. 'June is a good month to run it,' advised Tim, 'when the river is lower.' But he was talking about running it with long, thin mahogany boats, powered by 55 h.p. outboards, or simply balsa rafts. These were regularly used by the people of this hill town to reach the major centre of Rurrenabaque downstream. I wondered if a craft built of reeds would get through.

At the end of July, Jim Masters and his team returned from examining the cataracts in Brazil. We all met in La Paz, where Jim reported that, with the exception of three or four rapids, the cataracts could be overcome. The rest would have to be portaged around. We had also examined alternative routes to the Amazon from southern Bolivia, but at the end of a morning's conference I said, 'OK, so we'll investigate this "Paititi" site and then take the Beni route to the ocean.'

The prefect of La Paz, German Velasco Cortés, was delighted by the decision. He kindly offered support for a full-scale expedition, and at a well-attended reception in the prefectura he presented us with a splendid medal. Erik and Máximo Catari pored over the maps and photos. 'Can you build a reed boat that will shoot these rapids?' I asked. For a while the Aymaras said nothing, then Erik nodded. 'I'm sure my ancestors did.'

Back in England, I eventually met Ross Salmon at his home in

Plymouth. Sadly, he was now blind and partially crippled, but he had good recall of his explorations. Yoli – in Britain again, to help with the organization of our new expedition – had come with me, and as soon as Ross heard her speak he seemed to come alive. 'You are Colombian?' he asked. 'And I believe you are of Inca descent.' 'Yes,' she replied in Spanish. 'I recognized the accent,' Ross added. He had farmed cattle in Colombia until the light aircraft he was piloting had collided with a vulture when coming in to land. Ross, the only survivor of the accident, was found in the jungle with almost every major bone broken. But after two years in English hospitals he had still had a burning ambition to seek the lost Inca empire. So he and Yoli had a long discussion in Spanish while I watched a remarkable video of a programme he had made for Westward TV. His advice was invaluable – especially about snakes. A bite from a bushmaster, not far from our search area, had once put him back in hospital for many weeks. He was a supreme survivor, having also been shot down by 'friendly' anti-aircraft guns over England while a pilot in the Fleet Air Arm in the Second World War as well as having been in several serious car crashes in Devon.

3

Into the Field

It was amusing and instructive to watch people's reactions. There were the Prudent, who said: 'This [going on an expedition into Brazil] is an extra-ordinarily foolish thing to do.' There were the Wise, who said: 'This is an extraordinarily foolish thing to do: but at least you will know better next time.' There were the Very Wise, who said, 'This is a foolish thing to do, but not nearly so foolish as it sounds.'

Peter Fleming, *Brazilian Adventure*, 1933

TO ASSEMBLE A full team, we needed tough jungle-bashers and boat-crew members as well as archaeologists, medical personnel and other scientists: quite a spectrum of talents. To find such people, I start by calling on a number of old friends who have taken part in previous expeditions. Foremost among these was Lieutenant-Colonel Ernie Durey, another retired Royal Engineer who, like Jim Masters, had slogged his way through the Darién rainforest from Panama to Colombia with me in 1972 and two years later had done much the same, from one end of the Congo river to the other with a team of sappers. Jim and Ernie were very old friends, and Jim cunningly sold the idea of Ernie's participation to Mrs Durey by saying, 'It would only be for a matter of three or four weeks.'

A Canadian Air Force captain, Ivan Wood, had been on SES expedi-tions in Romania and Nepal. Eric Niemi, the dependable and practical American biology teacher, had been with me in Central America, India and Mongolia, and barrister Caroline Ralph had accompanied us to Ethiopia. Perhaps the most unconventional role was that of Marigold Verity-Dick, a leading harpist, who became the expedition musicologist. She had several times joined us in this capacity in Asia and with *Kota Mama* in 1999, when her sweet evening recitals had soothed many a savage breast.

Richard Snailham was another very old friend, and had been with me in Zaire, Chile, Mongolia, Sierra Leone, Bolivia and several times in Ethiopia. We had met in 1965 at Sandhurst, when I had chatted over coffee in the mess to this newly appointed civilian lecturer. I was planning to take a large party of officer cadets to the Ethiopian Rift Valley, and needed a deputy. He turned out to be a good second in command, fell in love with Ethiopia, ran a bar efficiently, and wrote reams of press releases.

For the rest, the formation of the team is, in part, a bit like the one-time Conservative Party method of finding a leader – some members just seem to emerge. I meet them after lectures, they write in to the SES – we had about a hundred applications that way, some of them patently from nutcases – or they are friends of members or of previous expedition participants. We are a growing fraternity.

We have to guard against allowing rotten apples to get into the barrel. On *Kota Mama 2* in 1999 there were a few whose attitudes caused me unnecessary anguish, during and after the expedition. This time I wanted no moaners or extremists, no one with a personal agenda contrary to the overall aims. So everyone was interviewed and their background checked.

There was a wide age range in the new team: the youngest was nineteen, but I also had four septuagenarians and six of us were in our sixties. Ernie Durey said, 'It just shows how difficult it is to get sheltered accommodation these days.'

The British Army looks kindly on its people applying for places on potentially arduous overseas expeditions, for these represent a useful chance for soldiers to apply some of their existing skills and to learn others. This is what the army calls 'adventure training', and years before I had been much involved with it as an instructor at Sandhurst and as a leader of large-scale expeditions. In all, I had seventeen serving regular soldiers with me this time, including many members of my own regiment, the Royal Engineers, and some from the Royal Army Veterinary Corps.

Retired US Air Force major Bill Holmes became our information officer. A visiting fellow of Wolfson College, Oxford, and an expert on environmental law, he came up with some useful intelligence on Paititi and on ex-Nazi and neo-Nazi activity in South America. Paul Overton, a well-travelled former Royal Navy physical-training instructor, became my adjutant and settled down to work at Motcombe, with Jim, Melissa (our expeditions organizer), Anne (my PA), Anne-Marie (Melissa's assistant) and Sarah-Jane Lewis (our dynamic PR lady).

One of the most important ways of raising funds is through sponsorship. Some of us sported blue baseball hats with 'JPK' on the front. These proclaimed the backing given by J. P. Knight Ltd, Kentish tugowners, who sponsored the big trimaran. HSBC, the banking conglomerate, had insured all our craft in 1999, and, as there had been few claims, were happy to do so again. (The risks of a giant floating straw bale doing much damage to third parties was minimal.) We also took with us five HSBC staff – Craig Cocks, Carla Turner, Mike Lulham, Kaye Parker and Craig Churcher.

I wanted to have a traditional raft built in Bolivia to accompany our trimaran. It would be a useful comparison to see how six or seven logs of balsa jointed together would stand up to the buffeting on the way to the sea. It would be built in Guanay, and we were to call it *Southern Gailes* – not in a misspelling of our anticipated river weather, but to mark the generosity of a Scots company which designs and makes golf courses.

A chance meeting by Bill Holmes with Dr Vijith Kannangara on the London underground had resulted in our sponsorship by Affno, his Sri Lankan company specializing in e-business design and engineering. Affno was to set up and maintain a web site, which would enable audiences to follow our progress worldwide. It was also an important part of a programme to link schools in Great Britain with children in Bolivia and Brazil.

Funds have also to come from the participants themselves. Their subscriptions included flights out and back, board and lodging for four months (or a proportion of that time), and a share of all the other manifold expedition costs – stores transshipment, fuel, vehicle and boat hire, administration, and so on.

Jim Masters, Paul Overton and Ernie Durey, our quartermaster, were concerning themselves not only with personnel but with *matériel*. Supplies and equipment were rolling in. Boxes to fit on the backs of mules were made – each to be taken out, packed with kit, as personal baggage by expedition members. Outboard engines, generators, inflatable dinghies, paddles, canoe helmets and a Tirfor jack were obtained. Maps came from the Royal Engineers, three army radios were borrowed from the Royal Signals, and for internal communication we had Motorola UHF and VHF radios, with NERA satellite phones for long-distance work.

In April 2001 the Royal Oak in Motcombe was the setting for an important occasion: a final briefing for almost all the expedition's members, most of whom had not so far met one another. Some thirty-five were able to assemble – a bonanza for local Dorset bed-and-breakfast establishments on a chill, pre-season weekend. Using slides, I explained the achievements of our previous expeditions, then Richard Snailham spoke of Bolivia, Bill Holmes presented the research he had done on Paititi and the Nazis, and the vets described how the mules would be brought into play. The plan for the forthcoming phases was then outlined. Meanwhile the expedition's three doctors were interviewing everyone to find out our state of health and preclude any medical problems. T-shirts, insect repellent and sunblock were given out. The kind of kit we should all need was discussed, and ways of acquiring it from our preferred vendors were explained. Everyone now knew their role and how we intended to tackle the expedition.

A few weeks later friends including a number of diplomats and sponsors gathered at Canning House, the London centre for Latin American studies, to wish us well. Our epic jungle expedition that crossed the Darién Gap from Panama to Colombia in 1972 had enjoyed a similar send-off there. I prayed that *Kota Mama 3* would not prove such a test of men and material as that venture had been.

'There's talk of a revolution,' said Yoli, over the echoing phone line from La Paz. 'Roads to the Yungas are blocked by protesting coca farmers, so we can't get to Guanay. It's still raining, and Erik has had terrible difficulty drying the reeds for the boat. Our stores are still in customs, and it's going to take something like an Act of Parliament to grant you a gun licence. A mysterious Austrian – or perhaps he's a German – has been attacking Oswaldo and the expedition in the press. Furthermore, the director of DINAAR whom we dealt with last year has been sacked.'

Listening to this at our expedition base in Dorset, surrounded by signs about foot-and-mouth restrictions and wondering how we could replace the dehydrated meat rations that the disease now made it impossible to export, I thought, 'What else can go wrong?' 'But otherwise, everything is fine,' she went on, ever optimistic.

A week later, when she met me in La Paz, this extraordinary woman had overcome most of our problems, though the official permit for the shotgun with which to shoot giant rodents to supplement our rations was still awaited.

*

We descended on Bolivia in three waves: I went ahead, next came an advance party, and then the main body. Yoli was there already.

It was May 2001. My first days in La Paz were troubled ones. A disturbed sleep pattern, caused by the flight out, was made worse by the noisy protests of the coca farmers and the wail of sirens outside the Sucre Palace Hotel.

From the noise in the avenue below, I gathered that crowds of *campesinos* were being dispersed by baton-wielding police. Coca has long been a staple crop in Bolivia. The leaves of the coca bush, which grows along the eastern slopes of the Andes, are chewed by workers, usually with the addition of a little lime. This produces a minute quantity of cocaine to reduce hunger and combat fatigue. Coca is also infused in boiling water to make a mildly narcotic drink – *mate de coca* – which gives one a slight kick. This is quite legal, and is supplied in every hotel and café. However, the US government believed production was far in excess of domestic needs, and the future destinations of the vast surpluses were well known. Pressure on the Bolivian government had led to a ban on the growing of coca in the Yungas – hence the trouble.

With their customary efficiency, the police had cleared the avenue by the time the shops opened and I strolled across to a bookshop to see if any of Hans Ertl's publications might be available. Browsing among the packed shelves I had a strange feeling of being watched, but then a gringo in a sports jacket and cords was always bound to attract attention. I carried on my fruitless search. Leaving the store I glanced back. Half concealed by the shelves stood two men in black leather jackets, who turned away as soon as my eyes met their reflective sunglasses. When the nearer one's arm protruded from behind the bookcase, I saw on it a crimson armband with a white circle in which was emblazoned a black swastika. 'What do you think of that?' I whispered to Yoli, who had come to find me. 'I think we should move on, John,' she said quietly. Why were Nazi supporters in this shop I wondered? Perhaps they too were seeking books by Ertl.

Next day I had TV interviews and important meetings with high-ranking Bolivians during which it would be more productive if I stayed awake, so I got stuck into the *mate de coca*.

On 4 May the advance party flew in and the nightly disturbances continued. 'They should call this city La Guerra not La Paz,' commented Prince Leopold as he flew in from Geneva.

One of the most important meetings to be held was with the Bolivian archaeologists. DINAAR had now been restyled Unidad Nacional de Arqueología, or UNAR, which we now worked through on archaeological matters. Meeting Oswaldo there, I was introduced to his colleagues who were to accompany us. Juan Domingo Faldin, in his fifties, was said to have much experience in the jungle, whereas Ruden Plaza, a younger man, had good general skills. They would come with Oswaldo to the 'Paititi' site. A friend from Santa Cruz, Wilma Winkler, would join us later to study rock inscriptions, or petroglyphs, as we descended the Rio Beni. Unrolling our Royal Engineer-produced 3-D map and the Bolivian Air Force aerial photos, I pointed out that the investigation of the 'Paititi' site would be no picnic. 'We archaeologists are used to such conditions,' retorted Juan Domingo.

Hurrying from this meeting, we were just in time for another important event. Just a Drop is a charity run by the World Travel Market that helps to finance water projects in the developing nations. The trustees had kindly agreed to provide \$3,500 towards the cost of installing a distribution scheme for clean water at the village of Hampaturi Achachicala in the department of La Paz. As a member of the charity's board, I had felt this was a most worthwhile project and was delighted that Prince Leopold could present the cheque. The alcalde of La Paz received it, press photographers snapped away, and we felt that this was another small way in which the *Kota Mama* expedition could help the poor people of Bolivia.

At the Sucre Palace an e-mail from Melissa Dice at Motcombe awaited me. It said that the Royal Signals' radios had still not arrived. Somehow £60,000 worth of high-tech gear would have to be flown out by our generous sponsors, DHL.

Some things went right, however. Teddy Jauregui, a keen Anglophile who had once run a business in Britain, came forward to help. Before I got to La Paz he had told Yoli he was descended from a Lord Masters: 'Maybe I am second cousin, twice removed, to your Jim and Gerry,' he had said.

German Velasco Cortés, the prefect of La Paz and his assistant, Jorge Velarde, were friends too. They had lent us transport for the reconnaissance, and promised more now. Although Yoli had to deliver a telephonic rocket to some of the prefect's staff, two four-wheel-drive pickups and a huge Volvo lorry eventually rolled up at the hotel.

To skirt round the rebellious coca farmers' blockade on the road to Guanay I had devised a neat Plan B: go to Lake Titicaca and take a mountain track from there to Mapiri. This was neatly scotched when the alcalde of Mapiri reported landslides covering that track. So we had to hope that we could somehow get through on the route I had used during the reconnaissance. After climbing over the La Cumbre pass at 15,500 feet, we were halted as usual at the military checkpoint; but Yoli's authoritative-sounding '*¡Misión oficial!*' again worked well.

Then the fun began, as once again we descended the terrifying track to the Yungas. On average, twenty-six vehicles a year take an involuntary plunge over the precipice. The highest death toll ever in any single-vehicle crash occurred in 1983, when Carlos Pizarroso Inde drove his truck into the depths with over 100 passengers behind him. 'A metal memorial cross is probably more effective than a caution sign,' Jim thought.

At San Juan we passed under waterfalls. Passengers in open lorries get a dowsing here, but luckily we, in our closed car, remained dry.

A pleasant discovery was that our driver's name was Angel. 'We obviously have had a most diligent angel watching over us,' said Leopold as we stopped for a pee.

The locals also invoke divine aid for this journey: as we set off, a driver had sprinkled alcohol on his bus's bonnet from a small phial, and other passengers threw bread to the stray dogs that lined the route, believing them to be the reincarnated spirits of the road's previous victims.

We did not stay in the Hotel Panamericano at Guanay this time: Don Lucho offered us greater space and security in a high-walled compound with heavy iron gates. This became our base – Ernie Durey's empire – and we named it Fort Mogg after one of the SES's greatest supporters, General Sir John Mogg, a distinguished soldier and founder of the Army's 'adventure training' programme. Sadly, he died while this book was in preparation.

A few days later a second wave of members came down from La Paz, bringing our incoming numbers to forty-four. We had a growing nucleus of Bolivians, too: as well as Oswaldo, Juan Domingo, and Ruden Plaza there was José Luis Buitrago – Ernie Durey's English-speaking driver, procurer and Mr Fixit.

We were a fairly international party. In among the forty-four – soldiers, archaeologists, medics, bank staff and others – were the Belgian Prince Leopold d'Arenberg, the Americans Bill Holmes and Eric Niemi, the Canadian Ivan Wood, our Sri Lankan IT and communications chief, Peter Kannangara (Vijith's brother), and of course the Colombian Yoli, our chief liaison officer, with widespread and valuable contacts in high places. There were so many of us together – more than at any other time in the expedition – that we overspilled into a nearby house and two of Guanay's hotels. The going rate in them seemed to be $2 per night, and a recurring word in the guidebooks is 'basic'. We measured them in cockerels – how many there were picking around in the backyard. Ours were four-cockerel hotels.

Before dinner I established a pattern which was followed every evening for the next four months and gave a briefing. In the Army it was an 'O' Group; on camel treks in Kenya a *baraza*. Essentially it is the same thing. I would say where we were and what we had done that day (with some participation from those who had done it), what we were going to do on the morrow, who was going to do it, and when.

Ernie and his enthusiastic local helper, Francisca Torrez Martinez, produced a magnificent 'regimental dinner' (twenty-six of us were military or ex-military) to welcome the newcomers, and the food was washed down with Kohlberg, perhaps the best of Bolivia's eminently drinkable red wines.

The following morning brought the usual mix of good and bad news. In the Guanay council chamber the deputy alcalde told us that the cutters he had organized to clear a path for us to 'Paititi' were on their way there. But among them was the strange Austrian who had been attacking us in the press. He was said to be a *huaquero* or treasure-hunter, and had been included in the party because he told the authorities he was one of our expedition. He had asked the Guanay council for financial help, but they knew him too well and had refused. However, he claimed to have maps, photos and documents from Hans Ertl. 'Is this some fiendish Teutonic plot?' I asked Yoli. 'He seems to be making a hell of an effort to prevent the scientific exploration of the site.'

The deputy alcalde and the councillors were extremely keen to be able to announce the discovery of the legendary Paititi. They could clearly imagine coachloads of tourists pouring into their town. However, we stated quite firmly that we could make no promises. 'We'll survey the site, examine the ruins for archaeological evidence, and make a foot trail,' I said. Yoli translated, and signed a protocol document to this effect before shaking hands.

Another important component of the expedition was our community-aid team. This was co-ordinated by retired Dorset schoolteacher Shirley Critchley. Tireless and dedicated to helping wherever she could, she had raised money to buy seeds to replace crops lost in a disastrous flood which had struck Guanay earlier in the year and in a fire caused by the petrol station exploding. Arriving there now, she told me, 'I saw three teenagers sitting on mattresses that were still charred, doing their homework in the dark. They hadn't even a candle. Nobody seems to be clearing the debris up. I gave out some sewing kits that I'd been given by church groups in the Bournemouth area. They shared their meal with me.'

Yoli had already handed over a handsome donation from GlaxoSmith-Kline to rebuild the Guanay clinic. Unfortunately local rivalries surfaced. The authorities in Mapiri, in whose orbit 'Paititi' lay, felt left out. They asked us for $3,000 and a computer. An ugly little squabble developed, and I left it to the two councils to sort out. The Guanay alcalde later apologized, and we said we would do what we could to help Mapiri. In the end our medical team and dental surgeon worked long and hard there, and Prince Leopold talked to the local high school, Colegio Nacional Mixto Reverendo Padre 'Gotardo Kaiser', and generously donated $1,000.

Now it was time to send off a reconnaissance party to blaze a trail to the 'Paititi' site. Leopold was to lead this small group, with Drew Craig and a former sapper officer, Mike How, accompanied by three local men.

On 7 May Ernie drove them 50 miles, across several swollen rivers, to the roadhead in the village of Quilapituni. It took five hours. The village headman, Celso, looked crestfallen: mules, supposedly arranged by the alcalde of Guanay, had not materialized. Using some tact, Leopold secured five rather seedy-looking horses.

The next day his party reached Waricunca and set up a base camp. After a night of heavy rain the track running steeply down to Smith's Crossing on the Rio Chinijo was treacherous. Furthermore enormous ferns now made it impenetrable for the loaded packhorses. At the crossing, Drew Craig fell badly and twisted a knee. He had to limp painfully back up to the camp and stay there while Leopold and Mike forged on to the top of a spur – Leopold's Spur – and along the ridge to meet the path-cutters coming back from 'Paititi'.

This encounter boded ill. The dreaded Austrian was with them, and also the powerfully built unemployed gold miner Juan Blanco, who had been our guide on the 2000 reconnaissance to Incapampa. There was something about this intimidating fellow that rang alarm bells. Although he knew him well from the previous year, and spoke fluent Spanish, Leopold found he could glean no information about the site from Juan

Blanco, or from the Austrian. It was as if they were determined to hide everything from us.

'You must be aggressive to get the merchandise over' was Leopold's way of telling me, back at Guanay, that we needed to build an aerial ropeway to ferry stores over the Rio Chinijo at Smith's Crossing. 'From Waricunca down to the river loaded animals could pass, but once across you must ascend the spur on hands and knees. Maybe the engineers can make a way up it for animals.'

And he also had disquieting news of another kind. Quite contrary to our agreement, the alcalde's cutters, with Juan Blanco and the Austrian, had cleared a route from Incapampa down the extremely steep slope to the Chinijo which we had deemed impassable on the previous year's reconnaissance – not from Waricunca to Smith's Crossing, which I had recommended and which Leopold's team had shown to be a goer. They had fixed a *maroma* or wire rope across the Chinijo, and had cut a route steeply up the other side to the ridge and continued along to the 'Paititi' site.

Even here they seemed to be playing us false. Along the ridge to 'Paititi' there were two routes: one longer but over more or less flat ground to a point above the site; the other a switchback route over seven separate ravines, each one involving a severe scramble up and down. The latter was the route they had cut! It was almost as if they were determined to make the route hard for us – perhaps even to make us fail altogether.

One of the Guanay councillors who had been on the mountain with him told Yoli that the Austrian – called by Bolivians 'el alemán' (the German) – had said, 'This should fox the gringos. They'll never get up here.' Of course it did not fox the gringos, who, though slipping and sliding, sweating and puffing, eventually followed the path and, thanks to more disinterested guidance at the time, managed to turn off at the right place to get down to the ruins. In short, it was a highly satisfactory instance of local obstructionism taking on British determination and coming off a poor second. The more these people did to frustrate our plans, the more we wondered why. Perhaps they believed the legend that a great Inca treasure was concealed there, and that an Inca ruler had fashioned a long chain of gold which his people had carried away from the conquistadors and hidden in the jungle.

Yoli explained the route problem to the deputy alcalde, who promised to deal with Juan Blanco and the Austrian. My resolve to get to 'Paititi' was all the greater, even if we had to go through uncut territory.

But how to do it? The march was organized on the lines of an old-style assault on Everest. We had a base camp at Guanay with all our supplies (and in our case the chance of buying more in local shops). From there Ernie would push forward what stores he could to Quilapituni – up the Ice Fall to the Western Cwm as it were. Mules would carry more up to Waricunca, our South Col. Leopold's Spur was Hillary's Step. The only difference: nobody hangs around at the top of Everest, whereas we were proposing to work for a while at 'Paititi'. So more stores would have to be carried – by mule or man – to our objective. Our Sherpas would have to be Aymara or Quechua Indians.

4

To 'Worry Conker'

There were the Romantic, who appeared to believe that if everyone did this
sort of thing all the time the world's troubles would soon be over. There were
the Envious, who thanked God they were not coming; and there were the
other sort, who said with varying degrees of insincerity that they would give
anything to come.

Peter Fleming, *Brazilian Adventure*, 1933

ON 16 MAY, Tac HQ, as I called my small command group, was ready
to move forward with Warrant Officer Craig Halford, a Royal Engineer
clerk of works from the Gibraltar garrison, and his engineers. Yoli had
hired two local cooks, a man and a woman. 'We only have one spare tent.
Would you share it?' she asked tactfully. 'Oh yes,' grinned the lady. 'He
prefers boys. I am quite safe!' We also took from Guanay a rugged,
dwarfish Quechua Indian with a wide smile and a mouth full of broken
teeth. Carlos, who had spent years mining gold in cramped conditions,
was immensely strong. He proved to be a real Man Friday in the weeks
ahead.

We moved off to the crack of exploding fireworks – a normal Bolivian
farewell. The road was axle deep in mud, but we ploughed through to
Quilapituni and camped on its football ground. I knew this road well
from our 2000 reconnaissance.

On the reconnaissance it had been cold by night and dry by day and
I had worried about a possible shortage of drinking water. Now it rained
from time to time, turning the road into a skidpan, and the view across
the soccer pitch was more Passchendaele than White Hart Lane. Craig
Halford with his section of Royal Engineers had spent some hours
helping to dig out a stranded lorry. 'Nothing will reach this village until
it dries out,' he said gloomily. The convoy carrying the main body of the
expedition next day took almost seven hours to get there from Guanay,

being seriously embogged seven times and arriving wasp-bitten, mud-spattered and exhausted.

Alasdair Crosby, a journalist with the *Jersey Evening Post*, had sat on the top of the Mercedes 3-tonner and leaped down into the quagmire every now and then to help push it free. On the drier bits he likened the narrow road to the driveway of a substantial but run-down private property in Hampshire.

But Quilapituni did have electric power, and Mike Smith — another IT expert, and our communications officer in the field — plugged in his laptop and happily passed on e-mails. And Yoli, with a cellphone provided by ENTEL, the Bolivian phone company, was able to speak to Jim Masters, who was by Lake Titicaca supervising the construction of the reed boats. 'Snow is forecast,' he told her.

Another surprise was the unscheduled arrival of Oswaldo with two friends. 'We walk eight days from Sorata.' They had come along the Mapiri Trail ('only for hardcore trekkers'), which runs parallel to the Rio Chinijo through Incapampa to Mapiri. Oswaldo had injured his ribs in a fall, and our medical officer, Jo Brown, prescribed a few days' rest. But 'I must go to hospital,' insisted Oswaldo, and he disappeared on a truck to Guanay. We never saw our director of archaeology for the rest of the expedition, and thereafter I turned to the cheery young Scottish archaeologist Bruce Mann, for archaeological advice.

Our advanced base was to be established on the ridge at Waricunca. From there the Royal Engineers would push down to Smith's Crossing. Their first task was to build a 50-yard aerial ropeway over the river and then make a path up the extremely steep spur that we had named in honour of Leopold. With them as interpreter went James Culshaw, an amiable, fair-haired Nottingham University student from Jersey, who spoke fluent Spanish and was thus a vital member of the team. Craig Halford's team would then clear a track forward along the ridge for around 4 miles until it met the trail cut previously by the alcalde's workers. There was no way that I would contemplate using the steeply inclined route down from Incapampa to the Chinijo that had been cut for us.

I am not a great fan of mules or packhorses. Working with them is worse than trying to lead a troop of monkeys. I prefer elephants every time. Richard, however, has no such misgivings, and rides mules regularly with his tour groups in Ethiopia. And in this case packhorses and a few mules it had to be. At least we provided some employment, and thus revenue, by hiring muleteers and their animals from Quilapituni and Mapiri.

In Britain we had recruited a strong team to manage the animal-transport side. Katie Gledhill, a captain in the Royal Army Veterinary Corps, led it, assisted by Lance Corporal Vanessa Hamilton and three other volunteers (two of them HSBC bank staff enjoying something of a change from their branch duties). While the forward-base quartermaster – Andi Player, a builder from Poole – sorted out the stores, Katie and Vanessa, working in the drizzle, examined the pack animals. Only a few of the promised mules materialized. 'I was expecting flea-bitten, ropy, worm-ridden animals,' said Katie, 'but in fact they were in remarkably good condition, and the muleteers looked after them surprisingly well.'

For their owners, the animals represented a major asset, so they were looked after with the same degree of care that a self-employed trucker might lavish on his vehicle. But the nature of the country did cause difficulties: the mules got ticks in their ears, and some of them became lame, or were bitten by vampire bats, which would land near the animals at night and then waddle up to them to bite their legs.

The packhorses were much smaller than mules and could not carry our custom-built wooden boxes, so we had to improvise some sacks, made waterproof by being dipped in locally grown rubber. They smelt abominable, but kept our kit dry. However, the special mule boxes were still of value to keep our stores reasonably intact at the base.

The animals conveyed food and equipment up the 8½ miles to Waricunca in relays, and in small groups the rest of the team eventually marched there in five hours (including Alasdair Crosby, who insisted on spelling our destination 'Worry Conker'). A skeleton staff remained at Quilapituni under Andi Player, to look after the returning pack animals, load them up with supplies that Ernie had driven in from Guanay, and send them back up to Worry Conker.

Our route to Waricunca lay along the Mapiri Trail. In 1900 the entire Bolivian Army had marched down this old Inca road to lose a war with Brazil. Colonel Fawcett used it subsequently, but it then fell into decay until opened for trekkers in the 1950s. 'It will never compete with long-distance Himalayan trails,' said Alasdair, 'with their guest-houses and other tourist facilities.'

Bolivia has wild scenery, archaeological sites and truly Indian countryfolk, but lacks the amenities that are already evident in Peru. 'I'm glad it doesn't compete yet,' said Katie. 'The Inca Trail to Machu Picchu is like the Pennine Way on August Bank Holiday.'

The Mapiri Trail was hard going as, squelching along in the liquid clay, we climbed steadily. Juan Blanco, who had returned to us with instructions to be more helpful, killed a large, multicoloured snake with the butt of his rifle, but we were too intent on keeping upright to examine it. After a couple of hours we reached the Rio India, a small, clear stream where canteens could be refilled. In spite of the rain, our lack of water was still a worry.

Juan Domingo and Ruden Plaza, our Bolivian archaeologists from UNAR, found the going particularly hard, and it soon became obvious that their jungle experience was more limited than I had been led to believe. Our column therefore slowed down, and, fearing we might not reach water by nightfall, I pressed on alone to the San José saddle, leaving Paul Hortop, the lithe jungle-experienced warrant officer who was to administer our field camps, to bring up the rest.

At San José, I found the animal-transport team which had accompanied the engineers. Distressed by the conditions, the girls complained, 'We can't use animals like this.' Also, 'The muleteers can't understand us.' Obviously the need to learn some Spanish – stressed at our final briefing – had not been taken seriously enough. I pointed out that the animals were essential for our supply system, and they marched back down to Quilapituni to get another load. In fact Katie and Vanessa cheered up as the expedition progressed, and played a vital role.

By 4 p.m. the Bolivian archaeologists were in no fit state to go further, so we put up our tents on the narrow saddle, refilled our water bottles, and ate a hearty supper of rice and tuna. On this high ground, Yoli's cellphone came to life again. 'The prefectura's vehicles have still not reached Guanay,' she groaned. 'Ernie will find a way,' I grunted, erecting my pup tent. I was too tired to move when the rain, leaking through a hole freshly cut by ants in my small shelter, soaked my sleeping-bag. The same ants practically devoured the fly-sheet of the tent which we had lent to the unhappy archaeologists, who without Oswaldo had no tents of their own.

Low cloud enveloped us and penetrated everything, but with the sunrise it dispersed and by eight o'clock the next morning the temperature was in the nineties. The horses and mules seemed to sense that it was only a short march to the next stop and were unusually co-operative as they were loaded.

It took only seventy minutes along a steep-sided ridge to reach Waricunca, where in a broad jungle clearing James Culshaw greeted us at a blue tarpaulin which was now the advanced base. The engineers had already gone forward to Smith's Crossing, from where Craig Halford radioed me, 'I've sliced my hand open on a bamboo – they're as sharp as hell.' I couldn't afford to lose my engineer leader, and dispatched Jo Brown to stitch him up. Delighted by the thought of action, she heaved her heavy pack on to her back and set off at the double.

At 4,000 feet, Waricunca was a pleasant place for a camp site. Although the day-time temperatures were extremely hot – often exceeding 95 °F – the nights were cool and pleasant, and the clear skies meant that the dome of the heavens was spangled with bright stars from one horizon to the other. Bees, wasps, stinging insects and mosquitoes continued to be a nuisance during the day, but their comparative absence during the night-time hours was another reason to enjoy the cooler evenings. Down at Smith's Crossing, however, the sappers suffered badly from the wasps, which seemed to dance in Deet, the insect repellent we preferred.

In the days ahead Paul Hortop got advance base organized, and the flags of all the nations of our team flew from tall poles – including that of my homeland, Jersey. This little flag was given to me thirty years ago by the *Jersey Evening Post*, and I always carry it. I'm not a superstitious person, but it seems always to have brought me luck.

Down in the valley, Ernie drove supplies to Andi Player up at Quilapituni; Katie and her horses then ferried them up to Waricunca and down again to Smith's Crossing. Quickly stocks and personnel were built up rather as on a mountain expedition. However, for us the summit was the site at the Rio Tulani, and as this was two days' hard march from Smith's Crossing the food there would be limited and boring.

Spectacled bears and jaguars were known to prowl around the Waricunca area, and one jaguar was certainly attracted by the smell of the pack animals. 'Look at those paw-marks,' said Paul Hortop, a keen naturalist, pointing at the soft ground around the waterhole. The mules and horses appeared quite nervous about the proximity of this large predator, and it has to be said that they were not the only ones to be slightly apprehensive about moving too far away from the camp, though it was unlikely that a jaguar would attack humans. Nothing untoward happened, however, and Waricunca remained a peaceful and restful interlude on the journey, the unsaddled pack animals providing a pastoral element to the scene as they grazed undisturbed by the rumble of rocks being dynamited at the crossing-point in the gorge below.

We now had many friends from Quilapituni – probably thanks to the good work of the medics. 'I've found an Indian who knows the ruins well,' said Yoli, introducing me to Angel Quisbert. 'I have seen two monoliths at Paititi,' said the sad-looking young man. 'Then please come with us,' I replied. Muleteers and their animals were becoming more readily available from Quilapituni, and several of the muleteers' wives were also helping us. One – Benita – knew the folk-history of the lost city. 'It is at the top of the mountain,' she said. 'The buildings are of white stones, and it is guarded by serpents,' she told us as she stirred a pot of stew. 'And,' she continued, 'there is a golden bell in a cave, entwined by a large snake. That is the symbol of Paititi.'

Sitting outside my tent at Waricunca with a mug of *mate de coca*, I watched the first rays of the sun dapple the eternal snows of the Andes. I wondered how on earth we could get sufficient rations forward to sustain a large archaeological party. I was also worried about the meagre water supply at the advanced base. The small spring was in danger of drying up as men, mules and horses used it. We needed rain.

Down at the crossing-point, the explosive provided through the alcaldía of Guanay was proving old and unreliable and there were some unnerving misfires. These meant an anxious wait to see if the charge would go off, before a courageous soul had to go forward, pull out the detonator, and repeat the set-up. In spite of the sappers' efforts, however, on 20 May Craig reported that there was no way we could get horses or mules up Leopold's Spur. 'It will have to be porters,' I told Yoli. 'Please see how many Celso can produce.' Paul Hortop reckoned we could use sacks for manhandling stores, and Ernie scoured Guanay for rucksacks. 'All the food will have to be dehydrated,' I told him. Luckily we had a vast quantity of beef-flavoured lumps of *soya carne* and noodles, procured by Yoli in La Paz when we had been prevented from bringing dried-meat products from the UK. Although they were pretty unappetizing, they did fill one's belly. 'Oh for the dried-beef granules we had to leave in Dorset,' muttered Paul as he chewed at a solid hunk of soya. 'Well, Shackleton's men on Elephant Island ate nothing but seal blubber for four months,' said Alasdair philosophically. 'Worse things happen in war,' replied Paul, and as usual went about his thankless task with good grace. A veteran of expeditions in the jungles of Central America, this unflappable soldier was quite accustomed to administrative problems in the field.

The next supply train brought up a map that Drew Craig in Guanay had annotated with information furnished by the alcalde, who seemed to be insisting that the route his cutters had made – down the steep incline from Incapampa, over the Chinijo, and up the other side – was better than the one I had been contemplating. Ever since looking at it in 2000, I had set my face against this way – it appeared useless for animals and a great strain for men – but perhaps we had better re-examine it. So Paul Overton, one of the fittest of us all, took a small team a couple of miles along the Mapiri Trail to Incapampa.

'If, as I believe, this route is also impassable for mules,' I told Ernie at Guanay over the NERA satellite phone, 'the only alternative will again be to convert the muleteers to porters and get *them* to carry the supplies. But it'll mean far less can be taken to "Paititi", and I'm concerned about whether sufficient rations can be transported through such extremely difficult terrain.' 'Your shotgun is going to come in useful,' he replied – 'you can live on *jochi* for a time.' But so far these tasty rodents had proved elusive.

That the muleteers were to become porters was not the best of news for them. They had a lively fear of snakes, and promptly demanded more money before they would venture across the river into the dense jungles on the far side of the gorge.

Paul Overton's group had it easy at first. The Mapiri Trail was here a good path through airy uplands. Stone walls and ruined buildings flanked it in places, just visible in the undergrowth. This hillside had once been well populated. Two of his group set up camp at Incapampa and went for water, while Paul and two others – with Juan Blanco – set off down the steep slope, from the grassy heights, past old field walls, into thick rainforest, and finally to a near vertical scree of loose stones.

Paul found the wire rope that the alcalde's cutters had fixed over the fast-flowing river, but it had no traveller wheel to carry loads along it. (We later learned that this was hidden nearby, but Juan Blanco – a member of what we now called 'the opposition' – chose not to mention this.) Butterflies danced on the stony beach as Paul, with a rope round his waist, dived into the river. But the current was too powerful for him to reach the other side, and his colleagues had to pull him in. A bridge would have to be built if a crossing here was decided upon, but the wall of the gorge on the far side looked forbidding. Paul's team cooled off in the river, filled water bottles, and then hacked up back to Incapampa. There was little water there – they managed to filter out only one rather muddy litre – and after one night they returned somewhat depressed to Waricunca.

Meanwhile Mike How, who had already been to 'Paititi' with Leopold on the earlier reconnaissance, had pressed forward from Smith's Crossing to find and report back on the ruins about which we had been told by the alcalde. With him went the archaeologists, including Bruce Mann, the interpreter James Culshaw, and some engineers.

Unfortunately the two Bolivians failed to make it up Leopold's Spur and had to turn back to Smith's Crossing, where Yoli and I found them when we visited the camp there later in the day. Juan Domingo could not swim, and being hauled through the torrent, even in a life jacket, had completely unnerved him. So I sent them both up the trail to Waricunca until we could organize porters to help them reach the 'Paititi' site.

Going hand over hand through the swirling water to the camp on the other side was most refreshing, and my clothes got a good wash on the way. Apart from the bees, Smith's Crossing, with its crystal-clear water, was an idyllic spot.

As Yoli and I climbed back up the hillside, sweating profusely, we rounded a bend and were surprised to find the two archaeologists. Juan Domingo looked grey, and his voice was a whisper. Clearly he was in serious distress. 'Crikey, he's suffering from heat exhaustion, and Ruden is not far off it,' I hissed at Yoli. 'You must drink water,' she insisted. Ruden gave her a pitiful look. 'We have none. We could not drink the river water – it is too dirty.' Shaking her head in disbelief, Yoli passed them her canteen while I dug out some glucose tablets. Then I radioed for the Quechua Indian Carlos to come down from Waricunca to carry their packs. That evening they revived, but complained that the going was too hard. 'We are archaeologists, not explorers,' groaned Ruden, adding that he wanted to go home to look after his wife, who was pregnant. Yoli was hard put to it to dissuade him.

Back at Waricunca, Alasdair, Paul Hortop, Yoli and I talked around the fire. 'It seems obvious that this empty countryside was once well populated,' said Alasdair. 'Everywhere you look there are roads, the remains of walls, defensive ditches and ramparts.' 'It all reminds me of Tolkien's descriptions in *The Lord of the Rings* of vestiges of vanished civilizations still discernible in the Western Wild,' I said, 'and it seems eerie to be walking along a road made by another civilization many centuries ago.'

'I keep wondering,' went on Alasdair, 'Who were they? Against whom did they build their defences? And were those defences successful in keeping out the enemy, or did the enemy finally overwhelm them – slaughtering the guards before pushing on to pillage the homesteads and fields and finally advancing to throw down the proud city of Paititi?' 'When the invaders retired,' put in Paul, 'did the jungle then advance in its turn, swallowing up the farmland, and leaving nothing of the prosperous fields and villages except the stone shells of some of the larger buildings, the vestiges of mines, and the walls of fields cut into the steep hillsides?'

Although Paul Overton and his team had had no good news to report, Mike's group on the far bank were getting on much better. Despite difficult conditions, they had ascended Leopold's Spur and pushed on, crouching beneath the low-overhanging jungle undergrowth. That night they had pitched camp in a marshy area where there was nevertheless an adequate supply of fresh water. The expedition called the place Peccary Wallow, as it was a regular haunt of vicious wild pigs. These peccaries were not ideal drinking companions, but luckily none of them was feeling thirsty while Mike and his team were in occupation of their 'local'.

The next day, the forward party marched on through the jungle, picking up the trail cut by the men from Guanay. Early in the morning, as they were ascending a tree-smothered hill, Bruce Mann suddenly noticed stone walls covered in vegetation.

In the course of a rapid field study, Bruce found that the walls made an almost square building – '16 metres by 15 metres. The walls are 1.2 metres high and 40 centimetres thick,' he reported to me on the radio. Around the site were roughly circular rampart walls. He concluded it was an Inca fort, which might have been one of the outer defences of the city. Cheered by this discovery, the group pushed on. They needed something to cheer them, because they were approaching the area of the ravines.

By mid-afternoon they staggered into the last of them, where there was a giant waterfall that had been discovered by Leopold and Mike on their earlier reconnaissance. They knew now that the ruins lay not too far away, so, after only a short rest, they pushed on downstream and up the steep side of the river valley.

As they hacked away at the undergrowth with their machetes, man-made features suddenly came to light: a half-buried slab; steps; what looked like an ornamental pool. They had arrived, and a radio message was sent back to say that the site that the local people called 'Paititi' had been found. Now the archaeologists had to establish what it was.

Meanwhile it was a quiet and torpid afternoon back at Waricunca. The temperature was 90° in the shade, which tended to discourage much in the way of strenuous activity. I was in my tent, trying to work out the logistics of moving the expedition across the river gorge and into the jungle on the far side. Other members were asleep in their tents or writing up their diaries outside. Alasdair Crosby was sitting with a laptop computer on his knee, swearing steadily at the incomprehensible technology that was hindering him in his efforts to write a dispatch to his newspaper. Overhead, a large turkey vulture hovered, perhaps wondering if the recumbent bodies far below were something dead and tasty. Some movement must have persuaded it otherwise, and it flew off, doubtless rather annoyed.

Into this late-afternoon torpor intruded the sound of the radio crackling into life: it was Mike How reporting his party's finds. As I repeated the news, my colleagues shook off their lassitude and gathered round. Cheering broke out at the news that the 'Paititi' site had been located. 'Pity there's no champagne,' I said, after the end of the radio conversation. 'It'll have to be double *mate de coca* all round.'

Mike's news was just the information I needed to finalize the plan. Although he had reported a lack of water on the ridge, all our people and stores would move up via Smith's Crossing. It would be a long, hard haul, under the most trying conditions.

Around the fire that night, I gave out the orders for the assault and sent instructions to Craig Halford (whose wounded hand was now stitched and bandaged) to move his engineer section forward next day. Barry Igoe, a highly competent Irishman, would run Smith's Crossing. Paul Overton would organize teams of porters to supply us from there to the Rio Tulani. Tac HQ and the rest of the archaeological section would then march to the Tulani. The pack animals would continue to bring supplies up from the forward base at Quilapituni, and I hoped that Katie could get them to Smith's Crossing. The die was cast.

5

Meanwhile, Back at Fort Mogg

Some 70 km northwest of Caranavi is the gold mining town of Guanay, an interesting, friendly place at the junction of the Tipuani and Mapiri rivers. You can change cash with shopkeepers or gold dealers. Electricity is rationed – every ten minutes or so – and water is available before 1200 only.

Alan Murphy, *Bolivia Handbook*, 2000

WHILE ALL THESE journeys were unfolding, Ernie Durey was establishing himself as the dominant personality at Fort Mogg in Guanay. He presided over a mountain of food, most of which was destined to be conveyed up the trail to 'Paititi'.

He regularly went out himself with consignments – of noodles, packet soup, pasta, rice, potato powder, *soya carne* and the favourite – Aunt Jemima's Pancake Mix – to be taken by vehicle and mule to the end of the line at the Rio Tulani. Canned goods, bananas, huge sweet grapefruit (costing about 1p each) and other provisions went to the intermediate camps at Quilapituni, Waricunca and Smith's Crossing. In a shop near Fort Mogg, Ernie had spotted three tins of beef labelled, 'DONATED BY THE GOVERNMENT OF AUSTRIA FOR PROJECTS AND EMERGENCY OPERATIONS OF THE WORLD FOOD PROGRAMME. NOT FOR SALE.' After a search, a full cardboard box was found at the back of the shop, and Ernie said, 'I'll take more if you have them.' A few days later three more cases had been procured from La Paz. Months after, on the Amazon, we were still tucking into Austrian beef intended for hungry *campesinos*.

Ernie had two sterling helpers. His driver, José Luis Buitrago, battled almost daily over the 100 miles from Guanay to Quilapituni and back. With mule-boxes bouncing about in the rear, driver often became helmsman as the IMBEX pickup – half afloat – churned between the boulders across rivers. And Francisca Torrez Martinez, a small, sharp-featured

Altiplano woman, continued to be a tireless worker in the Fort Mogg kitchen. She came in to work at 4 a.m., and was often still clearing up at 10 p.m., after managing to conjure up a succession of palatable meals armed only with a ladle and a sharp knife.

Ernie seemed almost telepathically to know what we needed out in the field – which was just as well, because communication with the base was very difficult. The army's A320 radios had finally arrived, but we simply could not get them to work here. Only by the expensive but very reliable NERA satellite phone could I talk to him. Yoli would call the ENTEL office in Guanay and, in Spanish, ask them to send word to Fort Mogg that she would call again at a certain time. A small boy was then dispatched with a note to 'Coronel Ernesto'. This was translated by José Luis, and Ernie would go to the ENTEL office, where the attractive telephone girls would turn on a cooling fan especially for him. To transmit text and pictures for the web site, Peter Kannangara had to drive for two hours south-east to Caranavi and use the Internet site there.

Lonely Planet's *Bolivia* says of Guanay, 'This area and all points upriver are frontier territory, and you may be reminded of the USA's legendary Old West. Gold is legal tender in shops and saloons; gambling, prostitution and large hunks of beef appear to form the foundations of local culture.' *Barranquilleros* mine gold in the hills and pan for it in the Rio Mapiri, though on a much smaller scale than used to be the case. An enormous gold-ore-extracting dredger stands idle and rusting on the river bank just outside town; locals said that in its heyday this monster had extracted $300 million worth of gold from the river. Now that this source is exhausted, the only remaining gold is difficult to reach and often dangerous to extract. Banks and bars have closed down, and the population has dwindled to 16,000. Some shops still announce '*Se Compra Oro*' (We Buy Gold), and a few tough customers can be seen slipping in to sell the result of a week's backbreaking panning. It was difficult to be censorious about these men's once-a-month bout of boozing and whoring: safety standards in the mines are low, accidents occur frequently, and some miners died in collapsed shafts while we were there.

Guanay was a noisy little town. Dogs barked, cocks crew, goals in televised football matches were marked by firecrackers in the street, karaoke bars hung speakers at their doors, and happy-clappy ministers tried to out-evangelize each other. It seemed decayed in some places, incomplete in others. A new bridge crossing the Mapiri had only its central T-shaped section built, and one approach road seemed as if it would come straight out of a hillside.

Our community-aid team did what little it could: we offered medical and dental services, engineering advice, and sundry other sorts of help. Shirley Critchley co-ordinated all this and gave her time selflessly. Over many months she had collected unwanted spectacles from the Dorset area. A hundred pairs were distributed, but the demand was ten times that. Craig Halford designed flood defences, bridges, hospital buildings and a school extension. Prince Leopold became patron of two schools and spoke to their pupils. In Mapiri, people rushed to greet him like happy peasants in a Ruritanian operetta: '¡El Principe, El Principe!' they cried. Guanay High School was a shining light amid the town's general seediness. It had no computers, no whiteboards, no child-centred learning: just dedicated teachers and polite, well-behaved pupils in uniforms. Boys and girls all wore ties.

It was there that the first of our satellite phone links was made with a school in Dorset. Paul Overton had prearranged a date and time for the link. A hundred Guanay children stood attentively in rows.

'Hello, this is Paul Overton of the Scientific Exploration Society . . . I'm phoning from Bolivia . . . Yes, Bolivia . . . Is that Mrs Hallett? Oh? . . . Is she? Could she come to the phone please?' A pleading note crept in here. 'Could you please find her and find some pupils?' Chris Tarrant never has this problem on *Who Wants to be a Millionaire?* 'We have about a hundred Bolivian children waiting to talk to children at the school . . . I'll phone back in five minutes . . . Please find her . . . Please find some of your pupils . . .' Fortunately Mrs Hallett was run to earth and brought some of her children to talk to the Bolivians. There had been a misunderstanding about the time, but it all ended happily.

Dr Sam Allen, a specialist registrar in infectious diseases and tropical medicine at London's Royal Free Hospital and University College, led our medical team, which had brought a large quantity of medical supplies from Britain. Sam − of Armenian descent, small, neat, trimly bearded − had travelled in South America before, and had been keen to return. In Guanay he was specially intrigued to find a case of leishmaniasis, a disease of which he had made a close study and which had eaten away the cartilage of a Mapiri patient's nose.

Firecrackers and garlands of flowers welcomed Sam's team in Mapiri. They treated over 250 people, but could do little for the extreme cases: one poor woman, dying of cancer, was brought to the clinic in a wheelbarrow.

Graham Catchpole is a dental surgeon from Taunton and a keen Rotarian who enjoys both ocean and dinghy sailing. Apart from extracting teeth wherever he went, he was one of our most successful video cameramen. At Mapiri he found a town of 14,000 people with no dentist, and was consequently swamped with patients. Some teeth proved very difficult to remove. 'This was the first time I felt like a butcher,' he wrote in his log. In Guanay and Mapiri Graham took out 467 teeth, usually helped by the less squeamish expedition members, who, in the absence of a dentist's chair, held the patients' heads.

He found himself pulling teeth in some interesting locations: a downstairs toilet, a village football pitch, and, in Mapiri, a tiny, claustrophobic room with just one light-bulb and a table. 'Never had I such perspiration dripping off me. I preferred the toilet as a temporary surgery: the top of the cistern made a good, more or less clean place to lay out my dental instruments, and at least there was a good spittoon handy. At the football pitch I stretched a tarpaulin from the top of the goalpost to keep the flies and the sun off.'

Graham sometimes found the journey to Mapiri an arduous one. Once our Toyota car, climbing a hill in heavy rain, slid off the road into a ditch. Ernie, in an accompanying pickup, shouted to its driver, 'Stay there till the sun dries the road off. We'll take your three passengers.' He had five already, and eight could be accommodated only by Shirley Critchley and Francisca lying on top of the three, heads out of one window, feet through another. After a while field treasurer Geoffrey Hoskins said, 'I'm afraid my leg has gone to sleep. I've no feeling in it.' 'That's because it's my knee you've been squeezing for the last five minutes,' said Graham.

On expeditions, chivalry is sometimes wanting. Shirley and Francisca decided that, despite the torrential rain, it would be more comfortable to crouch under a plastic sheet in the back of the pickup. Later, Geoffrey: 'Don't you think we should invite the two ladies back into the front?' Graham: 'What's the point? They're soaking wet. Why make us wet too?'

One result of all this medical and dental work was a steady flow of information on archaeological sites. However, if one believed the touts who came daily to the gates of Fort Mogg, Guanay was surrounded by lost cities. 'Hey! Gringo, You Want a Nice Lost City?' as Alasdair Crosby's headline ran in the *Jersey Evening Post*. For a few thousand dollars they offered to lead Bill Holmes to many such sites. Wisely, he declined.

Missing from our team in Fort Mogg were the Masters brothers. They were with expedition friend and interpreter Teddy Jauregui on Lake Titicaca, supervising the construction of the reed trimaran *Kota Mama 3*. Erik and Máximo Catari and a friend called Kakasaka had been hard at work at Huatajata for a month, and on 26 May 2001 the last reed was tied in and the three great jaguar heads were fitted.

All that remained to do was to get them to Guanay. General Ejército Juan Hurtado Rosales, the commander of the Bolivian Army, had kindly offered to move them on trucks with a police escort down 'the most dangerous road in the world', though Jim wondered if all the arrangements would work out. Somehow they did, for that evening three army 10-tonners arrived at Huatajata, and next morning 200 gallons of fuel were delivered by Air BP, our leading Bolivian sponsor, whose general manager, Alejandro Serrate, had been acquainted with the *Kota Mama* project when he was assistant to the prefect in 2000 and was a most valued helper. Alejandro had been at a north of England school, but 'I've forgiven the British now,' he joked.

Darius Morgan, another supporter, hired us his crane, which also arrived, and in no time the hulls were loaded on the lorries. Their police escort was waiting on the northern rim of the La Paz valley, and with it the convoy climbed steadily to 15,500 feet. Crossing the Cordillera Real, it edged its way carefully down to the Yungas on a road now barely wider than the trucks. By 6.30 p.m. it was dark, and the journey continued using headlights. 'This was more comforting, as we could no longer see the precipice and doom staring at us,' said Gerry. Then at 8.30 p.m. they pulled in to a small truckers' hotel, where they found beds for £1 a night.

At 4.15 a.m. they woke up to much hooting of truck horns. The army drivers wanted to be off. Dressing quickly, Gerry tried the hotel door. 'Christ, it's locked,' he said. 'We can't wake the chap at this hour.'

He and Jim ran down into a yard and climbed a wall. There was a 12-foot drop on the other side. The second wall they climbed led into a pigsty whose occupants they succeeded in waking. Escaping from the squeals, they clambered over a balcony and began to move over the tin roof of the lower storey. But Gerry is a big man, and the metal sheeting started to give way. In the end the patron, now well awake, let them out.

The menfolk of Guanay, astonished at what had just rolled into their town, soon rallied to lift the three hulls off the trucks and into the Mapiri river.

6

To the Rio Tulani

There were the people whose geography was not their strong point, and who
either offered me letters of introduction to their cousins in Buenos Aires or
supposed that I would find a good many Aztec ruins.

Peter Fleming, *Brazilian Adventure*, 1933

ZIGZAGGING DOWNHILL FROM Waricunca to Smith's Crossing, Tac HQ
met Juan Blanco coming up, limping badly. With him were two other
porters, Angel and Elvin.

'I've twisted my knee,' he said. 'Need to go to hospital.'

'Did you let Dr Jo see it?' Yoli asked.

Jo Brown, Paul Overton and Steve Henry – a mail-room worker from
Nottingham who was now an assistant quartermaster – had been carrying water up Leopold's Spur to make a cache at the top for future
climbers when Juan Blanco had come down past them.

He made no reply, and as he had walked for five hours from the
'Paititi' site at the Rio Tulani I didn't think it could be a very serious
injury. However, he was being paid by the alcalde, so I could not stop
his leaving us. And, as he appeared to be in league with the Austrian, I
was glad to see the back of him. Always a divisive influence among the
Indians, he had clearly intimidated Angel and Elvin and it took Yoli a
little while to persuade them both to stay on.

As he left us, Juan Blanco handed me an envelope from Craig Halford.
It contained a well-drawn plan of the 'Paititi' site, at which his engineers
had now arrived.

It took an hour for Barry Igoe, now in charge at Smith's Crossing, to
get my party across the Chinijo. The kit was slung over the aerial
ropeway in the waterproof sacks, while we stripped off and hauled ourselves hand over hand along a climbing rope through the cool, rushing
water to the west bank. At this idyllic, if bee-infested, spot we washed

our clothes, got badly bitten, made camp, and ate pork noodles with what few bread rolls the soldier ants at Waricunca had left us.

In the morning there was apprehension in the air. We felt as mountaineers must feel at the foot of Everest's ice-fall. A tree-covered cliff towered above us, steep and snake-filled. Barry Igoe set off first, with Juan Domingo and Ruden Plaza and their personal sherpas to carry all their gear. Without this help our gallant archaeologists refused to go on. Five others carried food and equipment. I brought up the other half of the team a little later. The 50° slope was blanketed in rotting trees and lianas. We were grateful for the occasional safety rope that Craig Halford's men had put in, and for a felled tree which made a footbridge over a gully. Otherwise, gloved against thorns, we pulled ourselves up on roots and vines. The ground was loose, and we slid one step back for every two steps taken. For two gruelling hours sweat poured from us, until we reached the ten-litre water container that Paul Overton had positioned at the top of the spur. Machetes then had to be used on the bamboo along the top of the ridge, as we were not yet on the path that the alcalde's men had cut for us.

In the early afternoon Paul, his face strained with exhaustion, came towards me with a party of porters. He had been to the Rio Tulani, and was making his way back to Smith's crossing at a fast Indian pace to collect more supplies. Monkeys and birds chattered and squawked, parrots and macaws called raucously as we struggled on in a tunnel of vegetation, lit only by the occasional shaft of sunlight. Elizabeth Dix, our youngest archaeologist, marked the way with red ribbons.

Wiser now, we had shed much of our earlier loads. What seemed at the outset to be indispensable kit had been gradually dumped by most of us along the way from La Paz. I had even left behind my sleeping-bag, but was pleased to find one that Bruce Mann had left by the wayside. I used it en route in exchange for carrying it up for him. It grew dark at 4.30 p.m., and we camped by a spring in a muddy valley.

'Tucandera make you very ill,' said Carlos, who was ever by my side, as he brushed an inch-long fire-ant off my back.

The next day, Monday 28 May, was a bank holiday in Britain, but there was no let-up for Mike Lulham and Craig Churcher, the two HSBC men who were with us. An hour after the start we saw red ribbons marking the point where we joined the alcalde's cleared trail. It was like coming on to a motorway after miles of tortuous B-road. The wider trail would now take us down into and up out of seven ravines between us and 'Paititi'.

As we topped a ridge, Angel pointed to a line of stones crossing the path. '*Fortaleza*,' he said, and Juan and Ruden examined what was soon found to be a rectangular structure.

'It's pre-Columbian,' they averred.

'We must look at it later,' I counselled, for we still had a four-hour march ahead of us – much of it over spongy compost which my trekking-pole unhelpfully punched straight through.

'Must look up,' I muttered to myself as I crashed into yet another low branch which the broad brim of my Australian bush hat had prevented me from seeing. Heads and necks were bowed all round now, as the strain took its toll. Alasdair Crosby neatly likened this steeply undulating route to the profile of a bar of Toblerone chocolate, and at the top of each chunk we would collapse on to the mattress of mulch, oblivious of all but the more aggressive of insects crawling over us.

Up and down we scrambled, and by 12.15 p.m. we had reached the third ravine and paused for a biscuit and tuna snack beside a tumbling stream.

At some times we managed a speed of a couple of miles per hour, at others it was more like a couple of hours per mile. It was a hellish switchback. Sweat seemed to be squirting from my brow. Mike Smith twisted his leg painfully, and I shuddered at the possibility of a serious accident in this remote place, but manfully he carried on. Elvin, who had at one point gone ahead, returned and took up Alasdair's pack and set off with it into the forest. He had done this sort of thing before, and Yoli asked him why. 'Some day I will be old, and I hope someone will help me then.' In fact he was forty-eight, and older than most of the people he helped.

The distant sound of rushing water spurred us on, and soon I slid and slipped down into the seventh ravine and the Rio Tulani. Cascading into it was one of the most magnificent waterfalls I had ever seen. Framed by ferns, it tumbled in three steps for about 90 feet to join the Tulani – a shallow stream gushing between boulders and islands towards other waterfalls 300 yards downstream. The well-documented Inca reverence for falling water may have prompted them to select this site for a settlement, I thought. And here we did indeed see the first signs of ancient habitation. Stone walls overgrown with moss supported platforms on either side of the river. I felt my pulse quicken. The stress and strain of the march up were suddenly forgotten.

Along the river banks, the first arrivals had pitched their tents and lit their fire. Mike How and the sappers now sat about staring glumly into space. An unspoken question hung in the damp air: 'Where is it all, then?' Clearly they had expected to find much more dramatic buildings – pyramids, palaces, ramparts, temples. 'I was distinctly underwhelmed,' said Alasdair.

The site lay at the top of the steep slope above the river, but, although early reports had been encouraging, to the layman there was not much to see and everything was cloaked in dense vegetation and layers of leaf compost. It was a dark, dank and evil place. The Indians were uneasy, and morale was understandably low. But, having seen jungle-covered ruins of past civilizations before, I was not the least depressed. So after supper I launched into an 'Eve of Agincourt' pep talk to rally the team's spirits. Thankfully it was reasonably effective, and soon the enthusiasm of Bruce Mann – our senior archaeologist – was firing up even the most reluctant of his helpers.

My Henrician encouragements had steeled everyone for battle, and we studied the map that Drew Craig had sent up from Guanay. Bruce Mann seemed happy enough with the potential of the site and led an inspection the following morning. We climbed one of the revetted walls on to a platform. The sloping plateau was overgrown with rotting vegetation. Along a track cut by the engineers we came upon an astonishing sight: a heavy timber frame of a roofless single-storey building stood in a small clearing.

'This must be where Ertl lived,' said Bruce. In 1954–5 the German had spent eight months up here, even planting fruit trees and rice for future expeditions. He must have had reason to think that this was the lost city he sought, and envisaged a long stay. Why else sink 15-inch-square baulks of timber in the ground, lay a stone floor, and plant maize for breadmaking? Or had he other motives? He had brought a radio with him and talked lengthily into it in German, two of his porters later told us at Mapiri.

From the clearing, five giant slabs formed a descending stairway to a big boulder. Fresh digging round them suggested recent treasure-hunters. A path led from the stairway through a gorge cut by the Rio Tulani across which a huge tree had fallen. At the end of the path were steps which seemed to have been cut. 'Natural,' Juan Domingo said. But Angel told me, 'This is the place where people come to get power. And here is the meditation house,' indicating a cliff out of which a massive slab had slid to form an overhang. Alasdair was reminded of the anthropomorphic designations made by guides in French caves, who point to strangely shaped stalagmites and say, '*Voici la vierge blanche*' or '*Violà la tête de Napoleon.*'

'This looks like some feature in a water garden,' I said to Bruce. We were looking at a large, shallow, triangular pool 20 yards across, with low walls round two sides and the remains of a third. Two rock-lined channels covered with small plates of stone fed water into the pool. Rectangular house walls 4 feet high stood nearby, and a well-like shaft dropped down 10 feet into the clay. From the stone-lined entrance to a passage lower down issued clear water which ran into a stone-lined canal. All very mysterious.

Around the site stood slabs of rock; others had fallen flat. Mike Lulham cleaned some of their faces to check for inscriptions, though none were found. We next scaled a 60-foot-high mound. Ertl had described two such mounds, and claimed they were astronomically orientated. He said that on 28 December – a special day in the Inca calendar – he had climbed some stone steps and, lining up the tops of these two mounds with the highest point in the San Carlos range, 6 miles off, he had seen the sun rise exactly on that bearing. He concluded that this alignment indicated some form of sun worship. Although there was indeed a clear view to a summit in the distant mountains, an exhaustive search during the next few days failed to find any steps or terraces from which such an observation could have been made. Nor could we even find the second mound. And, although the one we did find was symmetrical, it appeared to be natural. But piles of stones and vestiges of walls were everywhere, and the distinction between man's work and nature's was a hard one to make. The more I saw the more mystified I became. 'It looks as if an earthquake has hit the place,' commented Mike Lulham.

Over six days, Juan Domingo and Ruden Plaza, with Bruce and Elizabeth, scoured the area. Small, unidentifiable pieces of pottery were found near Ertl's house, together with more modern detritus like a rusty Quaker Oats tin. The rectangular building yielded some tiny colonial shards indicating that it might be a Spanish construction. Using a simple plane table, our army surveyors, John Gorski and Karle Reid, made a plan of the site.

The relative lack of pottery suggested that perhaps no one had ever lived there – that it was a site visited only occasionally, for specific purposes. Ertl claimed to have discovered gold figurines hidden in a cave, and his book showed pictures of them, but Juan Domingo was not convinced that they were found at this site. 'Why did he not photograph them *in situ*?' he asked. 'After all, he was a professional photographer.'

'Perhaps he was trying to salt the claim,' suggested Craig Halford. Ertl had written that, according to Spanish chronicles, Inca people came to Paititi from the Altiplano each December 'through mountains covered by snow and bringing many gold objects of adoration and much jewellery to pay tribute to their god. I did not have any doubt,' he went on, 'that I was in the core of Paititi, the valley of the two hills.'

We were now at the end of a long line of communication, and soon food became a problem. The engineers cut down palms and extracted their hearts – good bulk, but tasteless. Carlos went looking for 'turkeys' and unfortunately shot a small, gorgeous, orange-feathered bird. The porters wolfed it down. To live off the country with a large party is not easy. Our noise seemed to have frightened off the tasty rodents, and the only mammal to disturb us went crashing off unseen into the jungle. 'Perhaps it was a spectacled bear. They are known in these parts,' pointed out Paul Hortop. With a large team of engineers, surveyors and archaeologists at 'Paititi' we were very dependent on resupply, and there had been general rejoicing when Paul had arrived from Waricunca with Graham Lydiatt, an assistant quartermaster on the expedition, and stocks of fresh food.

But morale soon dipped again. As well as being often hungry, we were all being comprehensively bitten, working in mud and mulch kept us permanently filthy, no sun could break through the forest canopy, and the absence of dry wood made it very difficult to keep a fire going.

The two Bolivian archaeologists seemed the most depressed. Their employers, once DINAAR, now UNAR, were to be disbanded, they said, and their pay was in jeopardy. 'Why can't you ask General Banzer to send a helicopter for us?' asked Juan Domingo. 'Then we can return here when the site has been cleared.' 'Can you imagine how your president would react to such a request?' I replied. 'I must go home – my wife is pregnant,' protested Ruden, 'Who's fault is that?' retorted Yoli impatiently, and gave them a pep talk about the honour of serving one's country. Eventually they agreed to stay, but I felt this was largely because they could not face the prospect of returning alone and unaided through the snake-infested forest.

That night we had a sing-song around the fire. The porters sang lustily, while the British did their best – which was not brilliant. The Bolivian archaeologists did not join in, and the porters much preferred listening to Elizabeth chatting – they greatly admired her blonde hair.

On 2 June a fascinating discovery cheered us up. Carlos told me he had found a set of steps leading into a yawning chasm into which tumbled both a waterfall from the high cliff to the north and another created by the Rio Tulani itself. With Carlos holding on to me by a length of cord I slid out cautiously to the lip of the rock ledge over which the river raced to the fall. The roaring water and spray gave the place a frightening appearance, and anyone falling in would have the greatest difficulty in getting out. A false step here would have sent one plunging into what we named the Devil's Cauldron.

Alasdair Crosby crawled carefully over to join me as I inspected the face of this vertical-sided pit through my binoculars. Suddenly I caught sight of figures carved on the wet, black rock of the wall opposite. They read 1790, or perhaps 1750. 'Look at that,' I shouted to Alasdair above the roar of the falls, and passed him my binoculars. 'It must be a date,' he replied. 'Perhaps it was put there by a Spanish exploring party.'

Returning with Bruce and Mike, we brought ropes and slings. Belayed to a tree by Mike, Bruce inched his way along a slimy ledge above the chasm until he was right at the figures. 'It is 1750,' he called out, but then his voice was drowned. However, on his return he reported that all the other marks on the rock were natural except one. That was a carving of a bell-shaped object. 'Was there a serpent entwined around it?' I asked, but apparently there was not. Who had carved the figures? Were they a date? This was another loose piece in the jigsaw. Perhaps a Spanish colonist trying to unravel the secrets of Paititi had fallen to his death here. Indeed, to go further would require technical climbing equipment and skill.

High up on the side of Cerro Paititi, Mike had found a section of wall, so we clambered out of the Tulani valley to see it. An hour's jungle mountaineering brought us to a stream beside which the wall stood. After clearing the vegetation, the wall turned out to be part of an enclosed space lined with rocks. At one end two slabs overlapped to form a V through which water had been channelled. At first I thought it must be a simple hut, but then Carlos said, '*Han trabajado con oro aquí*' (They have worked with gold here). As a miner himself he had used similar constructions, but there was no doubt that this one was very old. Nearby,

Carlos picked up rock that he said was closely identified with gold deposits, so it seemed that this was an ancient mining site. Possibly we had found a kind of sluice, but we could find nothing to indicate when it had last been used. In fact walls and cut stones littered the jungle all around the Tulani site, but it would take an army months to clear the soil and leaf mould away.

The strange absence of ceramics or anything datable at the Rio Tulani was a mystery. Our Indian helpers were convinced this was the legendary city, but we needed proof – or at least something by which to date its occupation. So on the evening of 5 June, as the full moon rose above the distant hills and its light filtered through the trees, I got Celso and his men to tell us what they knew of the whole area and its history.

Quilapituni, they said, had been established about 1850 by an isolated group of Aymara farmers. Celso described their agriculture and religions and the highlight of their year, the feast of San Juan, which takes place in June. Houses and carts are decorated and sprinkled with wine or beer to bring good fortune. The people dance the Sampoña and sing and drink for three days. The climax comes on the 24th of the month, when they tell fortunes. This is done by pouring molten tin into cold water. The shapes in which the metal solidifies foretell the future – an interesting version of the tea-leaf method used in Britain. In fact metal plays an important part in Aymara folklore, but Celso emphasized that, although there is much gold in the area, his people do not seek it.

Gradually I brought the subject round to the Rio Tulani site. 'This place is haunted,' said the chief, lowering his voice. 'At night, voices can be heard in the forest. Once, much gold was here, and the bell symbol you have found carved on the rock face proves this is Paititi.' As we had seen, he pointed out, the site was guarded by hordes of snakes that congregate in this valley. Elvin interjected, 'Ertl was driven from Cerro Paititi by the snakes.' I had to admit that the German did go on about them rather a lot in his book, and we had ourselves come across a respectable tally. Paul Overton had nearly put his hand on one while climbing Leopold's Spur, and on arrival at the Rio Tulani Craig Halford had shot a four-foot fer-de-lance which sapper corporal John Dolman had barbecued for supper. His fellow corporal Nathan Leavold had pronounced it tasty enough. 'A bit like soused herring,' others had said.

As the moon rose higher and its light flooded into the ravine, Celso lowered his voice still more, as if to avoid being overheard. 'This may be a place where people came to worship the devil and increase their power over others. They could even get the power to move blocks of stone,' he said. There was silence for a moment while Yoli passed round an infusion of hot, sweet *mate de coca*. 'Many big stones have been moved in recent years,' continued Celso. The others, the whites of their eyes showing up in the moonlight, nodded their heads in agreement. 'The monolith has gone,' moaned one. 'Perhaps Juan Blanco has hidden it,' said another.

Conversation then turned to the fort. 'We think there is an Inca trail close to it,' said Elvin. 'I have a fine stone axe from Incapampa which I will show you, and a metal one discovered near Quilapituni.' 'The fort may have been a transit area for the city,' suggested Celso. Their testimony was vague, fantastical and full of wishful thinking. They seemed to be doing their utmost to convince me that this eerie place was indeed the legendary city.

As Yoli was having to translate everything, the session took several hours; but finally we rose. I yawned and was about to go off to bed when Celso made a few remarks about a place he called San Lorenzo, to the west of Incapampa. 'It is an old canton,' he said. 'People died out there because the water was polluted with lead.'

Going down to the river to collect my shirt, which I had left drying in an earlier brief patch of sun, I was startled by a deep groan from the water. Listening carefully, I heard it again. 'Blimey, it's the Indians' night voices,' I said to myself – 'boulders rubbing together in the fast-flowing stream.' I'd heard them once before, beside a glacier in Alaska.

To ease the food situation by the Rio Tulani, I had decided to thin out numbers by sending two parties back down the trail: Paul Hortop and the archaeologists to have a closer look at the *fortaleza* we had walked through on the way up, and some of the engineers under Craig Halford down the alcalde's route to the Rio Chinijo below Incapampa to see if, as Paul Overton thought, the river could be crossed there. By these two means I could also please Juan Domingo and Ruden Plaza by getting them a little further down the line towards the comforts they so craved and perhaps find a route out for us all which would avoid a potentially dangerous descent of Leopold's Spur.

Juan Domingo soon found pottery at the fort, which we had always thought could be an Inca outpost of 'Paititi', and Craig Halford radioed to say that the Chinijo was bridgeable. I decided we would all go back that way – albeit still with a tough descent and then a gruelling climb up to Incapampa. Once at Incapampa there would be just time to send off an archaeological team on the seven-hour hike along the Mapiri Trail to the ruins at San Lorenzo that Celso had mentioned.

The ever active Mike How said he would give San Lorenzo a go. Craig Churcher, archaeologist Elizabeth Dix and Celso himself made up the team, with a packhorse to carry water led by Israel the muleteer. 'You'll only have time for a rapid survey,' I told them. 'Scout around, and if it looks good we can come back another year.'

On 5 June John and Karle, our surveyors, completed the mapping of the Tulani site. Mike Smith and Bruce photographed the structures, and I took a last look round. We decided to name the waterfall the Velasco Falls, in honour of the prefect of La Paz. That night I gazed up at the tumbling water. In the moonlight the grotto that it created had a strange mystical air. Even the frogs were silent, and I could well imagine the religious significance that this eerie place had had for the ancient inhabitants, whoever they were.

7

Going Back Down

There were the Men Who Had Done A Certain Amount of That Sort of Thing In Their Time, You Know and these imparted to me elaborate stratagems for getting the better of ants and told me that monkeys made excellent eating, and so for that matter did lizards, and parrots; they all tasted rather like chicken.

Peter Fleming, *Brazilian Adventure*, 1933

GOING BACK DOWN is often harder and more dangerous than climbing up. Certainly our way out across the ravines was as gruelling as before – and was not made any easier by the wear and tear that the track had suffered during our stay at Tulani. Heaving ourselves up and down, every pore oozing sweat, we scrambled through the compost.

A cry rang out behind me, followed by the crash of something falling through the bushes. 'What's up?' 'It's Greg!' someone shouted. 'The track's collapsed and he's fallen through.' Thankfully Greg Alonso – one of our assistant archaeologists – survived his 18-foot tumble with only a few bruises and scratches.

As the day grew hotter, tiny monkeys feeding on the blossoms above us chattered in alarm as we passed, and the great electric-blue butterflies flitted ahead of our column. Some of the porters swigged local alcohol, and they all chewed coca incessantly to give them strength – or to perhaps numb the pain of their loads.

The last two ravines were dry, so, knowing there was no water at the fort, we filled our canteens with crystal-clear liquid at the fifth one.

A short, stiff climb out of the last ravine took us into the bamboo thicket that grew on the ridge, and soon we smelt the smoke of Paul Hortop's campfire at the *fortaleza*. 'We're getting fitter. Did that in three hours twenty minutes,' smiled Yoli as we reached the ridge and the trail flattened out.

The walls of the fort were now exposed, and appeared to be much better constructed than those at Tulani. Faced stone had been used, in the Inca tradition. Juan Domingo seemed pleased with the results. 'Inca,' he said confidently, showing me some pottery. 'I think it's an inn, not a fort – probably used by traders travelling up from the river.' 'If it was a pub, the beer ran out 600 years ago,' remarked Greg. Ertl had talked of another ruin 200 yards away, but, though we searched all day, the dense jungle and bamboo obscured everything. However, the soft moss that blanketed the ruins did have one advantage: it provided a superbly comfortable mattress when my tent was pitched on it.

Hidden from view, 2,000 feet below, on the Rio Chinijo, Craig Halford's bridge was progressing slowly. Jo had gone down to treat a couple of minor injuries, and Sam Allen, who had earlier joined us from advanced base, now provided medical cover for the main party. I was still worried about having a serious casualty in this treacherous terrain. Sam was an asset in many ways. He is an excellent cook, and his culinary efforts did much to raise spirits. Paul Overton had joined us again, looking rather old behind his shaggy grey beard. However, it gave him a measure of protection from the wretched bees that had returned to the attack. We all got stung and, remembering a near-fatality from a hornet sting on the Darién expedition in 1972, I hoped we had no one with an allergy to them.

Melissa Dice, at expedition base in Dorset, used e-mail and the satellite phone to keep me informed of the progress of arrangements in Brazil some 1,000 miles away to the east. We were due there in a month's time, and much remained to be done before setting out on our epic voyage.

Next day we spoke by satellite phone to Ballard School in Dorset, where Coralie Critchley taught. She had worked with me on Operation Raleigh – our follow-up to Operation Drake – and now introduced her young son, Christian, over the telephone. Christian asked me how his granny, Shirley, was getting on. What an odd world, I thought, when grandmothers can dash off on expeditions and talk to their grandchildren from the depths of the rainforest.

'Who won the election?' asked someone.

'I don't know. Nor do I much care,' said another.

Apparently this broadly reflected the view of the British electorate, a much reduced number of whom had re-elected Tony Blair in June 2001. More of our interest was focused on the progress of Craig Halford's bridge, which was now nearly finished. In fact Mike How's group, heading for San Lorenzo, had crossed it already.

As Tac HQ were about to leave the fort the rains struck. The descent to the Chinijo became more than normally hazardous. We slid downhill, ducking under low trees and clambering over massive trunks which blocked the way. Vines snapped and sent us slithering uncontrollably. 'If we get everyone down this cliff without a broken leg,' I said to Yoli, 'it will be a miracle.' But we did. Near the bottom the track was supported by ancient retaining walls of faced stone, and there were terrace walls and broad platforms. Everywhere one looked there were signs of an earlier civilization – but the two Bolivian archaeologists were too far sunk in misery to notice.

Craig Halford's engineers had worked hard on the bridge. A 60-foot length had been cut from a tree felled nearby. It didn't quite reach the far bank, so they had built a pier of stones for it to rest on. On top of it they had nailed short slats of wood to make a safer walkway, and had rigged a cord handrail. But crossing it would still be perilous: the Chinijo surged underneath, and good balance was required.

In pouring rain I said, 'I name this bridge Halford's Bridge,' and with my machete I sliced through a coloured ribbon tied across by Dr Jo Brown. Juan Domingo then donned a life-jacket and nervously made his way over. To have fallen off with a heavy pack would have been to invite drowning. Without a pack one might have been washed swiftly under the useless *maroma* cable 50 yards downstream and very soon carried to Smith's Crossing.

'Don't look down at the water,' cautioned Jo as I set off. That, of course, was an invitation to do so, but I nevertheless made it across. The ensuing wet season would probably see the giant log borne away on the flood, but at least I could get our expedition over it.

The steep ascent to Incapampa was then a challenge of a different kind. Rainwater was infused with perspiration in our sodden clothing, which clung tightly to our bodies as we toiled up. The sun struck the treetops, the temperature rose, and biting flies attacked. Panting and pausing, we seemed to make the seemingly endless ascent in a Turkish bath. In the later stages terraced walls were seen again, and eventually we came to the section we had found and cleared the previous year. 'Oswaldo says this is Inca,' I told Juan Domingo. 'I don't know,' he replied, gasping for air. At the top we stood in the bright sunlight and steamed like front-row forwards on a rugby field. Then the bees homed in on our white sweat stains.

Three packhorses, carrying our kit, enabled us to reach Waricunca within the hour. 'Good news first, or bad?' the radio operator asked me when we got there.

'Paul Overton at the fort says that some of our porters returning there from Incapampa came in looking bedraggled. They said that the bridge had collapsed, and that one of them had fallen in the river and had been pulled out by the others only just in time.'

The story, as often happens, had developed in the transmission. It turned out that the bridge was still in place, although one porter, having fortified himself with industrial alcohol a touch too liberally before committing himself to the crossing, had indeed fallen off, but was soon saved.

The good news came from San Lorenzo. Mike How and his group had found extensive ruins. 'It's there all right,' said Craig Churcher, a happy banker on this sunny afternoon.

Elizabeth showed me a sketch she had made. 'It's very near the Mapiri Trail. Essentially it's two enclosures, one of which is paved. One is 20 yards by 20, and the other 30 by 7. Just low walls, but a very fine set of four stone steps linking them. Outside them there's a drain and a wall, and a lemon grove and cemetery a little way off. I'm pretty sure they're Inca,' she said.

'It's much more impressive than "Paititi",' added Craig. 'Perhaps we can return next year,' I said and, seeing the flicker of interest in my eyes, some of those around me grinned.

Katie had sent up mules and packhorses to aid the final withdrawal. The muleteers seemed glad to be out of Quilapituni, where the vampire bats had been attacking their animals. They seemed to prefer the abundant grazing at Waricunca, despite the local jaguars. Nevertheless, some carried rusty shotguns.

As soon as the sun had dried the track after the heavy morning rain, I hurried on down to Quilapituni with the Bolivian archaeologists. Sad evidence of the work of *huaqueros* was seen at a small cemetery: human bones, broken pieces of coffin, and a board marked 1944 where grave-robbers had been busy.

Plodding on, eyes down and watching my step, I suddenly saw something that made me jump sideways. A pace ahead, coiled as if ready to strike, was a large yellow-and-black bushmaster right in the middle of the track. I stood quite still, but it didn't move and, recovering from my shock, I saw that it was dead. This reptile – a member of one of the most feared species in South America – had obviously been killed by an Indian ahead of us. Nevertheless it was a timely reminder that danger is always lurking where you least expect it.

Jolted back to reality by my Motorola, I heard Bruce's voice. He reported the discovery of more pottery in the fort. 'It may even be a pre-Inca site,' he said. That was good news indeed.

Ernie awaited us at Quilapituni with beer and good cheer. While Yoli paid off the Indians, he regaled me with a host of stories about his logistic battles.

As the expedition members gathered for supper, the village families appeared and looked on as the gringos finished their meal. Mike Smith made a hit with the children. He had brought with him from England lots of balloons that could be blown up and twisted into shapes such as sausage-dogs or bunches of flowers: the children had never seen anything like it. It was fun, and touching, to see how such a small expense could produce so much pleasure.

Ernie created a cocktail, and a party atmosphere quickly developed. Then after an hour it began to rain – softly at first, and then harder, until the concrete-dry ground of that afternoon turned into swamp. Everyone crowded under the banana-leaf roofing, and the event became surreal: a mixture of children's party, cocktail reception and heavy drinking session.

Later Elvin appeared at the door of my tent. 'This is for you,' he said, pressing a beautiful, polished stone axe-head into my hand. 'I find it at Incapampa. Thank you for what you have done for our village.' We said our farewells in the rain, and I promised to do our best to help the little community in the future.

There were quite a few people who woke up the next morning to find that their tents had half collapsed around them: the tent pegs had not been sufficiently pushed in the day before, and had come out of the earth. Mud – the thick, heavy red clay of Bolivia – was everywhere and had got into everything. It was also still drizzling.

These were not the best circumstances in which to decamp: muddy tents were rolled up into muddy rucksacks, and these were then hauled aboard a truck that had been sent by the alcalde to transport us to Mapiri. It was open-top, and there was not an inch of space available by the time everyone had clambered on board.

We waved goodbye to the sad-looking people of Quilapituni, who had gathered to see us off, and the truck sailed along the dirt track for about 500 yards before getting stuck in the mud. It was the same old story: everyone leaped down, shoved, avoided the flying ooze as best they could, trudged after the truck through the worst stretch and then climbed up again, before repeating the whole performance ten minutes later.

Several hours of pushing and shoving brought us down the zigzag track into Mapiri. Nestling on the banks of the river, neat houses and well-stocked shops gave the impression of order. The cobbled streets may have been copied from Inca roads, but the church was spacious and modern. Two Colombian lady missionaries, who seemed to play a leading part in the town's affairs, made us and especially Yoli, their compatriot, very welcome. The alcalde insisted on providing a steak-and-chips lunch for all of us. Nothing could have been better. He also produced two interesting men.

Primitivo Ramos had been on Hans Ertl's first expedition in 1954. Deeply tanned and heavily lined, he looked an old man as he rose slowly from his chair to be introduced. However, I learned that he and I were the same age. 'But you are tall,' he said. 'That makes you look younger.' He told me that the expedition he was on had lasted three months, and that as far as he knew he was the only member still living. However, there was also someone who had been on Ertl's second expedition. 'I have not seen Julian Piza since those days, even though he lives here. We can try to find him,' Primitivo told us.

Coca-Cola was served as Yoli questioned Primitivo. 'What did Ertl find?' she asked. 'He found a stone house and, about 100 metres away, six old graves. I do not know whose they were; there was no date. There were also two canals leading into a pool.' 'Did Ertl excavate?' Primitivo shook his head. 'He did no excavation!'

He went on to tell us that contact with Ertl had been limited: 'He did not speak Spanish.' And the Germans – five in all, including a woman – had kept very much to themselves. 'We porters lived in the stone house and put up poles to support a roof.' I remembered the 15-inch post-holes we had found. Ertl seemed to have had plenty of money, but was very sensitive and secretive about his tent: 'We were forbidden to approach Ertl's tent or to disturb him,' Primitivo went on.

'What was he looking for?' asked Yoli. 'A lost city, of course – but he found nothing,' replied Primitivo. He also described to us a large, heavy metal case with holes in it which the porters had carried all the way to the Rio Tulani. Apparently the Germans had said it was to house the golden bell of Paititi when they found it. They were going to put live snakes in the box with it, as a deterrent to thieves.

Yoli asked him about snakes, but Primitivo could recall seeing only one small brown specimen in a tree. He said they were no problem – which contradicted Ertl's account.

Yoli pressed him again about the results of Ertl's expedition, but he remained adamant that nothing had been found. Nor did he know about the figures we had seen inscribed in the chasm. He had never seen Ertl again after the expedition, but had recently been approached by the strange Austrian/German, who had sought information and asked him to come on an expedition to Paititi.

Next day Julian Piza arrived and, sitting with Primitivo, told his tale. On the second expedition, which had lasted from February to September 1955, there had been fifteen Germans, only one of whom spoke Spanish. They saw the stone buildings and snakes. The rains were heavy. The Germans did some excavation, but he thought that all they took away were some soil samples. Everyone slept in tents, and the workers were never allowed near the Germans' tents. No house was built by Ertl while Piza was there. At times the Germans became very depressed, complaining, 'Why is it we cannot discover Paititi?' They believed that if they could find and touch the golden bell all would be revealed to them. They had not explored the lower part of the Rio Tulani gorge, but had seen something on the mountain. They talked to Piza of piles of white stones, and said they had to leave the area because of snakes and violent thunderstorms.

'*Mi coronel*, the Germans told us the place was haunted, and there was much talk of mysterious and enchanted grottos,' said Señor Piza. When a worker was bitten by a snake, the Germans gave him a remedy to drink which apparently worked! As we were about to leave, Piza said, 'Ertl had a radio, and often talked to someone outside the expedition area in German.' Yoli asked about artefacts and discoveries, but Julian Piza had not seen the Germans find anything.

Another few pieces of the jigsaw had emerged, but I was still puzzled. What had been Ertl's real mission?

'Where are you going now?' asked the old man. 'To the Atlantic,' I replied, eager to be on our way. Julian Piza looked perplexed. 'The ocean,' said Yoli, pointing eastward. 'That must be very far from Mapiri,' he commented. 'I have never seen the sea.'

I started to draw a map, but Yoli touched my arm. 'The alcalde wants us to attend a short ceremony,' she said. 'But we have to leave . . . ' I started to protest. It was no good, however: the school band was already warming up in the *alcaldía* garden, where many of the townsfolk were now gathered. Elaborate garlands of fresh blooms were placed around Yoli, Elizabeth and myself as we were served with glasses of the ubiquitous Coca-Cola and listened to the children attack their instruments noisily, tunelessly and with magnificent enthusiasm. The beaming alcalde welcomed us in ringing tones, while the expedition members looked bemused. What had we done for Mapiri? Then we remembered the work that Shirley Critchley and the medical team had carried out here.

Knowing that we must hurry on to Guanay, I made a short response. But then the band struck up again and a local lady swept me off my feet – having difficulty with the oversized garland, which I discarded. 'You must wear it until you leave town,' hissed Yoli. 'It's insulting to remove it.' So I put it back on and danced around looking like an exhibit at the Chelsea Flower Show.

As we all pranced around, an elderly stranger in a battered trilby edged his way towards me. Speaking quickly in guttural Quechua, he seemed to be trying to tell me something. It was impossible to understand what he said, but one word stuck in my memory: 'Akakor'. It didn't sound Spanish. I turned to ask Yoli to interpret, but she was whirling around with the alcalde and when I looked back the man had gone. I couldn't be sure but I was pretty certain the word was 'Akakor', and I jotted it down in my log. If this was it, its significance would become apparent only much later.

Paul Overton eventually organized an elaborate dance which owed something to the hokey-cokey plus a little more to the Dashing White Sergeant and the conga. After forty-five minutes we managed to break away, promising to do our utmost to return to help this friendly community.

The band, blowing fit to waken the dead, led us to the river, where Eddy Loaiza – a Guanay entrepreneur who built and operated boats – had organized mahogany boats. There was only just enough room for all of us plus our kit in the two slim craft. Locals, looking for a free lift, tried to board and had to be rebuffed, but we managed to get Celso on, for I needed to talk to him in more detail in Guanay. Finally, at 12.30 p.m., the boat edged into the current and we swept past the band, whose members were still trying to burst their lungs. Within minutes the town and our new friends had disappeared.

According to Eddy, in the wet season, navigation upriver was possible in mahogany boats right up to a village called Urkupine Tarapo, near Consata, and small boats could come down from points even further away. Thus within about 30 miles of Lake Titicaca there was a way to the Atlantic. I felt that at last we might be following in the wake of the early navigators.

Cruising down the silt-laden river with the jungle closing in again, we watched gold-panners in battered straw hats slaving away in the hot sun on the sandy banks. Each prospector seemed to control a small area of mud. Some had small Heath-Robinson-style sluices; the more advanced used motorized pumps. Blue plastic sheeting at the edge of the trees provided modest shelter, beside which women in soiled clothing attended cooking-fires. Naked children romped in the water, and some floated along on old inner tubes. It must have been an extremely hard way to earn a living, but the lure of gold is such that, even with a depressed price, men were prepared to follow this tedious profession in the hope of the big find.

Passing through the wavelets of a few small rapids, we pressed on – still in our garlands. Katie, sitting on a bow, her long blonde hair streaming out behind, became a living figurehead. For the first time in months I relaxed and thought back over the previous extraordinary six weeks.

I mused on what the Rio Tulani site might have been, with its water – ponds, flumes and sluices – everywhere. John Hemming, lately director of the Royal Geographical Society and an acknowledged expert on South America, describes in *The Conquest of the Incas* how rocks, hills, springs and caves round Cuzco, in Peru, had had a magical significance. I felt it likely that the site we had reached was not, as Juan Blanco had called it, a city but a centre for ritual, a shrine, a place of water-worship – and a good area for mining gold too. Perhaps all those ponds were made for sacred ablutions. The people who farmed the extensive terracing maybe lived once in the surrounding forest. It could still have been one of the last refuges of the dispersed Inca after the fall of Vilcabamba to the Spanish in 1572, but I was convinced that the Spaniards had been there too.

We had read and reread Ertl's account, but in many cases his descriptions just did not fit the ground. He had spent almost a year at the site, much of it in the appalling conditions of the rainy season, yet had had no archaeologist. Nobody at UNAR in La Paz knew what had become of the golden ornaments he photographed and claimed to have found in 'Paititi'. His workers had told us he had found nothing and had done no excavating, but he had taken soil samples. Indeed, he seemed obsessed with the place, making two expeditions there. Why was he so secretive, and to whom was he speaking in German on his radio? Why had he constructed such a robust house? As our craft shot some rapids, I put all this to Yoli. 'Perhaps he planned to live there,' she said. 'Where people have lived before could make a good settlement, and if he wanted privacy there was no better place.' As an economist, she certainly had a point.

Naturally enough, many in our party were disappointed not to find Inca treasures or the remains of fantastic buildings, and the question remained: What could have been the reasons for the lack of artefacts or recognizable buildings? Had everything transportable already been carried away by generations of treasure-hunters? Had an earthquake or an enemy so comprehensively destroyed the city that nothing now remained? And why was the mysterious Austrian trying to prevent us carrying out a scientific study?

It is quite possible that there were in fact artefacts and buildings on the extensive area of the site that remained unexcavated and undisturbed under its jungle covering, and it would be good to think that the Bolivian government will follow up our work and take further steps to clear the site at 'Paititi'. But with only some twelve trained archaeologists in the country, and apparently little or no money to pay them, it seems unlikely that this will happen in the foreseeable future. Over half the ruins at the country's best-known site at Tiwanaku remain to be excavated, even though they are only a taxi ride away from La Paz, so, it is probably safe to say that nothing further will be done at somewhere as inaccessible as the Rio Tulani unless some other crazy gringos take it on. Indeed, it is a pleasant fancy to imagine that, perhaps in fifty to a hundred years' time, an expedition may light upon this book, read the description of Paititi, and then follow in our tracks to the site.

'When are you going to brief everyone on the plan for Phase Two?' asked Yoli, forcing me to leave the puzzle of Paititi behind for the time being and concentrate my mind on the forthcoming 3,000-mile voyage.

Three hours later we rounded a bend, passed the rusty giant dredger, and went under the unfinished bridge and into Guanay. There, riding at her moorings, was *Kota Mama 3*, with masts and sails rigged. It was my first sight of the trimaran and, although I knew what to expect, the initial impression was of a small craft sitting low in the water with her three jaguar figureheads bobbing about as if in conversation. Beside her floated *Southern Gailes*, the traditional balsa raft, about 33 feet long by 5 feet wide – not nearly so impressive, but every bit as river-worthy. Though for two years I had eaten, slept and dreamed the plan to sail to the Atlantic, this was the moment when it all seemed real.

After a frustrating wait, Jim Masters was now eager to greet the new team members who were flying in that day from Britain and to get on with the sailing.

The heat at the lower altitude made us all lethargic, but there was much to be done before our departure. To urge us on, the enthusiastic Guanay school band was practising 'God Save the Queen' and 'Rule, Britannia!' almost continuously in a hall next door. Even the most patriotic found it a bit much to leap to attention twenty times an hour. However, the versatile Graham Catchpole – an accomplished pianist – put the final touches to the renderings and the rehearsals grew fewer.

The councillors came with more tales of the opposition's intrigues and the news that the Austrian had got money from the prefectura to take an expedition to 'Paititi' later that month. It was all very odd, but I had other matters to think about.

Before leaving Guanay, I gave a final speech to the councillors and townspeople at a public meeting in the *alcaldía*. Describing our discoveries, with Yoli translating, I urged them to protect the site from treasure-hunters, pointing out that if they wished to attract tourists they would need to keep the trail open. I had already advised the alcalde of Mapiri that a guidebook about the area in Spanish and English was essential. However I was not optimistic that, in the midst of all their various problems, they would follow our advice, or that tourists would flood in.

Hoping that we would return, a number of people pressed projects on us. All carefully typed up in clean folders, they required varying sums of money. Were we the only source of aid for the people of this region? I wondered. Or did they do this, more in hope than expectation, to all gringos?

The mountains around were in ferment. The coca farmers were protesting again, and the government – its patience exhausted – had sent in the army. Protesters had been shot and barricades torn down. Near Lake Titicaca the Bolivian Navy had played its part, but had spared the demonstrators and shot a donkey instead. This unrest prevented the prefect and General Hurtado from attending our launch; but, as all we needed was now in place, our plans went ahead.

We were packing up when Bill Holmes was given another story about Paititi. An earnest and apparently sincere gentleman named Napoleón Quintanilla described how mysterious lights had been seen and bells had been heard ringing by a party working on Cerro Paititi in the 1950s. 'Could this Napoleón be related to the chap that Monika Ertl killed?' I asked Bill, but he had no idea.

Napoleón Quintanilla's tale was similar to others we had heard, but a colleague of his – a dentist named Vladimir – gave an account which really fascinated me. He had heard of the existence of a tunnel behind a waterfall at the Rio Tulani site. Inside this was said to be a small statue or sculpture, possibly of Inca origin. It was set on an island in the middle of a small pool into which led stone steps that appeared to continue down to another chamber under the water. To the best of Vladimir's knowledge no one had investigated further, and to do so would probably need diving equipment. It sounded like a description of a sacred grotto or shrine, and my mind went back to the Devil's Cauldron. However, was this account factual or, like so many tales in this remote region, simply a myth?

8

Guanay to Rurrenabaque

Very best wishes on the launch of *KM3* and for a safe passage to the Atlantic. 'The winds and waves are always on the side of the ablest navigators' (Edward Gibbon, 1737–94). Good hunting!

Message from Richard Knight, *KM3*'s sponsor, 14 June 2001

Now THE NEW phase began. At Guanay the expedition underwent a sea-change. Not only were there new personnel – sixteen team members flew home from La Paz, and seven Brits, an American, a Canadian and a couple of Bolivians joined – there were also new aims and new modes of transport. No longer would small parties be penetrating upland rainforest, shuttling back and forth along trails with mules, porters and packhorses. Now a smaller team would be all together, confined to a fleet of small boats that would thread its way down a long succession of ever-widening rivers whose very names changed confusingly as we progressed – Mapiri, Kaka, Beni, Mamoré, Madeira, Amazon. Previously it had been wet and dank. Now it would be wet but hotter.

We were tasked to pass through the little-studied Beni region of Bolivia, with its whisper of a possible far-flung 'Paititi', and to investigate it as far as time would allow. Then we would see how the reed trimaran and the balsa raft fared in the Mamoré–Madeira rapids and on the long haul down to the Atlantic.

Saturday 16 June dawned dry, but with a leaden sky that foretold a change in the weather. *Kota Mama 3* (*KM3*) rocked gently at her mooring, with *Southern Gailes* bobbing alongside. A few yards up the beach Eddy Loaiza's two mahogany boats – freshly painted with orange, blue and white designs – had the appearance of South Seas war canoes. In recent days a new craft had been added to the fleet: Eddy's *chata*, a square, flat-bottomed barge, some 42 feet long and 12 feet wide, with a blue plastic canopy and sporting a prominent loo which hung out over the stern. This was to be the support boat, carrying our HQ and much of Ernie's stores. And as tenders we had two Avon inflatables, with two men in each.

The flags of all nations represented in this phase were rigged to *KM3*. The Bolivian standard flew highest, then came the others: of Brazil, Great Britain, Colombia, Sri Lanka, the USA and, of course, my Jersey flag. The flag of St George was there too, and J. P. Knight's blue house flag and Air BP's banners. And on the sterns of the trimaran and the raft the red ensign fluttered proudly in the gentle breeze coming up the valley from the swampy flatlands of the Beni.

Among incoming members were Dr Marco Antonio Prado, sent by the Bolivian Ministry of Health to help us for the first week, and Patricio Crooker, a photojournalist sponsored by Air BP. Patricio, black of beard and roguish by nature, was a descendant of a British navigator who had served in Chile in the nineteenth century, presumably with either the Royal Navy or the Chilean. He wrote and illustrated excellent articles for *Escape*, the colour magazine of the Bolivian broadsheet *La Razón*, and would be with us all the way to Belém, where the Amazon meets the Atlantic. Alasdair Crosby had been doing much the same for the *Jersey Evening Post*, but now left with the outgoing group. He later reported seeing Juan Domingo 'smiling – very uncharacteristically – as he and his colleague climbed happily into a taxi . . . to be whisked far away to La Paz'. Alas, Wilma Winkler's son had been injured in a car accident, so she could not join us for the petroglyph survey, but she faxed through all the background information that Bruce Mann and Elizabeth Dix would need. Thereafter we kept in touch by e-mail.

Bill Holmes was putting up his maps and measuring distances. Peter Kannangara, who had now taken over from Mike Smith as communications officer, set up the radios and carefully stowed the satellite phones and the precious Affno computer in a padded mule-box. Yoli checked a hundred little details, while Ernie's team heaved aboard crates of bully beef, porridge and Gatorade (a high-energy powder to put in water).

As admiral of our fleet and one of the few who had ever sailed a reed boat, Jim gave *KM3* a final check. 'Three thousand miles to Belém,' he grinned – 'that's about the same as London to Cairo.'

Next morning *le tout Guanay* gathered along the strand two hours before our departure time. Women set up stalls to sell cold drinks and fruit. The alcalde and his staff and various town councillors shook hands and patted backs all round.

Philip Kittelson came from Caranavi to give part of the service of dedication in English. The son of Lutheran missionaries from Michigan but
born in Bolivia, he was the alcalde of Caranavi as well as minister there,
and we had met him on our way to Guanay previously. Press and television jostled for position. BBC TV in the person of Richard Drax, who
was now joining our team, interviewed many of us. Máximo Catari had
come down from Lake Titicaca and was dressed in his scarlet Aymara
cloak and woolly hat. I even saw two policemen.

Not seen – though said to be in Guanay at the time – was the sinister
Austrian who seemed to have been spending the last several weeks trying
to thwart our efforts to get to 'Paititi'. We later discovered he was one
Sigfried Trippolt, and, under the heading 'THE RUINS OF GREAT
PAITITI HAVE BEEN FOUND' the 2 September 2001 edition of the
La Paz newspaper *La Prensa* reported his claim, in a talk he gave in La
Paz, to have discovered the mythical city near Guanay. 'Archaeologists,
geologists and anthropologists confirmed the existence of the ruins of a
Pre-Colombian [*sic*] city in the vicinity of Cerro Paititi,' the article stated,
and added explicitly that Trippolt had not found gold but 'is now in
search of [it]'. It was evident to us now that this *huaquero* had feared that
we might find something before he could get up there again himself.

Trippolt had clearly taken up the mantle of Hans Ertl – making an
interesting Austro-German nexus – and now saw 'Paititi' as his own
domain. British-led interlopers keep out! He credited Ertl with the discovery of 'the city' in 1955, though, in line with our own views, he
admitted that 'many of Ertl's claims were fraudulent'. Sadly, his own discoveries, made in April 2001, were a touch speculative and not very con-
vincing – 'roads, streets and city squares covered by vegetation'. Where
were all these, we wondered? He was sponsored to some extent by the
prefectura of La Paz and the alcalde of Guanay, as we had been, although
he seems to have fallen out with the alcalde over money. This could
account for the low profile that he and his henchman Juan Blanco maintained during the high jinks that now attended our departure.

At 11.30 a.m. the high-school band marched on to the beach and
struck up with the Bolivian national anthem – 'its length', said Alasdair,
'suggesting some extended opera chorus.' One verse of 'God Save the
Queen' was followed by an astonished silence, as if no one could believe
a national anthem could be so short. Lengthy speeches by the alcalde and
his deputy, stressing the need for international friendship and more
tourism in Bolivia, earned polite applause, and I was given a magnificent

model of a balsa raft crafted locally in solid gold. Glimpsing Jim looking wearily at his wristwatch, ever impatient to be pressing on, I made my speech sincere but brief and ended with '¡*Viva Bolivia!*', which seemed to go down well.

Philip's dedication was also short and his address appropriate. He urged us all to place service before self in the testing time that lay ahead – and, most practically, to get more long poles with which to fend off rocks.

The English-speaking crews gave a lusty rendering of 'Eternal Father, Strong to Save' and there should then have followed the *challa de embarcaciones*, when wine would have been sprinkled on the boats, but Philip declined to participate in such a heathen tradition. In any case, the boats were now beginning to move. The crowds, swollen to several thousand strong, surged forward clasping our hands and thrusting up babies to be kissed, making it difficult for me to reach my support vessel. I doubted if Francisco de Orellana had had such a send-off when he set out down the Amazon headwaters on his pioneering journey to the Atlantic in 1542. I bade a last farewell to the alcalde and climbed aboard the *chata*. Yoli handed me the loudhailer and we shouted, '*Karurkama*' – Aymara for 'Until the next time'. The crowd, many of Indian origin, roared back with pleasure, firecrackers exploded, the school band struck up 'Rule, Britannia!', and *KM3* was pushed slowly out into the river.

Gathering our boats in its grip, the stream carried us towards the first rapids.

Like many departures, this one was chaotic. In 1998 at a frontier town on the Rio Desaguadero our three reed boats had cast off from the Bolivian bank, drifted across the river, and gone aground among reeds on the Peruvian side. Now there was a faster current, and immediately a bed of shingle became visible downstream. *KM3* executed a 270° turn in full view of the townsfolk and then drifted abeam towards it. Geoffrey Hoskins somehow fell overboard.

As we eventually raced downstream the jungle was still with us, for the Amazon rainforest – one of the world's most varied habitats in flora and fauna – spreads right across the continent, from the slopes of the Andes to the mouth of the giant river itself. At 'Paititi' we had tramped through cloud forest, with its orchids and bromeliads attracting iridescent humming-birds and colourful butterflies. Now we descended through gorges to enter a zone of older forest tightly packed along the river banks, behind which stretched endless swamps. We were to find taller trees and palms growing in the areas that flood during the rains – the *várzea* – and on the drier grounds the great hardwoods for which South America is famous.

As the landscape changed, so did the people. Although the Beni is now only sparsely populated, it was once inhabited by one of the earliest civilizations in South America. There have been suggestions that these people were the ancestors of the Andean cultures, and there would certainly have been trade between the two regions.

The soil of the Beni region is not very porous, so when the torrential rains cascade down from the mountains they flood the area for as long as four months. To exist in this water world, the Beni people constructed mounds linked to each other by canals and causeways. The mounds are usually built in groups of three or four, and oil-company geologists thought they were evidence of an early civilization, so in 1961 William Denevan, now professor emeritus of geography at the University of Wisconsin, Madison, took a helicopter over the vast Llanos de Mojos plain through which the Beni flows and saw in these savannah lands 'what seemed to be the remains of transportation canals, pyramid-like mounds, elevated causeways, raised agricultural fields and clusters of odd zigzagging ridges . . . I *knew* these things were not natural. You just don't have that kind of straight line in nature.'

Clark L. Erickson of the University of Pennsylvania, Philadelphia, reckoned that this part of the Beni had seen 'some of the densest populations and the most elaborate cultures in the Amazon'. Beginning between 3,000 and 5,000 years ago, these all ended between AD 1400 and 1700 at the time of, but not connected with, the influx of Europeans. An anthropologist at Tulane University in New Orleans, William Balée, agrees that much in this savannah region is man-made: the *várzea* and the bluffs above it were host to an important civilization.

Denevan, Erickson and Balée have their detractors, but in the 1990s Erickson led teams on a series of excavations of *lomas* or mounds in the Beni. Ibibate is 30 miles east of Trinidad, the capital of Beni province. 'Big mound' in the local Indian tongue, it rises 50 feet above the surrounding flatlands and was found to be full of potsherds to a depth of 30 feet. Apparently the builders of these mounds raised parcels of land to grow crops above the annual flood level. Linked by causeways and bordered by canals, the mounds grew higher as garbage accumulated. The zigzag earthen walls were fish weirs, signs of a form of pisciculture, and were piled high with snail shells (of the edible gastropod genus *Pomacea*) discarded after meals, just as we found on the banks of the Rio Paraguay in 1999. As Erickson concluded, 'The whole landscape has been organized and designed.'

The late Kenneth Lee, an American geologist, made a study of this culture, and came up with some staggering conclusions. According to Ross Salmon, who accompanied Lee on field trips, he had measured one of these mounds and estimated that it was 1,300 feet in diameter, rising to a height of 30 feet. He calculated that as many as 1,000 people had lived on the mound, and 200 could be available at any one time for construction work while the rest would have been employed on farming and hunting. It might have taken ten years to build such a mound, assuming it was possible to work on it only during the dry season.

Satellite photographs have revealed 40,000 of these mounds in Bolivia and Ecuador, and many more in Brazil, Colombia and Venezuela. It seems that an early civilization of at least 500,000 had existed in the Beni. Ross Salmon had been impressed by the 'technological brilliance of the indigenous stone age Indians', and pointed out that 'South America has millions of square kilometres of land with a potential to grow food for a hungry world'.

The air photos also showed that in ancient times it would have been possible to travel by canoe along canals and rivers throughout the region, and eventually reach the coast.

Dr Victor Bustos, an eminent Chilean archaeologist who has devoted much time to investigating the Beni cultures, has observed that pottery found in the mounds shows many similarities in pattern and colour with that found in the Andes. He feels that there could well be a link between the two areas of civilization. Working with him in the Beni, Ross Salmon had dug up knives and arrowheads of bone and granite. Stone of this type was not to be found locally.

Around Guanay there is plenty of stone, and within an hour of leaving we found evidence of early men on black rocks polished smooth by the action of river silt. Bruce and Elizabeth were soon busy recording petroglyphs – classic geometric patterns, snakes, stick-men, squiggles – some of them below the present water level.

Tomachi on the Rio Kaka was our first night's camp. After a warm welcome – floral arches and confetti – our medico-dental team began a pattern that it was to follow all the way to Belém: physical examinations, treatment and/or advice, teeth extractions. Dr Marco Antonio Prado dealt most efficiently with a villager who had an epileptic fit while dancing for us.

Most of us slept ashore in mosquito-proof tents, but, having no time to erect mine, I huddled up among the stores on the deck of the *chata*. Vivid lightning flickered throughout the night and rain came at dawn. As forecast, the cold front hit us and the temperature dropped from 77° to less than 54 °F in a few hours.

Pulling on waterproofs, we prepared to tackle Retama, the only rapid of any size before Esperanza, 800 miles away. We knew about this from the 2000 reconnaissance, when the British miner Tim Williams had shown me a video of the cataract. Then, when we had arrived in May, Eddy Loaiza had taken Jim and me to see Retama for real. I had been apprehensive about the 6-foot rollers breaking around the massive central boulder. '*Kota Mama* will go through all right,' Jim had said, 'but until I know what the river level is in June I won't know whether to tackle it as a complete trimaran or take each hull through separately.' Advised of the many big rapids, the Cataris had built the boat with this important capability.

Speeding down river in a mahogany boat, Jim now took the skipper and helmsman of *KM3* to have a look at the rapid. On the left side a tower-shaped rock rose vertically from the river. In the centre of the stream the huge boulder divided the river in two. The roughest water was to the right of the boulder.

Eddy's two mahogany boats went down the cataract first with no problems. Then the *chata*'s deck flexed and creaked as she wobbled through the rolling brown waves. As the helmsman brought her round in the calmer water below, I remarked to Bill Holmes, 'You wouldn't think a floating shoebox like this could handle rapids.'

Matt Wilkinson, the newly arrived sapper captain who was *KM3*'s skipper, now disposed his crew over the two outriggers. Jim had decided to keep the trimaran configuration and not split up the hulls. 'They're coming now,' he said as he crouched like a rowing coach in the bows of one of Eddy's boats. Then we saw the paddles flashing in unison as *KM3* and *Southern Gailes* appeared from behind the giant boulder and approached the lip of the rapid. The reed boat's jaguar heads bobbed up and down as the three hulls rose and fell independently. It was behaving just as we had hoped, and gave us confidence that this was the right design for the job. 'Now I know – early men could have come down on reed rafts in the same way,' said Richard Drax as he shifted his video camera's position.

Matt and his twelve-strong crew had worked well together, and it was not without significance that half of them were from the same army unit – the 9th Parachute Squadron RE. It had been this same unit that Jim Masters had joined in 1948 when it was formed.

'Do you think General Hurtado is having an eye kept on us,' I asked Yoli as two Bolivian Army helicopters came over us for the third time.

'No, I think he's out looking for coca farmers,' she said.

Sometimes even in remote places the prospect of something exotic, colourful, little seen, fails to come up to expectations in reality. The Musetenes Indians from the village of Muchanes had invited us to a traditional ceremony and display of dancing at the junction of the Kaka and Beni rivers. They had even sent a typewritten letter. On the morning of 18 June we found about ten of them in grubby western clothing on a windswept sandbank putting up some stalls from which to sell simple hand-crafted goods. Their pet animals skittered about – a coati, with narrow snout, sharp claws, and the distinctive long furry tail with buff-coloured rings; a monkey; some parrots; and a young white-lipped peccary. A sounder of these peccaries once charged through my camp in the Darién in 1972, scattering horses and obliging us to shin up trees in most undignified fashion. As I picked this one up it screamed with rage and clacked its yellow teeth as if it feared to let down its fellows in the Panama forests.

Graham extracted his five-hundredth tooth on the trip as we waited for the ceremony, but something seemed to have gone wrong and nothing happened. However, an Indian told Bruce Mann he had found pottery and seen a large complete pot about half an hour away. In moments Bruce was off, accompanied by Elizabeth, Bill Holmes, Steve Henry and our photographers. Indians have little concept of time, however, and the journey took thirty minutes by canoe, then another one and a half hours, initially up a dry river bed, then climbing up a 6-foot embankment to hack through a forest with machetes, followed by a long wade up an arroyo waist deep in water. By now the jungle and bamboo were dense. Things did not look at all promising until, glancing at the sandbanks in midstream, Bruce saw pottery fragments. Soon the shards became larger and more numerous, and some of them were painted.

Rounding a sharp bend, Bruce glanced up at the right bank, which rose for some 10 feet along a 200-yard section of the stream. There, projecting from the sandy brown soil, were a number of pots. 'Burial urns,' said Bruce. He could hardly believe it. 'It's a cemetery. What a find!' A number of the urns were being eroded out of the vertical face by the stream, and at the foot of the bank pottery fragments were scattered.

Clambering up the vertical face, hanging on by his fingernails, Bruce examined the pots. Six urns were in good condition and consisted of one pot placed within another. They were 24 to 32 inches in height and 20 to 24 inches in diameter. Inside could be seen human bones that appeared to have been put in after cleansing rather than inserted as a complete corpse. Small bowls and grave goods were clearly visible. Climbing higher, Bruce reached the top of the bank, where tree roots held the surface together. Pushing through the undergrowth, he searched for signs of stonework or buildings, but there were none. He guessed that the cemetery extended up to 200 yards from the stream. Perhaps the people buried here had lived in wooden huts, but from the size of the graveyard it must have been a large settlement.

Later, back on the *chata*, bubbling with excitement, he told me, 'I wasn't expecting such an important discovery quite like this, so close to the river. It's the first evidence I've found of a major civilization here. The petroglyphs indicated human activity in the area, but this pottery is the work of an advanced culture. Such a large cemetery indicates a higher density of population.'

A few days later we heard of some stone ruins deep in the forest. Apparently, similar pottery had been found there. There was no time to visit the site, but Bruce said, 'If those ruins could be linked to the cemetery this could do much to show interaction between the peoples of the highland and lowland regions.'

The site was still largely intact, but now the tree roots and the stream were eroding it quickly. The Indians had spoken of looters coming upriver in boats.

Bruce e-mailed Wilma in Santa Cruz and received a reply that said the site was new, probably a thousand years old, and pretty important. 'Can't the SES get an expedition back here quickly to work on this site before it vanishes?' asked Bruce.

It gave me the germ of an idea for the future.

Entering one of the final gorges of the eastern Andean foothills we came upon the great Madidi National Park – though, apart from the presence of a couple of scruffy but helpful wardens who came to visit us in a tin boat, one would not have known it. In fact this latest Bolivian reserve covers 4.7 million acres, with Andean glaciers reaching 19,000 feet on its western edge, dense rain forest at the east, and pampas in the north. This vast boomerang-shaped swathe of territory has one of the most diverse populations of flora and fauna in South America. Hardly had it been gazetted when it became threatened by a proposal to create a hydroelectric dam in the Susi canyon south of Rurrenabaque, involving flooding over 1,000 square miles, much of it in the park. Illegal logging and hunting have also to be brought under control, and we were to find evidence of indiscriminate looting of the park's archaeological sites.

As we headed downriver there seemed to be plenty of wildlife: black caymans, spectacled caymans and the large rodents called capybara were regularly seen on the banks or swimming near our camps. Peter Kannangara, sitting at his laptop, pulled on another sweater. 'I can't believe this is the Amazon basin in June,' he said. It was 48 °F and there was a high wind-chill factor.

For the most part, life for the crew on *KM3* was fairly monotonous. The balsa raft was poled occasionally, but more often it was towed alongside the *chata*. As the wind was usually contrary, it was only on rare occasions that the trimaran could use her sails; otherwise she was propelled by either a 15 or a 25 h.p. Mariner outboard, which droned noisily away and pushed her along at around 6 m.p.h. Jim felt it was critical to reach the Madeira–Mamoré cataract region by early July, to catch the ideal water levels. The weather had been suitable for the initial land-based journey to 'Paititi' only from mid-May, and so we now had three weeks in which to reach the Esperanza cataract. Allowing for stops and problems, this meant we ought to average 50 miles per day. However, to our satisfaction, the reed hulls remained in good shape and did not seem to be absorbing much water.

Most of those who were not permanent members of *KM3*'s crew were invited on board for a day every now and then. It was generally a fairly restful experience, but on one occasion Yoli, Eric Niemi, Geoffrey Hoskins and Dr Marco Antonio Prado had a rude awakening when the hull on which they languished struck a submerged log which thrust it high in the air, tipping all four of them into the river.

We passed through the last canyon, left the mountains behind, and approached Rurrenabaque – the last large town before we entered the flat expanse of the Beni lowlands.

The naval commandant sent a smart lieutenant upriver to meet us and warn us of the ceremonial which lay in store there.

Rurre, as locals know it, has grown from the sleepy, malarial village in which two or three English traders lived in the 1920s and is now sustained by logging and tourism. All the guidebooks rhapsodize about it, and new road and air links with La Paz have made it the capital of the Bolivian Amazon. Karaoke bars and tour operators offering low-budget jungle trips now dot the centre of town, in which it is scarcely possible to get lost. Some of us, including Shirley Critchley, had already arrived there by truck from Guanay – spending thirty hours in a freezing-cold cab.

Once there, we took a shower at the characterful Hotel Berlin, the town's oldest and 'bottom of the barrel' (*Lonely Planet*) at $3 per night. But there are a few better hotels, and some of us found them.

We left Rurre on 21 June, and soon after that Bruce Mann, pushing ahead in an Avon, came upon one of the famous mounds as described by Lee, Denevan, Erickson and Balée. The Beni had sliced through it, and the 'Indiana Jones of Scotland' found it to be up to 15 feet high in the centre, and for some 300 yards we could see from its profile that there were two or three layers of occupation. Pottery was widely scattered along the shores, some with intriguing geometric designs, but none of it was painted. Eric Niemi, our sharp-eyed biologist, spotted the major find: a half-complete burial urn. This was another double pot, containing bones and also a small ceramic vessel for the deceased to use on the journey to the next life. The trees on top of the bank were very substantial, because the high ground does not flood and so the hardwoods flourish. We learned to look out for such tell-tale signs as an indication of sites in the future.

While the medical team was at work near here, a patient brought in a fine stone axe-head as a gift. It was of andesite, a highland rock not found in the Beni, and the tool was similar in design and composition to the one that Elvin had given me at Quilapituni. This seemed a firm pointer to there having been ancient trade routes along the river, either in raw materials or in finished products.

At Rurre, Eddy Loaiza had been called back to Guanay on urgent business. He had taken one of his mahogany boats and left Cristo Flores, his chief boatman, in charge. On 24 June Cristo came to see me, looking a touch hangdog.

'What we going to do? We only have gas for *chata* and mahogany boat for one more day.'

For a moment I was speechless. It was still 375 miles to Riberalta, the next big place.

'Eddy make little mistake,' said Cristo.

'You're damned right he did,' I replied angrily. 'Have you been given money to buy more – supposing we can find any?' He shook his head.

All had been going so smoothly. Now I was incandescent.

9

Rapid Work

It is necessary to understand . . . that we are not Bolivians here: we are orien-
talists. We are a different people from those of the Altiplano. I would not like
you to leave with a wrong impression.

Señor Arauz, a farmer near Santa Ana, to Peter Grieve
in *The Wilderness Voyage*, 1952

ERNIE HAD BOUGHT enough fuel for *KM3* and the two Avons in Rurre,
but it could not provide for the *chata* and the mahogany boat too, so Jim,
on learning that there was a Bolivian Navy post halfway to Riberalta at
Cavinas, set off there with Yoli and a fistful of bolivianos. We needed
1,150 litres but they could spare him only 140. I would have to send a
boat ahead, itself using up fuel, to buy more in Riberalta and return to
the fleet with it.

Suddenly everything seemed to be going awry. Somebody put
unmixed petrol in *KM3*'s motor, a carrying-handle on another motor
broke off, the mosquitoes were villainous, and an unlit speedboat, probably running drugs, came close to hitting the moored *KM3* one night.
We learned about the *narcotraficantes* from Sergeant Ferrufino of the
Bolivian Navy, stationed at Cavinas. His detachment of *Diablos Azules*,
or Blue Devils, aims to check the river-borne flow of cocaine from
Bolivia to Peru and Brazil, most of it by night. His humble outpost
offered some of us a roof and a shower, and he warned us not to travel
on the river after dark. 'Only *narcotraficantes* sail then,' he stressed, 'and
my men open fire on them without warning.'

Paul Overton picked a team of six to go to Riberalta in the mahogany boat for more fuel. Mike How would navigate, and Julio, one of
Eddy Loaiza's men, would drive, with the help of Don Pascal, our Beni
river pilot. Patricio Crooker would interpret, and Bas Barrow, a tough
engineer, contributed muscle.

Furnished with dollars and bolivianos, a map and four 200-litre oil drums (three of which were empty), they set off on a memorable journey. Sergeant Ferrufino radioed ahead to tell the navy that these night-birds were not drug-runners. Julio managed a speed of 6 m.p.h., with Paul in the bows sweeping the darkness with his torch. There was a moon, but semi-submerged trees and sandbars were still hard to see. Roles changed as sleep overtook them, one after the other. About 4.30 a.m. they hit a mudbank and stuck fast. The prospect of caymans discouraged any heroics over the side, but after a cold hour's wait Mike How braved the water. The caymans were still there, but somehow they seemed less of a threat in the early-morning light.

He shoved the boat free, and they sped on for two more hours until they sighted a house. Paul ran up the bank to it. The occupants displayed the usual Indian impassivity, as if it was commonplace for a gringo, NERA satellite phone in hand, to come bounding up to their door at dawn.

At Peña Amarilla there is a truck ferry across the Beni run by a tubby little man called Socrates. He generously let them have 40 litres of petrol, and his wife produced some cake.

In the early afternoon a moored passenger boat hailed them from the bank. 'Can you take this lady to the next village?' asked the captain, a friend of Eddy's.

A large blonde was helped into the mahogany boat carrying a sack. Once under way, she took from it a big green parrot, which hopped on to Paul's arm and side-stepped up it to sit on his shoulder, where it fell asleep. She opened the sack again and took out a second parrot, which made the same journey up his arm and fell asleep too.

'Long John Silver after a heavy lunch,' said Mike How, 'with his pieces of silver in his bum-bag.'

As the pied crow flies, the distance to Riberalta is probably half that which the meanders in the river caused Paul's team to cover. At all events, thanks to Socrates and his 40 litres, they reached the town with just 1 litre of fuel to spare.

Patricio Crooker sprang into action, and in no time the authorities were aware that some foreign newcomers had arrived. Three smartly uniformed naval officers appeared and offered assistance, and the manager of Patricio's father's lumber business helped them to find petrol quickly. The supply was at a small filling-station on the edge of town. More used to selling 1 or 2 litres at a time to the numerous motorcyclists, the pump attendant was nevertheless unfazed when a bunch of gringos in a pickup asked for two extra barrels and 1,200 litres. Having parted with 3,972 bolivianos ($440), they piled back into the pickup and set off for the muddy waterfront. Now the problem was to load the weighty barrels aboard the narrow mahogany boat – for their return journey against the current, it was vital to balance the load. To Paul's horror, two of the drums were leaking, but Don Pascal promptly filled the holes with soap and the naval duty officer turned out the guard to lift the barrels aboard.

'Three cheers for the Bolivian Navy,' said Paul as he headed for the best hotel in town. The Colonial offered a bed, and at the restaurant next door a huge meal restored their energy.

Against the current and with such a hazardous cargo, the return voyage was much slower. At nightfall they were greeted by Socrates and his wife with drinks and a fish supper. Knowing the fleet were desperate for the fuel, they pressed on by the light of the moon, eyes straining into the gloom. Shivering in the cold night air, they scanned the banks for signs of our boats. Mike had calculated they should reach the fleet by 2 a.m. and at 1.30 a.m., to his intense relief, Paul saw our riding-lights. There was a great reception, for they had done a splendid job.

While ashore at Cavinas, Yoli had met a local historian, Alfredo Taro, who told her how 20,000 Inca had come down the Madre de Dios and Beni rivers from the highlands about AD 1700. 'Some came from Cuzco,' he said, 'others from the Altiplano. They settled along the Beni as far as Riberalta, where they built a fortified town.' He went on to explain that these migrants had been escaping from the Spanish conquistadors and had wished to find a place to re-establish themselves. Many died in floods and possibly in the rapids upriver. They were not used to the hot, humid climate, and diseases such as malaria and yellow fever took their toll. Only 5,000 survived, and those may have returned to the highlands or disappeared into the Beni region. 'There are ruins of their city and tunnels at Las Piedras, near Riberalta, and also at a place named Portachuelo, further upstream,' he said. As we progressed, more people gave similar accounts – and, after all, 'Las Piedras' does mean 'the stones'.

This was exciting information, and we decided to search for these sites. Was there another Paititi? We had heard so many rumours of lost cities that I was not optimistic. Furthermore, we had seen no evidence of stone buildings in the region. If such a place existed, why had UNAR not told us of it?

As usual, much of our intelligence came from our medical team's patients. The three doctors and our dentist gave assistance wherever it was needed, and often this took them to some very odd places. The most unusual was a huge raft of 600 cedar and mahogany logs being brought downstream. A young man aboard this heaving platform had a double-abscessed front tooth. Without hesitation, Graham, our intrepid dental surgeon, went aboard, moving like a lumberjack from log to log. Perched on the most stable part, he proceeded with some difficulty to extract the tooth.

While Graham operated, the raft-men told us about dangerous encounters along the river. There were accounts of people being taken by aggressive caymans, though all the ones we saw seemed keen to avoid humans. The alcalde of Fortaleza, a Yugoslav who had fled the Nazis, gave us a horrible account of a 15-foot cayman that took a young boy at his village. Seizing his gun, the boy's father had tried to save the child by shooting the reptile, but tragically he had killed his son instead.

Snakebite was another problem, and as most locals went about barefoot it was not surprising that a number were bitten. However, there were few fatalities. Nevertheless, we kept a watch for snakes, and one morning a puzzling track was discovered around our tents on a sandbank. It ran around the biologist's tent and then down to the river before doubling back some 200 yards to a pile of logs. A snake hunt began. 'Never seen anything quite like this,' admitted Eric Niemi. 'Seems the snake may have been pushing itself along with its scales.' The series of small puncture marks in the sand was a mystery. 'I think it is two rats walking side by side with sharp claws,' suggested a Bolivian crew member. Then Ivan Wood found the culprit under his tent flap. It was a large crab.

Between villages Graham and our medical team – Sam Allen, Jo Brown and Michelle Phillips – had little to do except what the army calls 'personal administration'. On board the *chata*, Shirley Critchley was one of the busiest – mending clothes, purifying water with her smart First Need filter pump, even doing others' washing: always a help in some capacity or other. Peter Kannangara found he had an increasing load of e-mails to deal with as we neared Brazil. The Affno web site constantly needed digital pictures for the 'local boy' stories that we had to send to regional newspapers.

In the mahogany boat Ernie and Francisca, helped by whoever was available, peeled vegetables, gutted fish, and produced superb lunches – eaten on the move. Four of us scurried about in the two Avons, delivering food and fuel to the other craft.

Yoli had to translate our evening briefing to the Spanish-speaking local crews and help with liaison at all points during the day. Francisca even tried to teach herself English with a dictionary Shirley had given her.

Only on *KM3* was life a little tedious. When not on watch or at the helm, the crew could only read or sleep. The novelty of rainforested banks, villages or the occasional riverboat soon wore off. In this respect, for some it was rather like an ocean voyage, and the only relief came when we stopped at a village large enough to have a shop that sold beer. Then the crew would swarm ashore, deplete the stocks, and enjoy a game of football. Attempts to involve the soldiers in the wildlife studies and archaeological work did not succeed. However, Matt Pickup, a parachute engineer from Torquay and a keen fisherman, was up until the small hours on many nights and landed some good catches.

Most people we met en route were friendly, but at Portachuelo we were treated with some reserve. Yoli had arranged for us to visit the village and for Graham to do some dentistry there. Thus we were slightly surprised to be met by locals armed with guns and machetes. It had transpired they had previously been badly treated by unscrupulous foreigners, though we did not get to the bottom of this.

While Graham performed extractions, Yoli went off to find the eighty-year-old village sage, Pedro Machuquiri. Although blind, very deaf and recovering from malaria, he told her that he had been a neighbour of the Napare tribe, who until a few years before had lived between the Beni and Madre de Dios rivers. Within memory they had practised cannibalism, but no longer did so. According to the old man, the tribe had split as a result of being converted to Christianity by missionaries. While about 100 had adopted civilized ways, the rest – numbering up to 400 – had gone to live deep in the forest, where they avoided contact with everyone, including their former fellows. I had often heard of similar results from over-zealous Christianization. We knew of a tribe in the Paraguayan Chaco who still did everything possible to avoid contact with the world outside, and there were tragic tales of the unfortunate results of one particular mission organization trying to convert them.

The Napare were known as ferocious warriors, and still used bows and arrows – sometimes aggressively. Although we had been told they were white-skinned, Yoli's informant corrected me, stating that they were dark-coloured but with unusually grey hair. The Napare religious ceremonies before a hunt involved dancing and the consumption of large quantities of 'chicha', made from fermented plantains. To strengthen the genes, the most successful hunter was given the most beautiful woman.

The only meat they ate was *jochi* and monkey, so we presumed that this was all they hunted. Apparently they did not eat salt. The women were said to be naked except for a small apron, but the men wore a colourful sleeveless knee-length tunic called a *kushma* and painted their faces red and black. On their heads they wore a band with two large feathers – one red and one yellow – at the front and black ones at the side. When the Napare had grown more aggressive, Pedro Machuquiri and his family had feared for their lives and left the vicinity.

On 30 June we reached Las Piedras, near Riberalta, and camped nearby. Bruce Mann then led us on an archaeological reconnaissance to see if we could locate the ruins. The modern village was well developed, with a soccer pitch and grandstand, shop and school. Yoli had already got rough directions to the 'stones', but as everyone was attending an important football match there was no one to guide us. So we walked up a long dirt road, sprayed with dust by passing motorcycles (no car was to be seen) as the population rushed to the match.

It was getting late when we turned off on a jungle path which led to a thatched hut in a clearing. An old Indian lady sat there with her pigs and chickens. 'Yes,' she said, waving her arm vaguely at the jungle, 'there are ruins.' At first she declined to show us the way, but Yoli's charm eventually won her over and, clutching her faded dress, she padded off into the forest. We followed, crossing a large, wide, dry ditch. The light was fading fast and I doubted that we would see much in the gathering gloom. Then the old girl stopped and pointed with her toe to a line of black stones. 'Quite definitely walls,' said Bruce. We pushed on in the twilight. There were more walls and a few cut stones, all of an igneous rock not unlike pumice. When it was too dark for photography, we reached a mound whose centre had been hollowed out and, the old lady explained, dynamited by treasure-hunters. As a girl, she remembered it having a fine doorway of squared stone. Some of the walls were over 6 feet in height. Bruce managed to find pottery, Elizabeth made a quick sketch, and then we had to leave.

'That was quite extraordinary,' said Bruce as we walked back. 'I never expected to find stone walls like those in a lowland savannah area. We really must look at them more thoroughly.'

'Well, I think we could,' I said. 'Maybe next year.'

Later I met the volatile Dr Said Zeitum López, rector of the

University of Bolivian Amazonas, and his colleagues, who told me all they knew about the site we had hastily visited. The oral history handed down related that this was the furthest east the Incas had come. He believed that, during a period of civil war, in 1460 the Inca Yupanqui had brought 10,000 people down the Madre de Dios river system. They sought to conquer the Beni tribes, and had fought many different groups during their journey. 'We have been trying to get the government to send experts to explore the site,' he said, 'but UNAR are not interested in Amazonas.'

I could see now that the exploration of the Beni archaeological sites was of a higher priority than our other tasks in South America, so I began to plan making this a part of the next *Kota Mama* expedition. Bruce and Elizabeth were to make even more exciting discoveries in this area.

My elation at this latest archaeological success was tempered by an incident that illustrated one of the problems of running multidisciplinary expeditions. The crew of *KM3*, many of whom were soldiers, were becoming increasingly bored by the monotonous journey from Rurrenabaque. Naturally enough, most looked forward eagerly to the next major settlement and its beer and girls. However, before arriving at any large town it was necessary for me to liaise with the authorities and then make an entry in the customary manner. South America is more formal than Britain, and to do otherwise might have caused offence. Not everyone understood the importance of this, and nor did they like the idea of delaying arrival at the bright lights for any longer than necessary. That night, after a few drinks, a handful set off for Riberalta. They went in one of the Avons in the pitch dark and without lights. This was quite contrary to my instructions and the advice of the Blue Devils, and extremely foolhardy.

Yoli, whose job was to liaise with local authorities, was greatly concerned, for she knew well that the anti-narcotics squads did not hesitate to fire on unidentified craft and also that none of this party spoke Spanish. Aroused from their beds and themselves risking being mistaken for drug-runners, Jim and Paul set off in pursuit in the other Avon.

They found the inflatable moored at the foot of a high bank, fortunately still with its valuable outboard engine. As a precaution, they untethered it and towed it back to the camp behind their own, leaving the drinkers to find themselves a bed with whatever money they might have left. Jim went into Riberalta in advance of the main party the next day and, finding the soldiers in a hotel, pointed out the error of their ways in no uncertain manner. When the rest of us arrived, those involved in the incident apologized, and this storm in a teacup was then forgotten. But it did focus my attention on the problem of how to keep both the musclemen and the specialists happy when they had such different interests.

The soldiers who did much of the hard grafting felt they weren't being rewarded, but old soldiers like Jim and Ernie, who also worked extremely long hours – getting up as early as 4.30 a.m. to light the cookers for breakfast – seldom complained. Both being over seventy, they were an example to us all. But Ernie could understand the younger soldiers' attitude: 'We're a different generation, John,' he said with a smile as he stirred the porridge. He could also understand the importance of the HQ group, who often worked hard extracting teeth from locals, running clinics, preparing archaeological reports, dealing with the numerous e-mail messages, or just struggling with the logistic nightmares that occurred almost daily.

Whenever we reached a large town there were civic receptions, presentations and send-offs to be undergone, and to maintain a good public image it was vital that we took part with good grace. Not all our team appreciated the importance of these time-consuming events, which necessarily were always conducted in Spanish.

There was a classic example at Riberalta: the naval and civil authorities gave us a resounding welcome while we paused for forty-eight hours to rest and replenish. This enabled me to make a dash to Guayaramerín on the border, to prepare for our entry to Brazil. Yoli and Shirley came to help me, as it promised to be a busy time. I would have to be back with the fleet the next day, leaving the two ladies to untie the bureaucratic knots.

We drove down the dusty road, took the ferry across the Rio Yata, and went straight to the house of Dr Hortensia de Bravo on the outskirts of Guayaramerín. She was a local dentist who had been a great help to Jim on the 2000 recce and had agreed to be a contact for new expedition arrivals in the area. It was 9 p.m. when we arrived, but supper awaited and afterwards Hortensia, jolly and helpful in spite of an impending attack of malaria, was immediately on her phone – confirming air flights, calling the local naval commandant, and alerting other functionaries to our arrival.

A breakfast meeting with naval officers and their forceful commandant, Capitán de Marina Armando Ayala Cerruto, who ran Bolivia's largest naval district, the 3rd 'Madera', proved extremely useful. The Bolivian consul in Guajará-Mirim, across the Rio Mamoré in Brazil, was present, along with a tough-looking lieutenant called José Velasquez, in command of the Blue Devils. With an impressive scar on his short neck – probably from a bullet wound – he had an enormous job to do. The United States has said in no uncertain terms that if Bolivia does not curb the traffic of cocaine northward to Brazil all aid to the country will cease. Teniente Velasquez has a fleet of fast patrol boats called Piranhas with American M60 machine-guns, but then so have the *narcotraficantes*. With great good humour Capitán Ayala gave us every assistance, and we tried to help him in return: he wanted some work done on a new floating clinic that the navy was readying for service, and we had the necessary tradesmen among our sappers.

My thoughts were concentrated on the imminent problem of navigating the Esperanza cataract when Yoli handed me a Bolivian newspaper. 'Read this on your way back,' she said. 'The German at Guanay is attacking us again.' On 1 July *La Prensa* – the rival publication to *La Razón*, whose colour magazine was carrying Patricio Crooker's articles about our expedition – had published a piece alleging that we had claimed to have discovered Paititi and the associated fort (or was it an inn?). 'Rubbish!' I retorted. 'We have never claimed this.' 'The article is by a treasure-hunter called Sigfried Trippolt,' said Yoli. 'He seems upset that no mention has been made of Ertl's earlier visit to the site.' At that time we had no interest in bringing Ertl or his past role with the Nazi party into the story, and to avoid any embarrassment to the Bolivian authorities we had made no public mention of him. Indeed, we had not issued *any* statements about our work at 'Paititi' to the Bolivian newspapers, although we kept the prefectura of La Paz fully informed and the Bolivian archaeologists had signed a report on the project which we all agreed.

In its article, *La Prensa* was asking for a response, but we were now almost in Brazil and I had no wish to be drawn into a political conflict. So I said, 'The government are fully informed of our work. We did what we were asked to do, and we must leave it to the prefectura and the Vice-Ministry of Culture and UNAR to respond if they wish to. After all, they are our partners in this project.' With that, I climbed into a battered Toyota taxi and ordered, '*Riberalta rapido por favor, señor.*' The driver flashed his gold teeth and, with a '*Si, mi coronel,*' slammed the bone-shaker into gear and took off in a cloud of red dust.

As we sped along the jungle-flanked track I glanced at my papers, tried to write notes on the day's meetings, and finalized the plan for the Esperanza cataract. My eyes flickered across Trippolt's article. 'What on earth are these strange people up to?' I thought. 'We come here to do an archaeological survey, bring medical and financial aid to a remote community, advise a devastated town on flood prevention, and find ourselves being criticized by a treasure-hunter who seems to be obsessed with what Hitler's photographer did half a century ago.' It was all very odd.

I was back in Riberalta by 12.15 p.m. I had told Jim to sail at noon even if I hadn't returned, but Ivan Wood was waiting with an Avon to rush me down the river to join the fleet. Now it was only 16 miles to the start of the major cataracts, where Eddy's boats would leave us and the HQ and part of the support team would become land-based until we reached Pôrto Velho in Brazil.

When a boat approaches the bank and there is no convenient bystander to catch a mooring line, some poor hand has to leap ashore with it. Ray Gargan, a sapper lance-corporal from Southampton, was our star performer in this respect. But the banks of the Beni are uniformly muddy, and on one occasion dangerously so. As *KM3* edged in close, Ray leaped – and sank up to his armpits like a spoon into chocolate mousse. Initial hilarity gave way to concern as his cries for help became more and more vibrato. But 'Hold it there while I get my camera!' shouted one crewman, and it was a moment or two before a thrown rope hauled Ray from the slime.

Mud constantly calved off the banks and on one occasion it caught some of us unawares. As a squall blew up, we found a timber mill at the top of a steep ramp down which cut logs were rolled into the river to be rafted downstream. As thunder crashed and lightning forked into the river, we sought the shelter of the mill. The rain lashed down as some of us fought a way up the muddy ramp, falling about like learner skiers. Others curled up damply on the *chata*. At dawn, the mill party had a hard time returning to their boats: the river level had dropped 6 feet and, as we watched, a massive fissure opened and the entire bank slid very slowly into the water.

While we were loosening the stretched mooring ropes to avoid being pulled high and dry on to the bank, Yoli came through on the satellite phone. A typically convoluted problem had blown up in Guayaramerín, where she was trying to get the expedition into Brazil. During early discussions with the Brazilian Ministry of Foreign Affairs it had been pointed out that foreign expeditions were not permitted to do scientific work without having a Brazilian partner. We had offered to provide facilities for Brazilian scientists to travel along the river with us and carry out studies; however, as nobody wished to take up this opportunity, we had no scientific partner. It was therefore decided that we should not undertake any scientific work in Brazil but simply concentrate on medical projects in co-operation with local mission organizations, assist two anthropologists from the University of Brasilia on a reconnaissance of the area, and study the boats' performance.

It had taken a while to get the Brazilian Navy to issue the necessary permit for the entry of the boats. Like the Argentinian Prefectura Naval during the 1999 *Kota Mama* expedition, it could not find a classification into which to fit a reed boat. At one time it had been suggested that, as we had a strong military membership, it should be a 'warship'. There may also have been another problem, for, although we flew a red ensign, *Kota Mama 3* had been registered by Yoli in Bolivia. Furthermore, in recent history certainly, no Bolivian vessel had entered Brazil via the cataracts of the Rio Madeira.

After much deliberation, the Brazilian Navy decided that *Kota Mama 3* should be classed as a craft for 'sport and recreation', and agreed to send a liaison officer to assist us. Captain Roger Turner, the then British naval attaché in Brasilia, had faxed me our permits, but somehow the instructions that reached the Brazilian embassy in La Paz were out of date and stated that we were a scientific expedition and must have a Brazilian scientific partner. This resulted in the Brazilian consul at Guayaramerín being instructed to allow us into Brazil only when we had a letter from the University of Brasilia saying that we were in partnership. Yoli's protests that we were not a scientific expedition and so did not need this were to no avail. The consul was adamant. He could allow us in only if his instructions were changed, and for this to happen we must have a letter from the university saying we were not a scientific expedition!

Numerous expensive phone calls were made to Roger at our embassy in Brasilia and to the Brazilian embassy in La Paz, but no one could be found with the necessary authority to unblock the logjam.

Eventually there was a simple solution. 'Why do you need the Brazilian consul's consent when you have a permit from the Brazilian Navy?' asked a high official in Bolivia who had better be nameless. 'All that is needed is the stamp of the Brazilian Federal Police on your passports.' So it was that a few days later Yoli and I found ourselves in the office of Dr Jerônimo José da Silva, the chief of the federal police over the river at Guajará-Mirim in Brazil. With us was José Velasquez, whose Blue Devils worked closely with the Brazilian police in the battle against drug-smugglers.

The smiling police chief gave us two hours of his time, personally checking each of the forty-five passports and the mandatory yellow-fever certificates before passing them to his secretary to be stamped. All the while he laughed and joked and in fractured English told us of his successes against the *narcotraficantes*. 'A most remarkable man,' said Yoli as we bade him farewell.

It was late afternoon when we left the air-conditioned sanctuary of police headquarters and my ENTEL mobile phone rang. 'This is Marcelo Mendes,' said the voice. 'I am in Guayaramerín.' 'Thank God!' I thought. Here in the nick of time was our Brazilian Navy liaison officer. A few days earlier he had greeted me by e-mail: 'Hello Col. Blashford. Here's Lt. Marcelo Mendes, the Brazilian Navy officer which is going to meet you're all in Guayará-Mirim in 4 July. I'm really exciting to be a part of the team expedition I guess because our contacts by fone were quite troblely, but Good bless you! See you soon. *Selva!!!* [Jungle!!!] Marcelo.' His command of English improved a hundredfold during the two months he was with us.

Marcelo, a tall and striking figure, looked every inch a marine officer. His firm handshake and well-organized baggage created a good impression. Here was a man you felt you could trust, and so it transpired. Immediately we set about the question of the mandatory inspection of *Kota Mama 3* by the Brazilian Navy. For weeks we had waded through a telephone-directory-sized set of regulations for foreign vessels entering Brazil. We had flares, riding-lights and lifebuoys, and HSBC in London had taken out special insurance to cover us against claims if our straw boat rammed anyone.

We also had to hire four-wheel-drive vehicles for Gerry Masters and his support group, and a large truck for Ernie's stores. This was far from easy, and we had still not solved the problem when darkness fell. We were just able to re-cross the Mamoré back to Bolivia in time for a dinner party at the home of Capitán and Señora Ayala.

An aerial reconnaissance of the Esperanza rapids had given Jim, Matt Wilkinson and myself the chance to see and photograph them closely, so that by the time the fleet arrived there we had a pretty good idea of the difficulties. On 5 July, using the photographs, Matt briefed his fifteen-strong crew on the challenge ahead. On his reconnaissance in July 2000, Jim had felt doubtful about our ability to run Esperanza. But from the air we could see that, although the waves were large, there were no obstructions in the cataract. It was thus decided to tackle it with *KM3* as a trimaran, albeit with masts and rigging removed. The crew donned helmets and life-jackets as the crowd grew on the waterfront of the nearby small town of Cachuela Esperanza.

The arrival of so many foreigners was quite an occasion for the little town, and the municipality did us proud. Within minutes of our arrival we were treated to a feast of fish and chips. Nothing could have been better.

'No one has ever survived the *cachuela*. There have been many deaths,' said the alcalde. 'Are you certain your boat can get through?' All I could do was smile confidently, but watching the tossing waves from the shore I did feel a little apprehensive. However, even after almost 800 miles, *KM3* was in very good shape, the crew had plenty of muscle, and the safety boats would be there to pick up anyone who was swept overboard.

Matt's briefing of his team was thorough, and as the Avons took up position below the drop we checked radio communication. Although I was pretty sure that *Southern Gailes* would go through, I felt it much more likely that early navigators would have paddled down the calmer water along the bank. Thus the balsa raft – like the Avons – had already been taken down the shallows at the edge of the river, by archaeologists Bruce and Elizabeth.

At 12.50 p.m. I sat with Patricio Crooker and Marcelo in José Velasquez's tin boat at one side of the cataract. The helmsman fought to keep his craft still in the turbulent water. Perched on rocks nearby, Graham Catchpole and Yoli waited with video and still cameras. 'Here she comes!' cried Patricio, his own cameras at the ready. As *KM3* came into view, we could see the three jaguar figureheads bobbing as the pad-dlers on the two outriggers strained every sinew, digging their blades deeper into the swirling water. 'Oh no, she's too far to starboard,' I thought, fearing she would go over a 20-foot-high waterfall. But helms-man Billy Baugh's course was true, and she came straight for the tongue.

At the top of the chute she seemed to hover, the three figureheads held high; then the trimaran pitched forward and raced down the slope to strike the stopper wave, sending spray cascading right over the craft as the jaguar heads reared up, their long white fangs gleaming in the bright sunlight. For a moment the Bolivian flag at the bow and the red ensign at the stern were all that could be seen above the flying water. Then the boat emerged unscathed with the crew paddling furiously as she spun around in the current before continuing through the lines of small waves. All along the bank cheering rang out. 'At last,' many will have thought, '*cachuela* Esperanza has been conquered.'

'History has been made today,' said the alcalde, pumping my hand when we returned to shore. Perhaps it had – or maybe we had just recreated it, for I wondered if any early navigator had managed to negotiate this formidable obstacle.

The reed boat was now making its way downstream towards Brazil, with Jim smiling happily and the crew self-consciously pleased with themselves.

While the trimaran had battled with the cataract, Ernie's logistic team and most of the HQ staff had been manhandling the 10 tons of stores and rations from Eddy's *chata* round the rapids to another *chata* that Yoli had managed to hire beyond the cataract. Piled high with cargo, and with Ernie perched on top, the rickety craft headed east for the Bolivian Navy post at Villa Bella.

KM3 and *Southern Gailes* were already well ahead, and Yoli, Marcelo and I sped on a naval skiff with José Velasquez to the sleepy little village of Vila Murtinho in Brazil, to arrange the landing of our stores in a new country the next day. Fearing that to cross at the nearest recognized point, from Guayaramerín to Guajará-Mirim, would be to poke a stick into a bureaucratic hornets' nest, I was pleased to have been told that Vila Murtinho would be the best place for us to enter with a minimum of fuss. It was something of a surprise, then, to find it seething with well-armed sailors and police.

'This is one of the main smuggling routes from Bolivia,' explained José. 'They even bring cars in here.'

'Don't worry,' Marcelo said, 'There will be no need to go to the customs people in Guajará-Mirim. I'll ask them to come here.' With an air of authority he immediately took command. The navy and the police responded with alacrity and prepared to welcome *Kota Mama*. I could see that Marcelo Mendes was going to prove very useful.

Returning to Cachuela Esperanza and then to Riberalta to tackle more administrative problems, we paused to take a last look at the rapids. On the foreshore stood a large crucifix inscribed to the memory of

Mancilla Suárez and her eleven servants, who had drowned in the *cachuela* Esperanza in 1893. Who was this unlucky lady? I wondered.

The monument above the rapids, we discovered, was in fact to the second wife of Don Nicolas Suárez, the greatest rubber baron of them all, whose centre of operations had been at Cachuela Esperanza. One of seven children, thrice married, father of eight, he lived from 1851 to 1940, and his astonishingly upswept white moustaches command attention on postcards. No smallholder, he had 12 million acres with over 10,000 workers, many of them Caripuña Indians. He also ran 500,000 cattle all over Beni province – a Bolivian contemporary of Australia's Sir Sidney Kidman – and traded in tobacco and Brazil nuts as well.

Some of his descendants still lived in the Rua Nicolas Suárez in Riberalta, and while we were there Richard had gone to talk to his granddaughter-in-law, the former Irma Steiner. After some time, Richard had tentatively broached the subject of her grandfather-in-law's second wife, Mancilla. Was it true, he asked (with Irma's son Miguel translating the sensitive bits), that her grandfather had engineered his wife's death by sending her in a boat down the Esperanza cataract? Had the incident recorded on the monument been contrived by Nicolas, eager to marry his mistress (and his wife's kinswoman), Judith Arias? The old lady had needed no time to ponder this: '*¡Falso!*' she said, and Richard had had to change the subject.

Perhaps it was just an accident. But Suárez was no angel. In fact it was said in Riberalta that he had made '*un pacto con el diablo*' and that when he died the devil took his body. His coffin was believed to be full of stones.

Whatever the truth, on 5 July 2001 we left the *cachuela* Esperanza and its memorial to the unfortunate Mancilla and sailed on down the Beni towards its junction with the Mamoré. Following the success at the supposedly impassable cataract, spirits were high. In José Velasquez's skiff, we raced past *KM3*, *Southern Gailes* and Ernie's heavily laden *chata* to Villa Bella on the Mamoré. Capitán Ayala had arranged for us to camp at this remote naval post – almost the most northerly point in Bolivia – and also to be shown the start of another dangerous set of rapids nearby.

The post's commander took us round the meagre facilities and introduced us to the 'restaurant' in the squalid village next door, where the owner promised good meals and a supply of beer at a modest price.

Having seen that the boats' crews were catered for in the best available comfort, I returned to Guayaramerín.

For those in the fleet it had been a hot ride, and Jim Masters and his tired crews were glad to establish themselves on the football pitch at the naval post, where the conscript ratings showed an interest in us and came to visit our camp. Alas, the supper we had organized turned out to be dismal, and on their return several people found their cameras and binoculars had gone missing. They were never recovered. Jim sensed a feeling of depression, and Villa Bella was becoming something of a low point in the expedition. 'I've had Bolivia,' someone said – 'let's try Brazil,' whose lights beckoned from the other side of the Mamoré.

That night there was a very heavy rainstorm. Jim had thought the floor of a thatched building a good bet, but had to move several times and still got soaked. Others ran into their tents over what soon became more a quagmire than a pitch. Nottinghamian Steve Henry, of an irrepressibly cheerful nature, 'found the entire scenario hilarious', for while Elizabeth Dix's tent 'began to let in water faster than Trent lock', he and Mike How, anticipating the rain, had moved under a porch in the naval barracks and were ultimately invited by ratings to transfer inside on to comfortable palliasses. These two were dry the next morning, but all the rest disconsolately sorted and packed their sodden kit for a day of important work on the Mamoré.

The irritation and recriminations that followed such an unpleasant night were as usual directed at the small HQ group, who some imagined to be having a good time in the big city while the workers huddled in their tents. However, we were not in fact living it up, but working hard in Guajará-Mirim to get the expedition legally into Brazil, while the sapper team under Gerry Masters and Eric Hay were cross-loading stores to the Brazil side of the river.

It was Friday 6 July. Black vultures were sitting high in the trees at Villa Bella. It was an uneasy time, and morale remained uncharacteristically low. Jim had come over to Brazil to see me as I was busy sorting out a host of administrative problems.

'John, can we talk about the boats for a few moments?' he said.

'I'm sorry, I can't talk to you just now,' I replied.

Jim took immediate umbrage. There were times when he felt that the efforts of the boats' teams – the *raison d'être* of the expedition, after all – were being ignored and undervalued. He had tried to raise people's flagging spirits, but I didn't know what a miserable night they had all had at the naval post across the river. Neither of us had enjoyed much sleep the last few days, and both our tempers frayed a little.

I always regret these brief moments of misunderstanding, and I know Jim does too. He later told Richard, 'They upset me as they upset him, I suppose.' But, although we have had the occasional run-in like this one over the forty years we have known one another, our comradeship is so firmly based that our irritation is soon past.

While Ernie was with the customs people, he heard that someone had cast loose the balsa raft. On long expeditions some things, either unused or awkward to handle, tend to become hate objects. Later in the journey it was the gas cookers – superfluous once we were on fully equipped support ships. But all quartermasters cherish their kit, and Ernie, furious at this wanton act, stormed out to find the culprit. He threatened to repatriate whoever had done it, but the soldiers stayed shtum. The raft was brought back and stayed with us to Belém. After that diversion the departure from Bolivia was carried out expeditiously and there was *não problema* entering Brazil.

Now we turned our attention to the notorious rapids on the Mamoré–Madeira. On the lower Mamoré (into which the Beni flows) and the Madeira, nineteen or twenty cataracts of varying degrees of severity (from grade 2 to grade 6 by today's reckoning) are to be found fairly close together over a distance of 325 miles. They have been known about by incoming colonists since the 1700s, but became a problem only when Bolivians in the mid-nineteenth century tried to develop a more direct route for their rubber to American and European markets. The rubber from the Beni and Acre regions – Pará rubber, as it was later called – was the best in the world and fetched good prices. It was worth taking laboriously on mule-back westward over the Andes and down to the Pacific coast, thence to be carried (in pre-Panama Canal days) round Cape Horn and up the South and North Atlantics. But how much better it would be if it could be got out down the Amazonian river system to Manaus or Pará (present-day Belém) and thus more swiftly by steamer to the workshops of the northern world.

The wild rubber trees in Nicolas Suárez's 12 million acres of rainforest were tapped by some of his huge workforce in a state of virtual slavery. Suárez developed a system of portages round three or four of the worst Mamoré–Madeira rapids and kept 400 of his men employed there. He took tolls from other users of his system, and sent his own rubber that way, making three round trips each year. It was a hazardous and wasteful system, however: each clumsy 10-ton barge with its crew of a dozen men had to shoot all the other rapids, and almost every year he lost almost 20 per cent of his rubber in the thunderous waves and vicious whirlpools. He also lost 20 per cent of his crewmen, but perhaps he regarded these as more expendable.

Now it was our turn. One of our Avons had caught on a nail while moored up to a derelict boat at Villa Bella and had become deflated. Billy Baugh and Eric Hay repaired it while Jim Masters, in the other Avon, led a team – Matt Wilkinson, Ivan Wood and Drew Craig – from Villa Bella to have a good look at the next three rapids we would encounter. The first five rapids on the Mamoré – Guajará-Mirim, Guajará-Acu, Bananeiras, Pau Grande and Lajes (to give all their names in Portuguese) – are further up the river, and as we had come in from the Beni we did not need to run them. But numbers 6 (Madeira), 7 (Misericordia) and 8 (Ribeirão) awaited us, and a further eleven or twelve thereafter.

The reconnaissance party moored upstream to a rock outcrop and assessed Madeira. They then put on their helmets and life-jackets again and ran down the rapid with little difficulty. They had found a good route for *KM3*. Then they dropped down Misericordia, and again it was *não problema*. But rapid number 8, Ribeirão, was in a different league – an Arsenal among Accrington Stanleys. The Mamoré is almost a mile wide here, and broken by tree- and shrub-covered islands into five channels. Which one should they take?

They moored upstream and walked to a vantage point. Jim and Drew Craig had been together on the reconnaissance in 2000, and had been told by the Bolivian Navy, who hunt for drug-smugglers on these waters, that there were viable routes down the right- and left-hand sides of Ribeirão but that their anti-*narcotraficantes* squadron had had two Zodiac inflatables flipped over in the larger of the two central cataracts. A few days earlier I had flown over Ribeirão in a light plane from Guayeramerín with Jim, Matt, Drew and Billy Baugh, the helmsman, to let them see what they had to face. Jim had called up all his white-water know-how and had made a judgement: a middle route looked feasible in a broader-based craft with three flexible hulls.

Now Jim and his team were on the ground. They roped the Avon down from the upper part of the rapids to an island from which Graham Catchpole was to shoot some astonishing video footage of what happened to *KM3* the next day. They walked round the island and saw that there was a possible route down the principal central chute. To the left of it there were a large hole and a stopper wave, which would have to be avoided, but Jim and Matt seemed satisfied, if a mite apprehensive. They made their notes and drew sketches, and then checked out a place to moor after the cataract. As they fought their way back upriver, Madeira gave them a hard time and they had to tie up to an island and portage the Avon and its outboard engine up and round it – over a sandbar and rocks for 200 yards. They got back to camp, as Jim put it, 'late, soaked, dirty, tired and jittery'.

10

Lost and Found

God looks after little children and mad people.

Capitán Armando Ayala Cerruto

PAUL OVERTON HAD raised the crews' spirits a little by making a good breakfast of scrambled eggs and fresh bread, but there are always long and frustrating delays before big rapids can be run. Kit has to be checked and rechecked, and reconnaissances must be carried out. Most of the expedition members had two days' wait at Villa Bella, and the boats' crew spent them having their own look at the next three cataracts. Some of the fifteen people on *KM3* had never been down serious rapids, so it was important to show them what they were in for. While Tac HQ continued to tackle the administrative problems and seek vehicles for the bank support team, Brazilian customs men had to cross to the Bolivian shore to look at the reed boat which had so mystified their bureaucrats, all of which held us up for a while.

The first reconnaissance downriver had involved only Jim, Ivan, Matt and Drew, but now Matt Wilkinson arranged for all the personnel involved to get a sight of Ribeirão and the problems it presented. The choice of route that he and Jim had first considered to be best on the aerial reconnaissance was confirmed on all these subsequent inspections.

A big boat needs a lot of water, and there were two main chutes in the centre of Ribeirão. The one to the left seemed fairly gentle, but it led into shallows with exposed rocks beyond. As Matt said, 'If crew members had to jump out and push, they would be at risk of being crushed by 15 tons of tightly compacted reeds.' The other chute in the centre was bigger and had an enormous stopper wave at the bottom of it. It would not do to get caught in this: in a spill, crew members might be thrown overboard into a maelstrom of circulating currents. However,

about 20 yards to the right within this chute was a route which circum-
vented the stopper wave and the hole before it.

'We had about six trips with all the crew members,' said Matt, 'and I
showed everyone this chute, explained the route we were going to take,
where the safety boats would be, and what people would be required to
do at different times.'

While these confirmatory reconnaissances were going on, *KM3* set off
from Villa Bella just after noon, slipped without incident down the
Madeira and Misericordia rapids – 'We got a bit of a wetting,' said Jim –
and moored about 500 yards upstream of Ribeirão. Eric Niemi and Ivan
Wood had gone on ahead in an Avon inflatable and had run down the
edges of Ribeirão to position themselves below the cataract as a safety
boat. The other Avon was still out of action upstream, but was being
rapidly got ready after its puncture repair.

KM3 could set off once Matt had heard that Eric and Ivan, having
dropped Graham Catchpole and his video camera on a good island
vantage point by a huge eddy, were properly in place. But the reconnaissances had taken time, and it was now 4.15 p.m. Jim ruefully envisaged
setting up camp in darkness again, somewhere below Ribeirão.

Spirits were high among the crew, however. Many had been going
through their customary routine of sit-ups and press-ups, and as they
came within sight of the chute Drew Craig said he felt 'a rush of adrena-
lin coming through'. James Culshaw, with his camera wrapped in a
waterproof canoe-bag, was shooting away. They seemed to be lining up
well on previously selected landmarks, but about 100 yards short of the
actual rapid Matt realized that the boat was being pulled inexorably too
far to the left and towards the hole. Twelve of the crew members, who
had been paddling on the outriggers, now pulled in their legs and leaped
into the centre to hold on to the safety line. 'To the right! More to the
right!' Matt indicated to Billy Baugh on the engine. Billy rammed the
tiller over, but to no avail. Matt could not be heard above the din, so he
signalled again to Billy – this time to gun the engine as much as he could.

At least part of *KM3* seemed destined to go into the hole, and in the
event almost all of it did. Tons of waterlogged reed dropped 15 or 20 feet
sideways and down, and then rode up on to the crest of the stopper wave.
The bow of the port outrigger was torn from the other two hulls, the
tough nylon cordage snapping like floss, and the whole craft canted up
on its side and fell back further into the hole, throwing Matt and ten of
his crew into the heaving tumult.

Matt's mind raced. 'Someone might die here,' he thought. 'I could have said, "No, I'm sorry to have to tell you we're going to have to portage this." It had been my call that it would be OK to run it.' 'What a waste it would have been to lose someone,' he said later. 'Being a soldier, it's one thing if you're on an operation somewhere and you're doing some good. But it's totally another to be running down a river just to prove a scientific hypothesis and lose a life.'

In the river, he remembers thinking, 'The boat's the most buoyant thing, so hold on!' But then it capsized and fell on top of him. He was aware of the three hulls, now partly disconnected, churning around above him, and of an outboard motor that might still be running.

Myriad thoughts ran through the head of Jim Masters too. It had been in 1948 that he had joined the same sapper squadron that Matt was now in. Twenty years later he had been in charge of the boat party on my first big expedition, down the rapids of the Ethiopian Blue Nile. In the mid-1970s I had asked him to take on the same role in the Zaire River Expedition, and he had guided our fleet of inflatables down the Stanley Falls and through the even more heart-stopping series between Kinshasa and the Atlantic. In both these ventures he had several times been pitched from a boat into a swirling cataract. Up the Beni in Bolivia, the *Kota Mama* team had celebrated his seventy-third birthday, and now the prospect of a struggle for survival in surging waters loomed again.

'I was on my way to drowning,' he told Richard afterwards. 'Something hit me on the head. It can only have been the reed boat. Everything went very dark. I went down feet first and swallowed a good deal of the Madeira. That was the first moment I thought I'd gone. Then I fought my way upwards and it got lighter. When I surfaced I looked up and there was this socking great wall of water coming down on me from as high as that,' he said, pointing to the top of a nearby 10-foot-high generator shed. 'That was the second moment.'

Drew Craig also had premonitions of death. 'Today I nearly died again,' he said that same evening. 'Again?' we asked, and he told us how he had once nearly lost his life on the Upper Nile, rafting near Lake Victoria. Now, 'I was taking a picture of Ribeirão', he explained, 'when I was hit an almighty blow by water and thought, "This is the Nile once more." I was scared witless at first. Then I felt some buoyancy and opened my eyes to find it getting lighter. In moments I got a breath and felt a bit better about things.' Like Matt, he emerged into big waves, fought them for a while, then decided to relax and go with the flow.

Soon there was a scattering of plastic helmets bobbing about in the eddies. Graham Catchpole had video film of the whole incident – 'red-hot property' he called it – and he and those of us on the bank were frantically counting and recounting heads. It was an agonizing time before the total came to eleven. Four were seen floating away still on board *KM3*, now free of the rapid, and one of the eleven climbed on later.

Jim's concerns were for what he called the youngsters. Theirs, to his annoyance, were all for him. 'Where's Jim? Where's Jim?' was everyone's cry. James Culshaw pushed a canoe-bag over towards him to provide some flotation. 'I'm all right,' he shouted, struggling with his life-jacket, which had not been properly tied on and was now trying to work its way over his head.

I had just returned from seeking support vehicles in Guajará-Mirim as the accident happened. Gerry was talking to Ivan on the Motorola, and he turned to me saying simply, 'Capsize.' Seizing the radio, I took over.

The Avon rescue boat with Eric at the helm was running to and fro looking for survivors and taking them to a nearby island. On the beach, I told Corporals Ray Gargan and Eric Hay to get the other Avon on to the river as fast as could be, whatever the state of its repair. They jumped to with alacrity and sped out to the wreck. 'Are there any local boats here that we can use,' I shouted to Patricio, who set off to see what could be found.

There was another momentary worry for Matt when he was counting heads while still being carried down river. Paul Overton, Jim Masters and Matt himself – the three who had been on the central hull – were there, and he could see all the paddlers from the starboard outrigger. But where were the six from the ill-fated port hull?

An Avon came towards him, but as he and those around him were in a safe eddy he sent it over to look for the missing crew on the far side of *KM3*. It pulled Drew from the waves and a couple of others from whirlpools, and came back over to Matt, who was one of a group of seven now swimming towards the beach. 'How many have you got?' he shouted. 'Three more,' said Ivan. With the five on the reed boat, that made fifteen. 'Boy, was I relieved.'

'Eric Niemi and Ivan came past me with a full boat,' Jim said later, 'and Drew stood up and jumped in the river to give me his place. It was like he was standing up for an old lady in the Underground. He meant well, but I was a bit peeved.'

Bas Barrow was about the last to be accounted for. It even flashed across Matt's mind that he might have to go and tell Mr and Mrs Barrow

1. Mount Paititi, so named by local people but as yet unmapped

2. Lance-Corporal Vanessa Hamilton of the Royal Army Veterinary Corps with her pack-horses at Waricunca

3. Dr Sam Allen (*left*) and Paul Overton preparing a delicious meal of *soya carne* at The Fort

4. Royal Engineer Surveyors Lance-Corporal John Gorski and Sapper Karle Reid mapping the 'Paititi' site

6. Yolima Cipagauta examines the giant steps. Evidence of recent digging by treasure hunters was apparent

5. Deadly coral snakes were plentiful among the 'Paititi' ruins

7. Hans Ertl, aged 93, proudly holds his wartime photo

8. The heavy timber frame of Hans Ertl's house still stands after almost 50 years

9. Bruce Mann examines the mysterious carvings above the Devil's Cauldron

10. A Musetenes Indian child with her pet, a dangerous white-lipped peccary

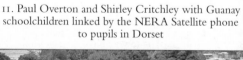

11. Paul Overton and Shirley Critchley with Guanay schoolchildren linked by the NERA Satellite phone to pupils in Dorset

12. Ivan Wood leads the team pulling *Kota Mama 3* up to the start point at Guanay

13. Captain Matt Wilkinson, Royal Engineers (*left*), and his crew on *Kota Mama 3*

14. *Kota Mama 3*, under full sail in the gorges near Rurrenabaque

15–20. Video footage of *Kota Mama 3*'s mishap at the Ribeirão cataract

21. After the mishap at Ribeirão we found *Kota Mama 3* tied up and relatively undamaged

22. Marigold Verity-Dick gives us a recital at the junction of the Madeira and Amazon rivers, in the presence of clouds of mosquitoes

23. Graham Catchpole, the dentist, hard at work

24. The Brazilian Navy pays a call following the warning of river pirate activity. *Kota Mama 3*, now converted to a catamaran, is making good speed

25. (*below*) The balsa raft *Southern Gailes* off Belém

26. Captain Jim Masters disembarking in Belém at the completion of the voyage

that their son had gone. One of the St Helens soldier's legs had been trapped between two hulls, and he emerged limping badly.

On the beach I was equally relieved that the fifteen were safe. Jim staggered up the sand looking distinctly ashen, and said 'Sorry about that.' 'Don't worry, old friend,' I replied. 'Have you got the satellite phone?' I was pleased to hear that it had been rescued – at least we still had one of our vital means of communication. Through my binoculars I could see the wreck drifting slowly but ineluctably downriver. One outrigger was being towed astern, but all the hulls were upright and floating high out of the water. It was incredible that it was still intact. As dusk was approaching and nothing else could be done for *KM3*, I decided to take the five remaining crew off and leave the badly twisted boat, its engine lost and its jaguar heads askew, to the mercies of the Madeira and its remaining rapids.

One of the five, who had made abortive attempts to cast a line ashore and arrest *KM3*'s progress, was Michelle Phillips, our only female crew member. She alternated sailing days with Jo Brown, her doctor colleague, and it had been her turn on this fateful day. She came up the beach and took a cigarette from someone. 'My Anacondor moment,' she called it.

Barry Igoe swam ashore and rose from the water looking more like Michelangelo's David than Botticelli's Venus – in helmet, shirt and lifejacket, but no shorts. They too were floating slowly down towards Brazil.

What had gone wrong? I recalled from our Congo river experiences that, while a helmsman may set his sights on a particular point on the lip of a cataract, as he draws near it a powerful current will often carry him, crabwise and protesting, 20 or 30° off course to another tongue of swiftly moving water. This is what seemed to have happened to *KM3*.

Drew Craig said afterwards, 'We were 30 yards to the left of where we should have been.' He added, 'There are lots of things I could say about the choice of route. We should have spent longer looking at the left-hand side of the rapid.'

But hindsight is all very well. We had had the advice of the Bolivian *narcotraficante* hunters. There had been no dissension. Everyone had agreed the course of action, albeit with some misgivings. Some thought our seemingly easy passage of Esperanza a few days earlier had induced a sense of complacency; others said that the plan had been good enough but that we had been unlucky not to strike quite the right line.

At all events, the consequences appeared dire. The two Avons had tried and failed to lasso *KM3*. She had suffered the fate of countless unfortunate late-nineteenth-century bargeloads of rubber, and we had left $28,000 worth of reed boat to float off down the Madeira untenanted. Outboard engine, cameras, canoe-bags stuffed with personal possessions – all were gone. Our hopes of reaching the Atlantic seemed in jeopardy: the three hulls had been contorted and disfigured. And there were still eleven more rapids, three of them – Girão, Caldeirão do Inferno (Cauldron of Hell) and Teotónio – with serious reputations as graveyards, though we had planned to portage most of these anyway, and Jim had worked out a system for this during his reconnaissance the previous July.

7 July 2001. It had been a day of upsets: Tim Henman had been knocked out of the Wimbledon semi-finals by Goran Ivanisovic, and *KM3*, having overcome Esperanza, had been tested beyond her endurance in her second round.

Going around the survivors, I was relieved to find that none had serious injuries, but the only cause for good cheer as the crews huddled damply on the beach, trying to light wet cigarettes, was that all fifteen of them were together. All were badly shaken, but they were soon restored to a semblance of normality by swift medical attention and Shirley Critchley's tea. Another piece of good luck was that at the head of the beach there was the road from Guajará-Mirim to Abuna, with a roadhouse, the Casa do Doce, where we were able to sink a few beers and then either pitch tents or eject the chickens from an outbuilding, spread mats, and sleep. Sergeant Paul Cawkwell had damaged a ligament, and the next day his bound-up left ankle was the only visible reminder of our spill.

As the crew drowned their sorrows, Yoli set up the satellite phone. Bad news travels fast, and immediately I sent word to the expedition base in Dorset that, although our flagship had gone, everyone was safe and nobody was badly hurt. I then went to the quiet of my tent and thanked God that no one had been lost.

At the evening briefing, most of us were pretty depressed. 'I would say it's all over,' one stunned crew member said. 'I saw her turn over – she's finished. We can't go on.' Positive action was the only way to tackle this situation. '*Totora* is incredibly tough material, and the Cataris build strong boats,' I replied. 'Can you get me Capitán Benquique?' I asked Yoli. 'We need his plane at dawn.'

★

First light at Guayaramerín airport found me, Yoli, Matt and Graham (with his video camera) facing banks of mist drifting lazily across the runway. 'What rotten luck,' said Graham. 'Don't worry, the sun will burn it off in an hour, then we can try and find your boat,' said Capitán Benquique – who had piloted our reconnaissance plane over Ribeirão – and as he spoke a light breeze began to work in our favour.

We had prepared with care. Yoli carried the Motorola radio with which to speak to those on the beach and a GPS to plot the position of whatever we found. A small cloth bag with trailing ribbons was made up so that we could drop a message and a map to the camp, to describe the trimaran's location. We also carried one of the NERA satellite phones. I was reminded of another cloudy morning thirty-three years previously on the Blue Nile in Ethiopia when, following a capsize, one of our Avon inflatables had disappeared, upside down and heading for a massive waterfall. The crew had struggled ashore, but the boat was carrying expensive cameras in waterproof boxes. We were desperate to find her before she went over the thundering falls. The last to leave, SAS Corporal Ian Macleod, had switched on the SARBE emergency radio beacon. Our Army Air Corps Beaver aircraft could pick up the signals, and we had been flying for only ten minutes when the steady 'beep, beep, beep' of the beacon came through. It grew louder. Suddenly our pilot shouted, 'There she is,' and right beneath us, snagged on an island, was the craft. She had survived an enormous pounding but was intact, and we got her back.

KM3 had no such transmitter, but the river's banks were unforested and if she was afloat I was confident we would see her. 'If she's still drifting, every second counts if we're to recover her before the next major cataract,' I told Yoli. Impatiently, we paced the airport patio. Finally, at 8.15 a.m. we got airborne. The flat green jungle etched with fleecy clouds drifted past and then opened up as we passed Villa Bella. Minutes later the team waved as we roared above their tents on the beach at Ribeirão.

Beneath us the cataracts seemed innocuous, and for 15 miles we flew on over more rapids, seeing no sign of our lost boat or her wreckage. Looking left and right, more in hope than in expectation, I glanced at the Bolivian bank and saw something. 'Circle round,' I yelled to Capitán Benquique. Graham had his video camera at the ready. 'What is it?' asked Matt. 'There's something there.' *KM3* was tied to the bank, her figureheads proud. At first glance she looked as if nothing untoward had happened to her! We simply couldn't believe our eyes.

A Bolivian flag fluttered beside a cluster of white buildings, and uniformed figures were pointing inland as Capitán Benquique throttled back. A few hundred yards from the barracks, carved out of the jungle, was a short grass strip on which he made a perfect landing. 'Welcome to Nueva Esperanza,' smiled Sergeant Angel, giving me a crisp salute. 'We have your boat, but we thought you were all dead.' 'Nueva Esperanza means New Hope,' explained Yoli as we strode to the river bank. 'Pretty appropriate,' I thought – 'an Angel of New Hope.' And there she was. Apart from twisted sterns on the central hull and one outrigger, this amazing vessel had survived Ribeirão and another couple of rapids and was still afloat, with the figureheads looking straight at us. 'The red ensign's gone,' I said with regret. 'No, it hasn't,' replied Matt. 'I picked it up as I was swimming ashore.' Like many good soldiers, he had rescued the colours, and now they would fly again.

'How did you find her?' I asked as Sergeant Angel led me to the bank. It transpired that the previous night a conscript sailor named Andrés Mamani had been on guard, keeping an eye cocked for drug-traffickers, when out of the murk had come what in the moonlight he first took to be a tree. Or was it three gods coming out of a dark tunnel? He knew about the legend of a tunnel to the river bank from the ruined city of Las Piedras. Reacting swiftly, the Navy sent out a boat party to investigate. Whatever it was, they secured it and brought it in. This, however, was achieved only with difficulty: hauling three hulls with a small tin boat was not easy, and at this crucial moment the Bolivians ran out of petrol. However, a crewman leaped aboard *KM3* and found a fuel can roped to the hull. It still held petrol, and with it they topped up their own tank.

They radioed the next post, at Villa Bella, to ask, 'Do you know anything about three bundles of reeds floating downsteam, all tied together and with a tiger's head on each one?' To their surprise the reply was, 'Yes, and there should be fifteen gringos on board. They left here this morning.' The absence of gringos caused some consternation, but the mystery was soon resolved.

We rewarded the sharp-eyed Andrés Mamani with $12, which must have been the equivalent of several weeks' pay, and phoned the good news to the expedition. Once airborne again, Graham took more aerial shots of this resilient craft, and as we skimmed over our camp I dropped a message with a sketch map to show where *KM3* was located. 'Let's get a crew aboard and press on,' I wrote.

Great chunks of reed had been torn from *KM3*'s, bows, and she would need some restoration before tackling the rest of the voyage. Meanwhile she was tidied up and rerigged, and Billy Baugh, with a group that included Shirley Critchley, sailed her northward to the very tip of Bolivia, where the Rio Abunã joins the upper Madeira and where a shuttle service of pontoons carries Brazilian road traffic from the Rondônia province westward into Acre. And there she was tied up to the Bolivian bank to await further developments.

Marcelo Mendes was with me on one of these pontoons crossing the Madeira and got into conversation with the ferryman. He discovered that the tugboats which are attached to one side of the pontoons to drive them across against the fast current are occasionally taken out of the river on a low-loader, or *plancha*, to be inspected. Phoning Pôrto Velho, he reached the owner of this low-loader, one César Doerner. Senhor Doerner was anxious to secure a contract to do work for the Brazilian Navy, so Marcelo was able to get him to lift our reed boat to Pôrto Velho at no cost. This was a real stroke of good fortune.

On the appointed day, his powerful Volvo 340 crossed to the Acre side, where several tugs – including one called *Airton* (sic) *Senna* – were moored. Another of them, *Roberto Matheus*, brought *KM3* over the Abunã to be split into its three sections by our sappers and loaded. The Volvo reversed what seemed like a perilously long way down a concrete ramp into the river, and the centre section of *KM3* was floated over the *plancha*.

Irineu Luiz Mazocco, the black-stetsoned driver, flicked his cigarette end out of the cab, gunned the engine, and drew the reed hull, dripping and stinking, out of the Brown Windsor soup of the Abunã river. He then took it over the Madeira on the ferry, drove it to Pôrto Velho, and later came back for the two smaller hulls. In this laborious way our reed boat was portaged round the final rapids and slid once more into the Madeira below them. 'Well, it's saved us the horrific manual portage that we'd planned,' commented Paul Overton, remembering our many discussions back in Dorset.

The only task remaining was to repair the damage, and for this I reckoned we needed the original craftsman to set to work on it. Yoli called Máximo Catari in his Altiplano fastness at Huatajata. 'We need your help,' she shouted down the crackling line from the Abunã phone kiosk. 'We've had a small mishap with the trimaran and it needs some repairs.' There was a pause as the old Indian considered the matter, then he said,

'Do you need a new boat?' 'No, but we want replacement reeds, cords, and your skill to straighten out the sterns. I'll put pictures of the damage on our web site, so your son can see what's required.' Máximo grunted, '*Si*, I will come.'

Yoli wondered how the Aymara boat-builder would get on to a plane with all his kit and bundles of reeds, and she called Lloyd Aereo Boliviano to seek their co-operation. This occasioned another typical logistic puzzle: how to get an air ticket to our Aymara friend. Eventually Yoli had to go all the way to the airline office in Guayaramerín, hand over the bolivianos, and instruct it to inform La Paz that a ticket in the name of Máximo Catari had been duly paid for. So in good time his stocky figure came shambling over the Guayaramerín tarmac from an LAB plane. In the arrivals hall he allowed himself a rare smile as he saw on the carousel his sackful of *totora* reed from the marges of Lake Titicaca.

Jim and Gerry already knew Máximo well, having worked with him in 1999 and more recently having spent a couple of weeks with him helping to complete *KM3* at Lake Titicaca. Now, in the hot sun on a slipway in Pôrto Velho, they teamed up again to repair the reed trimaran. Máximo was his inscrutable self. In fact he knows little English and speaks only Spanish or Aymara, so they progressed with nods and grunts.

'We can't do a complete repair,' said Jim when I went to see how the work was coming on. 'Two hulls have been badly twisted and the main damage is internal,' he pointed out. 'Máximo says the reeds in the centre of the hull are fractured,' said Yoli, who was translating. 'This will affect her buoyancy, but he will replace some of the outer reeds and adjust the binding cords to straighten up the craft.' 'Will she sail another 1,600 miles?' I asked Máximo. Giving one of his characteristic grins, the old Aymara nodded. '*Claro, mi coronel – y mas alla*' ('Of course – and more'). Much of the work was cosmetic, and we knew the repairs would not last long, but considering the battering she had taken *KM3* looked pretty good. However, as she became more saturated with water the twists in the hulls were to return.

Repairs in ancient times would not have been too difficult. The *totora* of Lake Titicaca is by far the best, being thick with a hard outer skin, but similar reeds growing along the rivers could be utilized, and back in Britain Gerry was later to construct a boat from reeds cut on the Somerset levels.

11

Pots and Smoking Maria

When the railroad was finished in 1912 Bolivia was already shipping its goods
through a Chilean port and the Panama canal was nearly ready. Spirits inhabited the empty cars of the Madeira–Mamoré.

Marcos Faerman, 1979, quoted in Marcos Santilli, *Madeira–Mamoré*, 1988

AT THE SMALL Brazilian town of Abunã we found the Hotel Thalita, an
inexpensive, friendly place to stay while *KM3* was sorted out. So Ernie
quickly set up a base there with HQ group and the sapper team, some
of whom were now detached to help the Bolivian Navy in
Guayaramerín, where Capitán Ayala was hoping to fit out a hospital boat
for the local community.

João, the hotelier, was delighted to have so many gringos occupying
all his rooms. Normally the Thalita would only attract two or three
passing truck-drivers a night. His eyes lit upon one of the *Kota Mama*
presentation shields that we gave as gifts to important people. 'May I buy
one of your shields to display in my hotel, *Coronel*,' he asked hesitantly.
'We have never seen boats like yours here.' He had been so obliging and
helpful that I handed him one. '*Moito obrigado*,' he exclaimed with a wide
smile, lowering his head and grasping the souvenir. Then, turning to a
desk drawer, he removed some old files and from beneath brought out a
heavy brown-paper packet which he handed me saying simply, 'This is
my gift for you.' Peeling off the paper wrapping, I found myself staring
at a well-made stone axe-head. 'I find it at *cachoeira* Ribeirão, João
explained. 'I think it is very old.' The artefact – almost 5 inches long –
was grooved for bindings to a handle and weighed over a pound and a
half. 'It's an amazing specimen,' I said, thanking him profusely. Like the
axe-head given us earlier, it too seemed to be made of andesite, a stone
not found locally. 'It's probably come from the Andes,' commented Bruce
Mann when I showed it to him. He had seen several other specimens as

we came downriver. 'Perhaps this is proof that there was trade along these waterways in ancient times,' said Yoli.

Taking advantage of this unforeseen gap in the programme, our archaeologists had returned to the Las Piedras site near Riberalta. While the portaging and repairing of *KM3* were under way, I wanted to visit both them and the engineers working on the hospital boat.

I first drove off to Guajará-Mirim with Yoli, Richard and Alexandra Foley, a public-relations consultant who had just joined the expedition to assist with sponsorship. There we went over the Mamoré to Guayaramerín. Dismissed in guidebooks as merely the point at which adventurous travellers transit between Bolivia and Brazil, Guayaramerín, founded in 1888, indeed has little to draw the discerning visitor – despite now having a tourist office and a striking, tall blonde called Keyner Roca de Roca to run it. However, it must be said that the town has cleaned itself up a good deal of late, and now has an imposing Casa de Cultura – founded by our friend Hortensia de Bravo. We could not see Hortensia on this visit, as she had gone to Trinidad (the Bolivian town, not the Caribbean island) for malaria treatment, but I did meet Capitán Ayala again.

Unhappily, our team of sappers that had gone to fit out the hospital boat had nothing more than a five-a-side *futbol* match against the naval officers in prospect. The Navy had been unable to provide tools or materials with which to plumb in lavatory pedestals or to fashion wood-work. Capitán Ayala's effusive welcome ended with a promise that these would be supplied the next day – our team's penultimate in the area.

We were taken to the naval hospital, where a German-made sterilizer needed repair. I promised to let our dentist have a look at it – it was all I could do. The hospital was a drab and dingy place, and the four ratings lying at attention on their beds in their uniform blue pyjamas looked smart but not particularly happy. At least they had a doctor and nurses.

We then took a taxi for the 60 miles to Riberalta; with four up it is not expensive and much quicker than the local buses. Halfway there a good earth road led to a *balsa* (pontoon) which was to take us across the Rio Yata – a pleasant break which also provided a chance to buy crisps made from sliced plantains.

Riberalta, like Guayaramerín, is Suzuki City: there are very few cars. Everyone is on small motorbikes, many of which are moto-taxis. I had liked the look of the town during my earlier visits. Once the great rubber capital of northern Bolivia, it was founded in 1894 by the great-great-grandfather of one of our expedition's most amusing and knowledgeable members, Patricio Crooker. Patricio's ancestor, Juan L. Muñoz, was a cartographer sent by a Bolivian president to map the most north-easterly corners of the country in the days before the frontier with Brazil was properly drawn. He came to a high bank (Ribera-Alta) where the Madre de Dios flowed into the Beni, and began a settlement there.

Colonel Percy Fawcett had come to Riberalta in 1907, at the height of the rubber boom, to draw up plans for an iron floating dock in the Beni. Construction of the Madeira–Mamoré railway had resumed in that year, and Riberalta was to have been the terminus of a line from Pôrto Velho in Brazil. Had it not been for the collapse of the rubber boom in 1913, so that the Bolivian section of the line was never built, Riberalta would have been a thriving entrepôt for rubber produced in the Beni and Pando provinces.

Of course, there were people in this region long before Muñoz, Suárez and other early settlers like the Graverolle family, migrants from France, or Antonio Vaca Diez and Antenor Vasquez. Much earlier incomers and the sites they had occupied were the subject of a study by Bruce Mann and Elizabeth Dix in a team led by Mike How.

When we had first passed through Riberalta we had had time only for a brief evening visit to Las Piedras. Now, on a fleet of eight motorcycles, the archaeological team drove off to the river ferry upstream of the town. On the northern bank a walk into the rainforest eventually brought the party to the thatched house of Don Norberto, whose wife had previously shown Yoli and me the ruins.

With him as guide, we crossed into the trees over what seemed like a vallum or defensive wall such as might have surrounded an Iron Age fort in Britain. Inside the ramparts was thick secondary rainforest, but Bruce was able to show us a mound, now hollowed out, which Norberto's wife remembered as having once been a stone building with a lintelled door. We then came to a sharp edge of earth where there was a steep drop to a flat area where Bruce supposed the Beni had once run and perhaps still does in the months of flood. If so, this would have made an excellent defensive position. Finally we saw an impressive section of stone walling – not classic Inca in precision, but carefully made, over 6 feet high, and well preserved. As Dr Said Zeitum López had told us after our previous visit, a mid-fifteenth-century Inca civil uprising around Cuzco had driven many thousands of refugees into these lowlands. They are said to have headed for the lower Beni, and this could have been one of their fortified settlements.

Bruce and Elizabeth had done a proper survey of the Las Piedras site. They had traced its surrounding walls (of a local porous volcanic rock) for 600 yards and computed that they enclosed about 125 acres. They also found the tumbled remains of what was probably a stone bridge across the 23-foot-wide vallum. The central mound posed problems. There were numerous stories about it. Treasure-hunters in the 1950s had spent a month digging it out. The Bolivian Army was said to have blown it up in the 1980s – but for what reason? British troops exercising for many decades on Salisbury Plain have never found it necessary to blow round barrows up. Other treasure-seekers were said to have dug more recently. Locals seemed to remember it as rounded at the top, its surface covered with flat stone blocks like a Victorian ice-house. Bruce Mann concluded that the Inca Tupac Yupanqui might have built a fortification here at this strategic confluence of two big rivers.

Dr Said and the local people were eager for us to come back in ensuing years to examine Las Piedras and other places in the hope that some site clearance might both reveal pottery and organic material which would enable us to date its occupation and encourage tourism.

We went to another site close by – the shape of a light-bulb in plan, with its socket in the present bank of the Beni. A shallow earthwork encircled what may have been a defensible landing-stage. Again, excavation will be necessary to find out more.

A third site 2 miles west of Las Piedras was revealed to the archaeologists by our local helper, Juan, just as they were mounting their Suzuki 125s to leave. He told them of a friend's field full of pottery shards, so they drove over there. A smallholder called Angel Subetha said that he constantly turned up broken pots over an area of about 250 acres. In five minutes, digging only 4 inches down, Bruce Mann found fragments of pots and rims of nine different sorts of vessel, almost all a light tan in colour, similar to pots of the Amazonian culture. He and Elizabeth asked Angel to keep what he found until we came again.

The archaeological team had been fortunate in their domestic arrangements: arriving in northern Bolivia, they had had a chance encounter with a Riberalta lady who had said, 'You must all come and stay at my house.' Sure enough, Maria Klarer-Cuellar had rooms free to accommodate seven of them.

Our visiting group of four was lodged in the Hotel Colonial in Riberalta – itself a gem of its kind. A large entrance hall leads to a still bigger one hung with sombre paintings of forest and river by local artists.

This hall, furnished with fine pieces in dark wood, has three walls: on the fourth side is a lush tropical garden with walkways at its edges leading to rooms. Once the private town house of a well-to-do merchant, the Colonial has been a hotel under the relaxed, suave management of his son, Miguel Duran, since the 1970s.

Riberalta has other points of interest. Near a bust of Nicolas Suárez on a tall plinth, and overlooking the Beni, is a small, nineteenth-century steamer, the *Tahuamanu*, named after another river that, like the Madre de Dios, flows out of Peru. 'The first and last steamship on northern rivers,' a plaque said. The *Tahuamanu* had taken part in three wars: the two Acre wars of 1901–3 and the Chaco war of 1932–5, in all of which Bolivia lost swathes of territory – first the rubber-tree forests of Acre to Brazil, and then the searing-hot scrublands of the Chaco to Paraguay. A tall smokestack bore the Bolivian colours proudly, however, and Alex Foley and Richard noted that its engine had been made by Cochranes Ltd of Annan, Scotland.

As we were all about to leave the Hotel Colonial to find a restaurant, a spectral figure walked in from the dark street. It was Andrew Holt – a former sapper officer, now a freelance photographer, and an unorthodox member of this expedition. He had come out first to La Paz after Phase One had ended, but had had to fly home prematurely after the start of Phase Two. Enterprisingly, he came out in the early stages of Phase Three in late July, hoping to get footage of the reed boats in the rapids, and left again when we were a little way down the Rio Madeira. I found him pleasant, persuasive, determined, resourceful, but something of an enigma: diffident in manner, but intense in his enthusiasms – which included alternative religions and mind-altering substances.

The demands of photographers and film-makers can often strain the patience of expedition leaders, but Andrew was always so scrupulously polite in his requests that it was difficult to refuse him. However, I had to do so once or twice. He first arrived in Guanay as we were all coming away from the mountain. 'I want to go to Paititi,' he said. 'No chance,' I told him. 'It's four days march, and you'll never find the way unguided.' 'Well, I'll just go to Incapampa and look across at Paititi. I'll be all right on my own.' 'I wouldn't want you to risk it, Andrew. Besides, there's nobody there now.' We had moved down a couple of days ahead of schedule, and he had come just too late to see any more than the base camp.

After we had all left Rurrenabaque, he looked increasingly worried about his wife, who was ill in hospital in the UK. Suddenly he said, 'I have to go back now.' So we stopped a tiny *peke-peke* coming upriver and put him on it.

Andrew had made his decision to return to us after checking the expedition web site on the Internet. Of course this was always a few days behind events, so he bought an air ticket and flew to Pôrto Velho expecting to catch us grappling with the biggest of the Madeira–Mamoré rapids in mid-July. But the capsize at Ribeirão a few days before had meant that our running of the remaining nine cataracts in *KM3* (after Ribeirão she had gone down two rapids unmanned) and our planned manual portaging of the formidable falls at Girão, Caldeirão do Inferno and Teotónio would not take place, so he had missed another photo opportunity. But Andrew had a genius for using local transport and flushing us out wherever the expedition was, and now he was with us again, and lodged with the ever welcoming Maria.

After his quick call in at Riberalta, Andrew left the base camp at Abunã for Río Branco, capital of next-door Acre province. On the way to us he had met some people who told him of a religious community deep in the rainforest where adherents take a decoction called *ayahuasca* and subsequently see visions – not the sort you experience hallucinogenically, when you see something that is not there and believe that it is, but those when, with your mind in an altered state, you see beautiful things knowing that they are not there.

This sort of experience is meat and drink to Andrew, so he went to an Internet café and looked up Ceu do Mapia, the location of the community. He then took an overnight bus to Río Branco, a shared taxi for four hours to Boca do Acre, and a boat for two hours down and six hours up a narrow winding creek to come upon a wonderful, almost Alpine, village in a clearing in the forest: chalets, green gardens, neat fields.

At first, proposing to stay only two days, he was mistrusted. But fortunately for him there was to be a ceremony the night he arrived, in a big, hexagon-shaped hall. (Its symbolism seemed to be a mixture of the Star of David and the Christian cross, its gods part Christian and part natural – sky, stars and forest.) The presiding minister in the end welcomed him, but did not let him film. It was all mind-bending stuff: children sang and women danced, swaying sideways and marching to and fro, chanting all the while in Portuguese.

Andrew took his *ayahuasca*, which they called the Santo Daime, and had his visions. The drug usually induces vomiting, but on his empty stomach it just made him nauseous. As luck would have it, the next morning the community was in the rainforest collecting ingredients for the next group experience. The men cut tall vines, the women collected the appropriate leaves, and boys then beat the vines rhythmically to pulverize them. The result was a very powerful, grainy, dark-brown goo. At the end, Andrew said, he found the community (which included two Dutch women, an American, and a German) friendly, reasonable and normal.

He would probably have leaped at the chance to go with Shirley Critchley, our community-aid organizer, and the medical team when an opportunity came to visit 'Israel'. The officer at the Bolivian Navy post at Nueva Esperanza on the Mamoré had said he would take them to see a strange village community in the far north of the country. A doctor goes in once a month; otherwise visitors are discouraged. But Shirley – a great facilitator – managed to get an assurance that she, Sam and Graham would be admitted.

The community is part of an organization called AEMINPU – Asociación Evangélica de la Misión Israelita del Nuevo Pacto Universal, founded in Lima in 1968. Branches were established in Bolivia in 1982. Its members aim to follow the laws set down in the Old Testament, and to eschew many aspects of modernity – tobacco, for example, and alcohol. For the last fifteen months 250 of them had lived in a newly built village of eighty neatly aligned houses on the banks of the river. No road led to the community, so Shirley's group were taken over the Mamoré to Brazil by the Navy, then walked along the road and crossed back by boat to Bolivia. Veiled women were washing clothes in the river, and a delegation of robed men welcomed them on the high bank. They all walked to the school, where Graham and Sam began to work.

Shirley found that the members of the community had come from all parts of Bolivia – La Paz, Cochabamba, Potosí – to follow the laws of Moses. Long hair and beards are worn by the men (Leviticus 21:5), and the women go veiled – all to avoid punishment when the last trump sounds. Until that dire moment they will farm (Proverbs 28:19), build houses, breed chickens, and cook over open fires. The children have no toys or television and play no sport.

At 3 p.m. they all assembled at their church – men and women on different sides; well-behaved children in front. The Ten Commandments were read from *Primero* to *Decimo*, and responses were given. The three visitors were introduced and welcomed, and made reply. Hymns were sung, the women – wearing sky-blue, red or white veils – shaking tambourines with trailing ribbons. The only modern touch was a massive amplifier, through which, one hopes, the last trump will be relayed when it sounds. Shirley – *profesora* as they styled her – was pleased to find four teachers for the eighty children.

While *KM3* was being portaged and repaired, Matt Wilkinson asked if he could take some of his team in the two Avons to examine the rapids we had bypassed. Although this did not have a direct bearing on the expedition's main aim, I agreed, as I thought it might well add some useful information. So six men, with a bank support team of two, successfully ran most of these rapids between 12 and 15 July.

On the first day they had a look at then slipped down the unexceptional Pederneira and Paredão, rating them grades 2 and 3, and camped at the entrance of the Rio Mutum-Paraná. Next day Tres Irmãos also proved no problem, and things went easily until they came to Girão, a reputed monster. A portage of over half a mile through dense riverine forest would have been too laborious and time-consuming, so they deflated one Avon and carried it with the other to the nearby road. On the way they saw interesting petroglyphs – a rectangular grid of small circles – on a south-bank rock, and Matt was able to grade the falls at 5 on the south side and 5/6 on the north. The reconnaissance of 2000 by Jim Masters and his team and Drew Craig's resultant report were proving to be most accurate.

Matt's team put the boats in the water again just below the Cauldron of Hell, and then motored up to its foot to look at it. They then ran on downstream over Morrinhos to Teotónio. The previous leak in one of the inflatables was giving trouble again, so they portaged round Teotónio – quite easily accessible by road, and something of a tourist attraction now – and continued down to the final and most picturesque set of rapids at Santo Antônio and thus into Pôrto Velho. All agreed that it would have been one hell of a challenge to drag *KM3* around these impassable cataracts.

We were soon to learn that Pôrto Velho does not mean 'Old Port' (it dates only from 1907) but 'Port of the Old Man'. In that year one old man was scratching a solitary existence on the jungle-fringed banks of the Madeira 3 miles or so downstream of the Santo Antônio falls. Could he have been the American whom H. M. Tomlinson had met there on board the *Capella* in 1910? 'Boys, I'm old man Jim,' he had announced as he stood in the saloon in a widening pool of water. On his way out to the newly arrived packet in a canoe, he had been overturned in the darkness by floating logs, but fortunately he was fished out of the fast current by the first mate of the *Capella*. He explained that he had lived there since 1907, before Pôrto Velho even existed.

I was interested in how the bustling city that now welcomed us had been started in such an unpropitious location in the early 1900s. One factor had brought it into existence: the railway. Finally completed in 1912 to bypass the Mamoré–Madeira cataracts, the railway itself had a single justification: rubber.

Known even to the Indians whom Columbus encountered in Hispaniola in 1492, the sticky, milk-white latex from a particular Amazonian tree was adapted throughout South America for use not just as a bouncing toy for children, but in shoes, cloaks and even small syringes and pumps. In 1755 the King of Portugal sent his boots to Pará (now Belém) to be coated in 'gum elastic', and it was not long before *caoutch-ouc*, as the Indians of the Brazils (and the French) called it, had wider applications in the northern world. The great eighteenth-century chemist Dr Joseph Priestley created a pencil eraser and called it 'India-Rubber'. In 1823 Charles Macintosh patented a waterproof fabric which was essentially a sandwich of rubber between two layers of cloth, hence the name of the rainwear. The Guards, rather improbably, are said to have paraded before George IV in their rubber gear in the 1820s. In 1839 Charles Goodyear found a way of stopping rubber from going soft in hot weather and brittle in cold: vulcanization, which led to the production of pneumatic tyres – patented by a Belfast vet called John Dunlop in 1888. Edouard Michelin in 1892 made some tyres that were detachable from the wheel rims. And so it went on: more refinements, huger demand. Carriages began to run on rubberized wheels, and the vogue for bicycles in the second half of the nineteenth century and the later mania for cars led to a colossal surge in the call for rubber.

The best-quality latex came from the wild *Hevea brasiliensis*, which was found all over the Amazonian rainforests of northern Bolivia, Brazil, Peru, Ecuador and Colombia. The enterprising unemployed therefore flocked to the Amazon from the poorer provinces of Brazil and from the outer world. Soon even the Amazon's many vast tributaries seemed almost to be getting overcrowded by the incoming *seringueiros* (syringe-tree-men), who tapped their trees every morning and in the afternoons coagulated the latex into massive cannon-balls of rubber.

Entrepôts like Iquitos in Peru and Manaus and Pará in Brazil prospered and burgeoned, linked to the outside world by the elegant black-funnelled vessels of the Booth Steamship Company of Liverpool and their like. The Amazon is navigable by ocean-going ships as far as the foothills of the Andes in Peru, as are many of its tributaries, especially on its southern side.

Only Bolivian rubber was at a disadvantage: it had to be hauled on the backs of horses and llamas over the Andes to a Pacific port, or man-oeuvred on barges down the dangerous Mamoré–Madeira rapids, or painstakingly portaged round them.

Some Bolivians were interested in a better river route to the Atlantic long before the trade in wild rubber really took off. An engineer, José Augustin Palacios, navigated the Mamoré–Madeira rapids in 1846 and, in possibly the greatest understatement in the history of an enterprise given more to hope than to practicality, said, 'This inconvenience can be easily overcome.'

In 1851 American lieutenants Lardner Gibbon and Richard Herndon were sent by their government to check out the rapids. It took their team twelve grim days to hack its way from Guajará-Mirim to Santo Antônio. 'At the end of the afternoon [of 30 September] we reached the begin-ning of the cataract of Teotónio, the most terrific of them all,' wrote Lardner Gibbon, 'Here I was stricken by bilious fever and forced to bed . . . We were all emaciated, pallid, exhausted.' Back at home, they proposed a road of 180 miles around the rapids, and reckoned it would take fifty-nine days to carry trade goods from Baltimore to La Paz. This optimistic guesstimate allowed thirty days by steamer from the US eastern seaboard to Santo Antônio, seven to bypass the falls by the road, fourteen for mules to reach the foot of the Andes, and eight more up to the Bolivian capital. In those pre-Panama Canal days the trip usually took 180 days via the then Peruvian port of Arica and Cape Horn.

Ten years later Quentin Quevedo, a Bolivian general, evolved the idea of either a canal or a railway round the obstacles. The Brazilian engineer João Martins da Silva Coutinho in the same year proposed a railway some 280 miles long around the rapids. In 1861 railways in Brazil were already in the ascendant: canals had had their day. The Brazilian government warmed to the idea of a railway because it offered a link running exclu-sively in Brazilian territory between their Atlantic port of Pará (Belém) and the fertile and mineral-rich province of Mato Grosso. This was better than having to take the products of Mato Grosso southward down the Paraguay river and through the isolationist republic of Paraguay. The need for a northern route was reinforced when in 1865 Paraguay's unstable president, Francisco Solano López, declared war almost simultaneously on Brazil, Uruguay and Argentina.

It was during the war years, 1865–70, when the Mato Grosso was effectively cut off from the rest of the country, that Brazil began talks with Bolivia, whose own trade northward down the Madeira was increasing. This was mainly in sugar, cocoa, cigars, jerked beef, hides, tallow and live cattle, as well as rubber. Even though it involved sixty or seventy hazardous passages down the Madeira–Mamoré rapids every year, it had grown in value to about $120,000 by 1864.

A treaty in 1867 between Brazil and Bolivia guaranteed freedom of trade on each other's rivers and free use to Bolivia of whatever facility was to be built round the rapids. In 1867 the German brothers Josef and Franz Keller, both engineers, passed up the Madeira to Santo Antônio with a party of seventy-eight men and began an assault on the falls in seven canoes. They had hard times in Teotónio and the Cauldron of Hell, and lost a canoe at Ribeirão. The Kellers were over four months at the Madeira–Mamoré rapids and proposed both a canal 22 yards wide and 2 yards deep and a railway 200 miles long. But their costings were fanciful guesses, and they never properly looked at the land over which their railway was to run.

General Quevedo was sent as Bolivian ambassador to Mexico, and there was introduced to an American soldier of fortune, Colonel George Earl Church, a man of many facets who had worked on railways in New Jersey and Argentina and was in 1904 to become a vice-president of Britain's Royal Geographical Society. He had also fought on the side of the Union in the American Civil War, and afterwards went to Mexico ostensibly as a correspondent for the *New York Herald*. In fact General Ulysses S. Grant had sent him on a secret mission to further the cause of Mexico's displaced president, Benito Juárez, against the unpopular Emperor Maximilian, lately foisted on the country by the French.

In 1868 Church went to Bolivia and carried out a reconnaissance of the problem area by river. As Charles Gauld has written, 'Church was almost the sole survivor of a Bolivian expedition of twenty-six that shot the Madeira–Mamoré rapids in flood. He reached Belém a skeleton.' Subsequently he won the concession to tackle the problem of the rapids. The notorious, outrageous, unpredictable Bolivian president Mariano Melgarejo, who had just ceded a vast triangular segment of the Acre region to Brazil – allegedly in exchange for a horse – is said to have tested Church's mettle by having his cavalry ride full tilt up to him to see if he flinched. Church had stood his ground, and he next won the support of Emperor Dom Pedro II of Brazil, who named the railway the Estrada de Ferro do Madeira e Mamoré. Soon the National Bolivian Navigation Company was formed with a capital of £2 million, raised in London.

The operation began in 1872, when the British Public Works Construction Company sent out to Santo Antônio twenty-five engineers and a workforce, with material to build 22 miles of railway. Malaria, smallpox and the Caripuña Indians soon did for them. They built 2 miles of track, lost 200 lives, and in May 1873, ten months after their arrival, returned home, describing the area as 'a charnel-house . . . where men die like flies'.

But Church was a sticker, and he returned to the United States to secure a loan from the Philadelphia Steelworks (who would make the rails) for a contract with P. & T. Collins, experienced railroad-builders. So it was that in 1878 the *Mercedita* left Philadelphia for Pará with 210 men and 1,000 tons of gear. 'The first time in US history that an expedition has been sent from the US equipped with American money, material and brains for the execution of a great public work in a foreign country,' proclaimed the *New York Herald* on 3 January. Sadly, the report also said, 'No colored need apply.' Seventy had been taken on, but Brazil, a slave nation until 1888, had been unhappy to admit free blacks.

Santo Antônio was a huge disappointment to the Americans: a detachment of six idle Brazilian soldiers and the ruined barrack blocks of the British railworkers. Nothing more.

The rainforest proved almost impenetrable. An axe blow would bring down a shower of fire-ants on the woodcutter's head, and when a tree was parted from its stump it would remain upright, suspended by a tangle of vines and lianas. Mosquitoes, sweat bees, vampire bats, peccaries, piranhas, stealthy Indian archers – all contributed to a gradual debilitation of American morale. Quinine was in short supply, and almost a quarter of the workers died from malaria. Then their wages were cut and some began to try to escape, downriver or into the forest, not to be seen again. A second ship, the *Metropolis*, steamed from Philadelphia with 246 men, 500 tons of rails and machinery, and 200 of provisions, but foundered off North Carolina. A 4-4-0 locomotive named *Coronel Church* set off on the 3½ miles of completed track and leaped spectacularly off the rails. P. & T. Collins went bankrupt. The American venture, like the British one before it, had failed. The Brazilians themselves tried in 1882 and 1883, and failed too.

As the Americans were beating a disconsolate retreat in 1879, a war was breaking out on the other side of the Andes, as a result of which Bolivia suffered a blow to her national pride which she has not yet fully forgotten: she lost her Pacific coastline. From 1879 to 1883 she was, with Peru, involved in a war against Chile – a war which she had brought about herself by raising the cost of the licences needed by Chileans mining copper and nitrate on the Atacama coast of Bolivia's Litoral province.

Under the feckless President Hilarión Daza, the Bolivian Army was slow to mobilize and entered the War of the Pacific in a lackadaisical fashion. The Chileans swept north and took Cobija, Bolivia's Pacific port – a mean little place, but symbolically important – crossed into Peru, and pushed the frontier up beyond Arica.

Although in 2002 still twice the size of Spain, since independence in 1825 Bolivia has lost half of her original territory – most of it desert, mountain or rainforest. The loss of Litoral, however, reducing her to the present nine provinces, shut her off from the sea, and this *enclaustramiento* is still bitterly felt.

Chile compensated Bolivia in some measure by offering free use of the Pacific ports of Arica and Antofagasta, which she still enjoys, and built railways from them up on to the Altiplano to facilitate trade. But the fact that Bolivia was landlocked gave greater pertinence after the treaty of 1884 to her attempts to open new ways to the Atlantic.

In 1903 Bolivia lost more land. After a short war, she gave Brazil the rest of the Acre territory and in return Brazil undertook to resume the building of the Madeira–Mamoré railway and to carry it over the Mamoré into Bolivia to the fast expanding town of Riberalta – very much in the domain of Nicolas Suárez, Bolivia's greatest rubber producer.

To carry out this part of the Treaty of Petrópolis, the Brazilian government put the work out to tender. Joaquim Catramby's bid was accepted. He brought in Percival Farquhar, a forty-two-year-old Quaker from Pennsylvania, who set up the Madeira–Mamoré Railway Company with $11 million capital and subcontracted the construction work to the engineering firm of May, Jeckyll & Randolph. I had wondered why a street in Pôrto Velho was called Rua Farquhar. He was the town's virtual founder.

This second wave of Americans arrived in Santo Antônio in 1907.

Conditions at first were appalling. The undergrowth was so thick that visibility was often only 3 feet. American, Arab, Brazilian, British, Caribbean, German, Italian and Portuguese workers, aged from thirteen to seventy, were attacked by Caripuña Indians, clouds of mosquitoes, sweat bees, piums – buffalo gnats – and other flies. Diseases raged: typhoid, amoebic dysentery, blackwater fever, and above all malaria. Quinine at one time fetched £20 an ampoule. Later, under Farquhar's benign and far-sighted management, it was provided free and administered compulsorily before meals.

There was colossal drinking on pay nights, and the survivors shot each other up in sporadic gunfights. The operational HQ was moved from Santo Antônio 3 miles north to Pôrto Velho, where old man Jim lived. Weakened by fever, he mistrusted the Indians enough to dress a dummy, place it in his hammock, and spend the night in the corner of his hut, eyes open, nursing a gun. We had our own old man Jim, of course. Masters, like his namesake of 1912, had many spills in the Madeira, and developed a badly infected ear from an injury in the capsize at Ribeirão.

At their first sight of Pôrto Velho, new recruits mutinied or fled, appalled by the shrieks of beriberi sufferers in the makeshift hospitals. The company's recruiting officers, who earned a handsome commission on each hand hired, were banned by the authorities in Spain, Portugal and Italy.

Farquhar soon realized that the endemic sickness was counterproductive, and reforms began. He was a compassionate man, and organized a 300-bed hospital some way downriver below Santo Antônio at Candelária. Dr Carl Lovelace, with fifteen interns, drenched the stagnant water around the buildings with petrol and erected mosquito-proof porches as dormitories. On average there were 4,350 labourers on a monthly wage, of whom about 3,000 were fit for work at any one time. Ninety per cent of the workforce could expect to be hospitalized during their tour. A man's average work time would be about three months. But week by week under Farquhar's beneficent rule the survival rate increased.

Pôrto Velho was improved, along with the lifestyle of its inhabitants – in particular of the eighty Americans on the permanent payroll. Soon there were wharves for incoming ships (though when the *Capella* arrived on 30 January 1910 its purser, H. M. Tomlinson, could report only that 'a rough pier was being thrown out on palm boles to receive us, but it was not ready. We anchored in five fathoms, about thirty yards from the shore'). Before long the town had pure water in three large metal tanks on legs which still crown the hill by the river, a steam-powered electricity plant, telephones, a laundry, a steam bakery, movie house, ice machines, a printing press and a newspaper – the *Marconigram*.

The workers at base enjoyed minstrel shows, as well as turkey dinners on the Fourth of July, and they even played baseball on some Sunday afternoons. The old menu of 'sow's belly and beans' ended, and liver and bacon, Irish stew, and buckwheat cakes and syrup all became available. By 1910 herds of cattle on the hoof were carried up the Madeira by barges to a slaughterhouse – the *Capella* had brought sixty head up from Itacoatiara. Californian oranges, pears, potatoes and onions came in too.

But the work was still punishing and the toll in lives considerable. Over the five-year construction period 22,000 men were employed, of whom at least 3,600 died, on site or on the way home. One carpenter became a full-time coffin-maker. To keep the necessary numbers the recruiting officers' commission was upped, and sixty-eight Cretans earned one of them £8 a head. Every month 500 newcomers came ashore.

'The line must go through' became the watchword. Jaguars – or *tigres* as the locals called them – were shot out; the Caripuña Indians were protected on Farquhar's orders and fobbed off with beads and mirrors. Coal came from Swansea, steel from Pittsburgh, and sleepers of euca-lyptus wood – impervious to termites – from Taiwan and Australia. The £2¼ million estimated cost of the railway eventually quadrupled. But the line was built: 227 miles of it, rising 267 feet from Pôrto Velho to Guajará-Mirim.

And it was all virtually a waste of time: in one of the supreme ironies of history, no sooner had the railway been inaugurated than the world rubber boom ended. To make things worse, cheaper rubber from the neat plantations of South-East Asia undercut the more expensive South American wild rubber.

It was a Briton who had spelt ruin for the tappers, their *patrãoes* the opera-going toffs in Manaus – and the Estrada de Ferro do Madeira e Mamoré. In a parallel to the achievements of Sir Clements Markham, who between 1859 and 1862 smuggled quinine-bearing cinchona trees out of Peru for planting in India, Sir Henry Wickham, commissioned by the India Office in June 1876, had brought into Kew Gardens 7,000 *Hevea brasiliensis* seeds.

The India Office had sent Sir Joseph Hooker, then director of Kew, an 1872 report by James Collins, one-time curator of the Museum of the Pharmaceutical Society, praising *Hevea brasiliensis* as the best of the ninety-four species of rubber-bearing trees. Hooker was also told that the Foreign Office had asked HM consul at Pará to acquire some seeds for transmission to Kew for germination, and thence to Ceylon (Sri Lanka).

The consul approached rubber-exporter Henry Wickham, who cannily asked for £10 per thousand seeds – four times the going rate. He secured 7,000 seeds in the highlands by the Tapajós river, chartered an empty cargo boat homeward-bound to Liverpool, and, needlessly fearing their interception by Brazilian customs officials, got the seeds on board and conveyed them to Kew. About 2,400 of them germinated successfully, and the bulk of the seedlings were taken out to Colombo in 1877.

Oddly, the cultivation of the ensuing rubber trees by planters in Ceylon, and equally in Malaya, was slow to take off, and not until 1897–8 did demand accelerate rubber production there. But it was not long before a glut brought about a general collapse of the rubber price in 1913 – only the second year of operation of the Madeira–Mamoré railway.

Because of the slump, the Brazilians never finished pushing the line from Guajará-Mirim across the Mamoré to Riberalta. And so it was not until we entered Brazil at Guajará-Mirim that we first saw signs of the railway. Near the embarkation point for Bolivia stands the beautifully preserved 2-8-2 locomotive No. 17, *Hildegardo Nuñes*, and alongside the handsome Guajará-Mirim station buildings, now a museum, stands the 4-6-0 No. 20.

While we were based at the Hotel Thalita in Abunã, Richard and I walked along the line of the old track to look at a 2-6-0 in a very badly decomposed state. It had been much vandalized even in the last twenty years, and a termite nest now enveloped its nearside driving wheels. The former Abunã station buildings are still recognizable, with a worn 'EFMM' on a side wall. This station was at the end of the notorious Abunã strait, much subject to landslips and flooding, and stood where the route executes a 90° turn southwards.

On 10 July Richard approached the railway-terminal buildings at Pôrto Velho in high anticipation. Crowds were milling about in the extensive natural amphitheatre in which Farquhar had first set up his station, offices, repair shops, engine shed and marshalling yard.

A factory siren blared continually, and the sky was loud with the noise of firecrackers – an everyday occurrence in South America. He learned that this was, however, a special day: they were celebrating an anniversary of the railway's closure!

The massive metal sheds were still there, rusting and forlorn. A 4-6-2, No. 50, built by Baldwin's of Philadelphia, stood outside the former workshop, now a museum. Inside was the star exhibit – the first locomotive, also built by Baldwin's, the 4-4-0 *Coronel Church*, which had been brought out in 1878 and which Farquhar had found in 1907 with a tree growing out of its smokestack.

As *Capella* dropped anchor off Pôrto Velho in 1910, H. M. Tomlinson heard 'a violent scream in the forest near our bows . . . and a locomotive ran out from the base of the trees, still screaming'. Richard hoped for some similar signs of steam life: all the guidebooks say that there are tourist trips on the first few miles of track every Sunday. But No. 50, No. 18 on a turntable nearby, and other locomotives and rolling stock were all still.

In 1919 the Americans had handed over control of the equity to British investors, who ran the railway until the more serious worldwide economic debacle of 1929, when they passed it to the Brazilian government. It ran at a deficit until closure on 10 July 1972, when it was decided to lay a road along the line of the railway track and across its many bridges. There were some protests at this destruction of Brazil's national heritage, and on 5 May 1981 services for tourists were inaugurated when Manoel Soares Silva drove No. 15 along the surviving 5 miles of track out of Pôrto Velho as far as Teotónio and back. There was to be a restricted service also out of Guajará-Mirim. *A Ferrovia do Diabo*, the Devil's Railroad, lived again. It was billed as Maria Fumaça – Smoking Maria – in homage to the earlier railroad workers' adaptation of 'Madeira–Mamoré' to become 'Mad Maria'.

There is a Madeira–Mamoré Railway Society based in Castleford in Britain which works with the Associacão de Preservacão de Estrada de Ferro Madeira–Mamoré in Pôrto Velho. Together they are now resisting plans to develop the terminus site as a shopping-centre.

We eventually learned that a landslip up the line from Pôrto Velho had for several months brought the Sunday tourist services to a stop. It is to be hoped that the government of Rondônia province and the Secretariat for the National Historical and Artistic Heritage (SPHAN) can summon up enthusiasm and money to restore these services and protect what is left of a remarkable enterprise.

12

Some Madeira, My Dear

The pilot we engaged . . . called the Madeira the 'long cemetery'.

H. M. Tomlinson, *The Sea and the Jungle*, 1912

JIM MASTERS, WITH James Culshaw as interpreter, had gone into Pôrto Velho with the central hull of *KM3* on its low-loader. Several others, their time expired, had left the expedition via Guayaramerín or Pôrto Velho airports – including Captain Matt Wilkinson, *KM3*'s skipper, and Sergeant Paul Cawkwell, to serve with NATO forces in Macedonia. Still others were arriving from Britain to take part in Phase Four of the expedition: the journey down the Madeira and Amazon rivers to the sea. On 18 July the contingent in the Hotel Thalita at Abunã moved by bus to a sports complex by the Madeira at Pôrto Velho,where preparations for this phase could continue more efficiently. Marcelo, Paul Overton and I were occupied in procuring a suitable support vessel, Ernie Durey began to amass his stores, while Jim supervised Máximo Catari's repair work on *KM3*.

Pôrto Velho may be at the heart of a vast continent, but it is also a thriving port. All along the east bank of the Madeira are slipways to which powerful *empurradores* – pusher tugs rather than pullers – guide their rafts of barges. On the barges are trucks, tankers, trailers, containers, to be hauled up the slipways to the fuel storage tanks, warehouses or city depots. Warehouses and shipbuilding yards line the banks. Opposite our camp on a football field a giant *balsa* or ferry called *Brenda* – the identical sister of *Monica* and *Olivia*, which carry traffic over the Madeira at the Abunã river mouth and link Pôrto Velho and Río Branco, capitals of Rondônia and Acre – was being fitted out and given a good coat of orange paint.

Ports are not often pretty places, and the riparian road into Pôrto Velho is a grim stretch – though not perhaps such a vile place as Peter

Grieve described it half a century ago: 'A nest of ramshackle buildings with grey roofs, and then a rotting railway truck on a grass-grown track . . . an extensive hell of corrugated iron . . . much of it rust red and scabrous, under which dwelt the 5,000 inhabitants of the town.'

Three hundred thousand *Rondônianos* live there now and, if it is still an unprepossessing place, it is certainly big and thriving. Three of us tried its most expensive hotel, the gaunt, cavernous, modern Vila Rica, for a few days, but Richard was even luckier. Jim Masters had met a palaeontologist, an Argentinian teaching biology at the local college. Mario Alberto Cozzuol – short, bald and bearded – invited Richard to stay at his capacious, securely walled house in the outskirts in return for a lecture to his students. There was a moment of apprehension when, on being shown to his room, Richard saw hanging from strongpoints on the wall bunches of hooks, shackles, rings and chains. He wondered what sort of time he would be having. Tentatively asking whether these might be for weighing dolphins or other creatures that the professor might collect from the river, Mario told him it was where his mother-in-law slung her hammock when she came to stay. Mario taught Richard a great deal about Pôrto Velho, the dolphin and the Madeira river.

Meanwhile those not involved with preparation for the next phase of the expedition enjoyed the hospitality of the Aquarius Hotel. Emerson Castro, the general manager, had generously provided rooms at a huge discount, and indeed the friendly people of Pôrto Velho all made us most welcome. The local discos did a roaring trade as our crew loved their short stay in the first big city on our route.

Plans had been laid in Britain for us to collaborate with WorldVision, who have a ship which we believed we could deploy in support of *KM3*. It works the Amazon tributaries carrying out eye operations for the local people. Unfortunately we heard that it had a mechanical problem and would be under repair in Manaus until 28 July – far too late for us. Also they asked for a subvention of $10,000 for medical supplies. The arrangement fell apart. However, the Presbyterian Church of Manaus, with whom WorldVision were associated, was keen to assist our medical work along the river and kindly agreed to send a liaison officer with us.

As luck had it, I was next offered a boat by Reinaldo and Braulia Ribeiro, who came to our camp in the sports complex. They were from JOCUM – Jovem con um Misião, or Young People with a Mission – a worldwide organization founded in the USA in 1960 and with an office in Harpenden, Herts. Here, outside Pôrto Velho, there was a scattered community of 150 mostly Brazilian Christians, who look after twenty-seven of the separate ethnic groups living up the tributaries of the Madeira. JOCUM's land lay alongside the smart, modern buildings of the Summer Institute of Linguistics, a shadowy missionary society permitted entry by only a few Third World countries and once roundly slated by Norman Lewis in the *The Missionaries*. But JOCUM seemed to us to be gentle healers, facilitators and civilizers rather than fundamentalist soul-hunters. Kindly people, they even regretted having to kill a 28-foot anaconda that had eaten their cow!

We had a look at their boat, the *Sal y Luz*, but at 37 feet overall it was far too small. Nevertheless, one of their Brazilian missionaries, Nilton Corrêa de Cavalheiro, came with us as far as Humaitá, some 160 miles downriver, and was extremely helpful to our medical team, who were now preparing to do all they could to aid the more remote communities rarely visited by doctors and dentists.

'Perhaps we could hire a regular Amazonian ferry boat,' I suggested to Marcelo, and eventually we secured a splendid two-decker called the *Capitão Azevedo*, which could accompany and accommodate us as far as Santarém, where it would be necessary to charter a larger, more powerful, vessel that could cope with the rough seas near the mouth of the great river.

For two months we were based on the *Capitão Azevedo*. Small two-decker passenger ferries just like it ply the Amazon and its tributaries with cargo stacked on the lower deck – boxes of fruit, crates of Skol beer, corrugated roofing, once we even saw a car – while passengers swing in their hammocks on the upper deck. There are heads for males (*Ele*) and females (*Ela*), a galley and a bar, but cabins only for the crew.

A great many Amazon ferries, however, are dingy single-deckers with noisy two-stroke engines. They phut-phut along hung about with old tyres as fenders, washing flapping in the breeze, a couple of hammocks slung inside amidships, and a woman and child in the galley at the stern.

Large three-deckers were occasionally passed – more and more as we neared the bigger towns – with air-conditioned passenger cabins and modern appointments. One notable three-decker, the *Ana Maria VII* of Manaus, came alongside *KM3* at Humaitá with most of its passengers dancing a lively salsa on the open part of the top deck, music blasting out *fff* in true Brazilian fashion from four speakers each as big as a tea chest. Best remembered of the dancers was a large bald man gyrating with commendable nimbleness alongside an astonishingly underdressed *café-leite*-coloured nymphet.

The *Capitão Azevedo*, owned by João Azevedo da Silva, was built in Manaus in 1992 and was normally employed in taking up to fifty tourists at a time on short evening river cruises out of Pôrto Velho at 3 reals (about $1.40) a time, typically up to the last (or first) cataract at Santo Antônio. She was almost ideal for us: plenty of deck space to sling hammocks or spread a Therm-a-Rest and hang mosquito nets, good cooking facilities, refrigeration, white plastic chairs and tables, showers in the loos, her own plates and cutlery. Our only complaint was the low headroom. Ernie Durey and Patricio Crooker walked about unconcernedly; tall people like Graham Catchpole, Paul Overton and myself constantly struck heads on the ceiling or on a sharp central ridge on the upper-deck roof. Poor Bill Holmes, at 6 feet 6 inches, had to walk about like a case of severe kyphosis. 'I've got built-in sonar, like these river dolphin,' he said. 'Tall people get to have this.'

The expedition main body went aboard on Wednesday 25 July. Yoli, Peter Kannangara and I installed ourselves the evening before, to get the 'operations centre' properly established by converting the vessel's shop on the lower deck. Arriving next day, the rest of the team was slow to settle in and for a while things were a shambles. Ernie Durey, selflessly making a hot drink for everyone, tripped in the galley, fell, and cut his head badly. Fortunately two doctors were immediately on hand.

Joining us at this point were two charming Brazilian ladies, Doctora Eurípedes Dias da Cunía and her assistant, Marcia Leila de Castro Pereira, anthropologists at the University of Brasilia. They fitted in well, and in between their studies of the local population they lent a hand with all the shipboard chores. At our nightly conferences Eurípedes often gave us an interesting insight into the lives of those who lived along the river.

Our send-off from Pôrto Velho was in a lower key than usual. At Puerto Quijarro in 1999 we had had a Bolivian Navy band, the commandant of the local naval base and his chaplain. But Pôrto Velho was only a staging point on our long journey, and the ceremonial had quite rightly been at Guanay, our start point. Nevertheless, we were seen off by the bear-like Coronel Miguel J. C. Maltez, Chefe do Gabinete Militar, who had kindly provided a car and an armed driver during our stay. With him were the tiny, efficient-looking head of the Capitania Fluvial da Amazonia, Capitão Antonio Martins, and César Doerner of

Rodonave Navegãoes, who had so kindly provided the *plancha* and given us a splendid camp site at his sports club. We were all filmed, and I was interviewed by TV Rondônia Canal 4 and the press.

KM3 slipped her mooring at 9.30 a.m., and the *Capitão Azevedo* followed twenty minutes after. Several drums of fuel were lashed together on the lower decks – petrol for *KM3* and the Avon's outboards, and diesel for the support ship in the hold. We were running with the Madeira's own 4 m.p.h. current, but would still consume big quantities of fuel – though more would be available at the few small towns we should encounter: Humaitá, Manicoré, Novo Aripuanã, Borba, Nova Olinda do Norte and Itacoatiara.

We fuelled ourselves with local food at every opportunity. Bread, eggs, sausages, chicken, vegetables and fruit were plentifully available. We had brought with us numerous tins of the Austrian meat, powdered milk and potato, tinned fish, coffee, tea, soup, pasta, rice and soya. Vast quantities of beer, Coca-Cola, fizzy orange and a pleasant local variant called Guaraná were regularly carried aboard to be put in the fridge. We could become seriously dehydrated in the course of a day, and many 2-litre bottles of pop were imbibed without much recourse to *Ela* or *Ele*.

I must admit that we ate as well as Oxbridge crews do in the weeks before the Boat Race. Fighting cocks could not have fared better. This was mainly due to one man – Lieutenant-Colonel Ernest Durey. Ernie, our quartermaster, had a love-hate relationship with the tiny, stifling *cozinha* in which he so many times cooked, priding himself, with justice, on the quality and regularity of our meals, and yet loathing its oppressive heat. He slept nearby on a couple of mule-boxes filled with food, and so was easily able to rise at 4 a.m. – or 5 if it was an easy day ahead – to get the kettle on for morning coffee and, generally with the help of his old friend Jim Masters, prepare the breakfast and the takeaway lunch for the *KM3* and Avon crews. The reed boat's crew enjoyed porridge and a cooked dish of eggs, sausage and potato at 6.15 before they cast off from the mother ship for the day.

Poor H. M. Tomlinson on SS *Capella* fared far worse, though we shared with him a dependence on canned meat and butter:

> The dinner bell rang. Because the saloon is now hot beyond endurance, the steward has fixed a table on deck, and so, as we eat, we can see the jungle pass. That keeps some of our mind from dwelling on the dreary menu. The potatoes have begun to ferment. The meat is out of tins; sometimes it is served as fritters,

sometimes we recognize it in a hash, and sometimes, shameless, it appears without dress, a naked and shiny lump straight from its metal bed. Often the bread is sour. The butter too is out of tins. Feeding is not a joy but a duty.

Ernie always seemed to be slightly in the wars. 'Who's been playing noughts and crosses on your head?' asked James Culshaw once. Steristrips covered his scalp after a second bad fall, and he had another tumble going ashore at Itacoatiara. With a titanium hip on one side and a gammy knee on the other, he had a hard time moving about the ship, and especially getting off it. The *Capitão Azevedo* had a narrow, springy gangplank which he had to walk to reach an often muddy bank. It was also a hazard for some of the reed boat's crew when they returned in the small hours after depleting the local bars of their stocks of Antarctica lager. 'Rush it! Rush it!' I heard one crew member urging another. There was an anguished cry at Borba when James Culshaw fell with a splosh into the Madeira.

But these were rare occurrences, for the towns were far apart, and we looked forward to them after mile on mile of unrelieved jungle and the slow, hot drag of the now longer days on *KM3*. Under the blistering sun, pale British skins turned pink, bright red and then ever darkening shades of brown. The thermometer hovered in the nineties, and when we stopped the cooling breeze dropped away, leaving us dripping with sweat.

No sooner had the ship's cook, the captain's wife, Gorete, made breakfast for the *Capitão Azevedo*'s crew than Ernie would be setting to on our lunch – which might be soup, filled rolls (or, once, slices of pizza brought in a doggy bag from a local restaurant the previous evening), water melon, fruit salad, tea, cocoa or coffee. The evening meals were so varied as to be incapable of summary: sometimes Gorete prepared us something Brazilian; sometimes Michelle, Jenny Campbell (our newly arrived army nurse), Marigold (our harpist), Sam, Yoli or any permutation of these would produce a special dinner to give Ernie a rest, and for the same reason whenever we came to large town we would find a *churrascaria* and dine ashore. On high days and birthdays we would set tables and chairs on the upper deck and eat there. Fish were often caught over the side – I hooked some good surubí – but just as often a local tin boat would come up to *Capitão Azevedo* and, after some haggling, we would buy tambaqui, pacu or dorado. It would have been foolish to ignore this rich resource over which we floated daily. All in all, we ate as well as on any of the expeditions I can remember. The support-ship personnel showed a recognition – felt if unstated – that the privations of the reed-boat and Avon crews needed compensating for in the evenings.

Every now and then the support ship's tin boat would go ahead to see if there was any requirement in the villages for medical or dental attention. In that way Sam, Michelle, Jenny and Graham would be prepared and the sick villagers alerted. The tin boat could put the team ashore ahead of the rest of the fleet. We often arrived to meet the village chief smiling bravely after some extractions, his mouth full of bloody wadding. As before, this service proved a valuable way of making friends and getting information.

The constant high humidity was a problem for a group of people from Edinburgh, Taunton, Perth, Pittsburgh and similar temperate places. A shower a day was a necessity. The Victorian public-school code of character-building cold showers suddenly seemed like good sense; I had never before looked forward to and enjoyed a daily succession of them. The showers were in the loos, which, though often hotter than the rest of the ship (except its infernal hold), were clean and pleasant places. Richard once sat in the *Ele* looking out of the open wooden porthole at the dolphins looping up from the Madeira's murky depths. This was a memorable, unique experience. He mused about the other river denizens that might take advantage of the human faeces that streamed from the stern of our ship, and suddenly the term 'bottom feeder' took on new meaning.

Once, someone mischievously locked Yoli in the *Ela*. Richard went into the *Ele* next door with a view to climbing out of his porthole and along the ship's side to effect a rescue, but already she was out of her porthole and scrambling aloft. Ernie, enjoying a beer on the upper deck, was mightily surprised to be tapped on the shoulder and asked for help. Her slight, elfin figure was easily hauled inboard.

The water for the showers and loos came from the Madeira, which most of the time looked like asparagus soup with foul suds floating on the top. For our own consumption and cooking we had to collect cleaner stuff. Thrice we turned up less muddy tributaries – the Maici, the Marmelos and the Aripuanã, each with a sharply visible separation line – and filled our plastic jerricans and swam. Capitão José Pinto dived into the Marmelos from the top deck of his own ship.

These occasional swims, putting aside all thoughts of caymans or piranhas, were a joy. In the early stages Richard said he was so hot he wished he could climb into the refrigerator among all the Sukita orange bottles and Coca-Cola.

It was never possible to retire for the night comfortably cool. The atmosphere remained sticky and hot until at least midnight. We were a crowded ship too. Caroline Ralph said, 'We had eleven hammocks on the upper deck last night and less room between them than there was on HMS *Victory*.' The confinement sometimes led to tensions, as did our occasional water and power failures. One evening after supper and the evening briefing, Marigold Verity, our expedition harpist, who had entertained no fewer than four SES expeditions with her splendid folk harp, was giving a recital on the upper deck, accompanied by Marcelo on his guitar. The lights suddenly failed. Ernie, in the galley below, trying to prepare a takeaway early breakfast, was frustrated at the lack of notice people took of the power cut. Marigold, using her head-torch, played on in the darkness, and Ernie's pleas for assistance went unheard. Soon his strangled cry came: 'Why doesn't someone turn on the ******* generator?' As Marigold and Marcelo continued playing, Ernie kept time below by slamming mule-box lids and throwing saucepans about. He was given to such outbursts, but they were often synthetic and always short-lived. His good nature quickly shone through.

Our nights were punctuated by the fairly heavy river traffic. In Amazonia it is more comfortable to travel in the darkness hours, and many services are scheduled accordingly. Passenger ferries and *empurra-dores* abounded, scything the night air with their strong searchlight beams.

By day they were always an impressive sight. One powerful pusher vessel, its helmsman in a bridge lofty enough to see over the four or five barges ahead of him, with their deck cargoes of twenty or thirty lorry trailers and tankers, was only just managing to gain ground over the Amazon's strong stream. Another time, golfer Graham Catchpole said, 'Look at the length of that train of barges. Must be at least a drive and a nine iron.'

KM3 had to take special care to give these behemoths a wide berth. Fortunately the Madeira and the Amazon were broad and deep enough to take any amount of traffic. She was a difficult craft to steer, however, with her unusual configuration of three hulls tied together and the engine between two of them. Every day Jim Masters would invite a member or two from the HQ and support staff on board, and they generally made a hash of the first fifteen minutes of their hour on the helm.

Marigold was to spend a day on *KM3*. She went aboard with several pretty floral bags which filled half of one of the outriggers, and then settled herself against them rather as she might have seated herself in a punt from which to watch the Grand Challenge Cup at Henley. Skipper Pat Troy looked on with disdain. I suppose he was relieved she hadn't brought her harp. She was the only helmsperson actually to ram the support ship.

On that occasion she fell into a confusion which often overcomes inexperienced crew. In an attempt to correct an error, having pushed the tiller the wrong way, she pushed it even further the wrong way. The result was that, while *KM3* and the support ship were proceeding at a good rate on parallel courses, *KM3* suddenly slewed round and headed straight for the mother vessel. To her credit, Marigold foresaw the imminent collision, abandoned the helm, and rushed forward with a paddle to fend off. It was of no avail, and *KM3* struck the bigger ship abeam, flattening a jaguar's face and temporarily dislodging one of its teeth.

Life on *KM3* was very different to that on *Capitão Azevedo*. Nowhere on board was quite comfortable. Jim Masters, Admiral of the Fleet, sat on his mule-box at almost all times, watching the river ahead and astern and manning the radio. Marcelo, our Brazilian naval lieutenant, navigated, squatting near the massive chart book and the invaluable Silva GPS receiver. Barry Igoe kept an eye on the outboard motor's fuel tank and topped it up from time to time. The rest of the crew disposed themselves around the three hulls.

In mid-morning those crew not on duty crawled under a central awning to escape the sun's direct rays. Great quantities of water laced with Gatorade were consumed, some from a newly fashionable gadget rather like a colostomy bag, though larger. Designed to be placed in a rucksack, it has a tube attached through which the walker can drink en route. A lunch, packed by Ernie in the pre-dawn, was a pleasant break. The day's journey might be 50 to 65 miles and 9, 10, 11 or even 12 hours long – much of it in the middle of a vast river away from distant banks. Reading, sleeping, doing push-ups, sit-ups and pull-ups, and listening to portable CD-players all whiled away the time.

The only other problem was physical: there were no loos on *KM3*. 'I have a young man here who wants to do big jobs,' came Jim's voice over the radio in mock parental tones. For 'small ones' men could accommodate themselves reasonably easily over the aft end of an outrigger. For female visitors and what ex-Royal Marine Pat Troy called 'the morning George' the Avon was brought into play to convey people to the *Capitão Azevedo* or the shore, in some cases about a mile away.

Time spent on the reed boat felt like real travelling – the push of the bow waves, the flutter and snap of the flags overhead, and river water sluicing down between the hulls.

Jim Masters checked *KM3* daily to see how the reeds were standing up to the voyage, whether cords were chafed, and how the wooden fittings and masts were lasting. I could tell by his expression when he came aboard the support vessel if anything was amiss. However, at this stage our 'bale of straw' was doing pretty well. After the punishment she had taken at Ribeirão I was very impressed.

Sometimes *KM3* did not reunite with the mother ship in the evening. The crew would take cookers, food and tents and moor up independently on the bank or at a village. They liked to do this: it seemed more of an Amazon experience, and it also gave them a certain freedom of action. There was the usual jocular friction between the *KM3*/Avon workers and the HQ drones. Exaggeration takes over here: the front-line heroes regarded the support boat as never being properly supportive, and the effete softies in HQ regarded the boats' crews as noisy, beer-swilling space-fillers. It was good to separate once in a while, if only to enjoy a private moan.

On one occasion Drew Craig and James Culshaw walked upstream, put on life-jackets, and drifted in the Madeira's current back to *KM3*, dolphins surfacing all round them. There was a secluded bay nearby in which great pieces of undercut bank calved off, creating tidal waves and producing more mud to tip on to that huge submarine mountain far out in the Atlantic. Afterwards, the boats' crews were amazed to sit by São Roque's only TV and watch the German Grand Prix live.

Another village they found was Nazaré do Retiro – Nazareth for the Retired – which amused sixty-nine-year-old Pat Troy, although he probably won't be drawn from his Jersey lair.

It wasn't all joy, however. *KM3* camped on an insect-ridden football pitch in one place. Mosquitoes passed the word back to their base in the nearby swamp. The crew were in their tents by 8 p.m., awake at 2 a.m., and off, before the morning squadrons struck, at 6.

We shared the view of Robin Furneaux after his travels in the 1960s: 'Mosquitoes were the only creatures of the Amazon to live up to their evil reputation.' I can hardly write these words for insects of all sizes flying about, and more gyrating around the light above my head. Down below, near my ankles, lurks the almost silent *Anopheles maculipennis*. Each bite from the female implants thirty or forty malarial parasites into the bloodstream. In two weeks they become trillions. Other insects might bring yellow fever or dengue, about which warning notices were pasted up in villages alongside the ones about Aids. Dengue fever is on the increase, and there were 525 deaths from it in Britain in the first eight months of 2001. Most of these were the result of daytime mosquito bites in South-East Asia, although forty-seven occurred in Venezuela. In 1938 mosquitoes infected over 100,000 people in Brazil, 20,000 of whom died.

Some places were worse than others. In towns and big villages we suffered less and could dispense with our nets. The worst experience came at the confluence of the Madeira with the Amazon. The *Capitão Azevedo* agreed to meet *KM3* there, and the only spot from which she would be clearly visible was by a low, marshy island just in the stream of Amazon's darker waters. A pretty scene by daylight, it was the most grimly infested place yet. Every lamp collected a dancing troupe of insects so gregarious and malevolent that we had to eat in darkness. Afterwards there was a cheering, if bizarre, interlude. Marigold gave us another harp recital, this time swathed in a mosquito net, her music sheets lit by a head-torch, and all against a background of croaking frogs and a thumping generator.

It was a foul night for almost everyone. Richard, under his old army net, started itching just after midnight. Then came the awful realization: not only had he *been* bitten, but he was still *being* bitten. Somehow the bugs had found a chink and got in with him. The usual futile snatching at the air began. He lay on his Therm-a-Rest, an inert mass, virtually naked. *Anopheles maculipennis* must have thought it was Christmas. His only recourse then was to pull on a damp, sweaty T-shirt and trousers to reduce the available grazing ground. After two hours a light breeze got up and fitful sleep followed.

While we were on the Madeira a book came out called *Mosquito: A Natural History of Our Most Persistent and Deadly Foe*. The two authors – Andrew Spielman and Michael d'Antonio – apparently encourage their readers if not to love the mosquito then at least to admire it. They would have been hard put to it to win our sympathy.

I have always been driven by a sense of curiosity, and generally strive to find out what, in Kipling's phrase, lies 'beyond the ranges'. There are few ranges in the Amazon rainforest, but the main rivers have smaller tributaries some of which led to lakes – which intrigued me.

Near São Salvador on 29 July, Eric Niemi, our American biologist, took an afternoon reconnaissance to nearby Lago do Antônio. It looked promising, so at 9 p.m. Patricio, Bruce and Marcelo went with Eric on a night prowl. On the way upriver to the lake's entrance they picked out 126 caymans (*jacaré*) in their beam. 'I shouldn't trail your fingers in the water,' said Bruce to his neighbour. 'This isn't the Dee, you know.' 'Or when you get home you'll give your friends a high three,' said Eric.

On the small part of the lake they were able to cover in the time there were another seventy or so. It was the biggest concentration of caymans that any of them had ever seen – mostly Common Spectacled (*Caiman crocodilus*) but with, judging by their size, some Black (*Melanosuchus niger*).

We came to another lake on the following day. The map suggested that a narrow river led to a long stretch of water attached to the Madeira like an appendix – Lago Acará. A tin-boat reconnaissance by Yoli convinced skipper José that the *Capitão Azevedo* could manage it, and in the late afternoon we began the hour-long journey. At first we passed a few fisherman's dwellings, high on the banks, then through if not virginal then reasonably chaste forest. Caymans lurked in the reeds, dolphins surfaced languidly, and fish leaped in frenzy for their evening insects. As darkness fell I poured myself a glass of my favourite J&B Scotch and sat in the bows watching the bats come swooping to garner mouthfuls of the Coleoptera that the captain's powerful spotlight picked out. We entered the lake as the moon was rising, crossed it, and moored at a village. Tomorrow we would wake up to see where we were, and I would organize a wildlife count at dawn.

In the cool of the evening the medical team went to work. For an hour Richard was orderly to the dental surgeon, and he learned about elevators, luxators and extractors, with which Graham took out sixteen teeth. The patients ranged from a frightened, under-sized eleven-year-old to the number two of the village, Adonais Vaz, who, at seventy-two, was having his last five rotten teeth removed. We left him with Popeye's sunken cheeks, trying unsuccessfully not to smile. Ernie produced another excellent curry for supper.

13

Between the Banks

There is no land. One must travel by boat from one settlement to another. The
settlements are but islands, narrow footholds, widely sundered by vast gulfs of
jungle.

H. M. Tomlinson, *The Sea and the Jungle*, 1912

SO WE CARRIED on down the seemingly interminable Madeira, watching
the white-rumped swallows, washing up greasy plates in the galley,
manning the radio, writing our diaries, and taking our weekly Lariam or
gut-wrenching doxycycline anti-malarials. We looked out keenly for villages or the very occasional town to relieve the tedium of the unbroken
secondary rainforest on both sides of the river, often only a distant
smudge of grey-green atop a high bank strewn with tree trunks left
behind after the last annual flood.

In the upper Madeira the few bank-side houses were little more than
shacks. The villages – São Carlos, Santa Catarina, Calama, São Salvador,
Vencedor – were all spread along the river line with very little depth
inland. They enjoyed the tranquillity of having no road traffic, but
suffered the isolation of a place incapable of attracting much river trade.
The houses, which were on stilts, were interspersed with fruit trees of
many varieties – lemon, grapefruit, mango and others, *jambo*, *açai*,
cucurum, for which we could find no English name. There would be a
primitive schoolroom, with desks or benches, a chalkboard and little else;
a church – generally Catholic, sometimes evangelical, often Assembleia
de Deus – a football pitch; but no shops in the smaller villages.

If we stayed in a village we always played it at football – sometimes five-
a-side, sometimes eleven – with the *Capitão Azevedo* crew and some village
lads press-ganged into playing against their fellows. Previous expedition
experience – in Zaire, Panama and Kenya – had taught us that we have
better public relations with the local communities if we lose narrowly. On

most occasions in Bolivia and Brazil we overdid it. São Salvador, a tiny village, beat us 8–1. In fact we didn't have a victory in Brazil until hanging on to win 5–3 against Vencedor (a sweet triumph, since Vencedor means Conqueror).

The medical team and our dental surgeon, Graham Catchpole, went to work wherever possible. These communities have to take their sick a long way, and they neglect their teeth entirely. Graham extracted rotten and painful ones in schoolrooms, on the prow and bridge of boats, in a general store and on a log raft, as well as in a toilet. 'You can take teeth out anywhere,' he said later. His extraction count was now in the high eight hundreds.

Late one night Sam Allen examined Anilton Ramos, a local man who had been bitten on the leg by a potentially lethal Arafura File snake the previous morning. In his distant locality nothing had been done about it at first, but then the venom kicked in. Twelve hours later he was brought into São Carlos in great pain and with his leg grossly swollen. Sam treated him symptomatically, and probably saved his life.

Michelle and Sam usually had less dramatic cases, but often patients presented with conditions that could not be dealt with in a dusty school-room with limited instruments and medicine. For example, in Santa Catarina we found Ronalda, a six-year-old girl with a harelip and a severely cleft palate. Her mother told us how her little sister's hand had been damaged by a scorpion bite, perhaps permanently, and as if this weren't enough disaster for one family a brother had life-threatening per-nicious anaemia. All our sympathies were engaged by this little girl with a radiant smile, appealing eyes but gross disfigurement. Jim Masters was perhaps most affected of all. While still on the river he determined to do something about it, and back in the UK he began raising funds to pay for the two or three operations that Ronalda needed. Jim found out about an organization called Smile Train, which could arrange for cor-rective surgery in Brazil. Their hospital is at Campinas, near São Paulo, so the problem was to arrange for Ronalda and her mother to travel there and stay for the necessary time. Enough money was raised to cover the costs and a place offered at the hospital.

In Calama there were chest infections, gastric problems and girls with pregnancy complications. In Santa Catarina, Sam and Michelle de-wormed an entire school. In São Salvador, Sam – a specialist in tropical medicine – saw his first cases of South American trypanosomiasis (Chagas' disease), Madura foot and Weil's disease.

Geraldo Reinaldo de Lima, a Manaus schoolteacher and evangelical pastor sent by the Presbyterian Church, acted as the liaison officer and a valuable interpreter on most of these medical occasions. Indispensable in negotiations with the support-ship crew, he was with us from Pôrto Velho to Belém, and astonished us all by cracking open Brazil nuts with his teeth. (I can't even open them tidily with a nutcracker.)

The language problem was considerable, and not only for the medics. Portuguese is not Spanish, and it is certainly not English. Spoken fast, idiomatic Brazilian Portuguese is incomprehensible to outsiders. Written Portuguese is fairly easy to read for those with a classical education or some ability in Spanish, but to speak this sing-song tongue is of a high order of difficulty – something on a par with tackling Mandarin. So much depends on stress and intonation. I could only manage a few phrases, including 'A beer, please' and 'Thank you'. Richard, who has some facility with languages at a basic level and speaks some elementary Spanish, could only add, 'Very good', 'Ice cream, please' and 'Where is the Post Office?' – though he seemed to get more fluent after a glass or two of the local Antarctica lager.

The struggle with the language began early. At Abunã, four of us at a table, trying to get hot water, summoned a waitress – a typical *jolie-laide* fourteen-year-old, in short skirt and skimpy, lace-backed top. We tried *caldo, caliente* and *calor*, made little bubbling noises, pointed up at the sun, and whistled like kettles. But the girl stood mute and uncomprehending. It turned out that the word for hot sounded like 'caincher', so we were way off the mark.

At Juruti we moored opposite a board on which the local evangelical church advertised itself. Richard picked away at 'LOUVAI AO SENHOR PELOS SEUS ATOS PODEROSOS COM SOM DE TROMBETAS – SALMO 150 v.2.' With help from Marcelo, our Brazilian naval officer, he eventually teased it out as 'Praise the Lord for His mighty acts with the sound of trumpets.' What more mighty act, some of us thought, could the Lord have wrought than the Amazon on which we then floated?

I constantly encouraged the team to master some simple Portuguese. One way of learning was to translate the names of ferry boats like our own, which scurried up and down the river like the cockroaches which lived aboard them. They had names that were mostly religious in character – *São Sebastião, Santa Ana, Concepcão, Salmista*. We reckoned that *Bom Jesus, Cristo Vem, Anjo Gabriel* and *Com Deus Eu Vou* were anglicizable as *Good Jesus, Christ is Coming, Angel Gabriel* and *With God I Go*. *Cometa Halley* and *Elizabeth II* were refreshingly different.

Of course, Brazilians speaking English had our difficulty in reverse. One man at Santarém's nearby beach resort of Alter do Chão, trying to convince us that the Tupi Indians before the colonial period had had no prostitution, said, 'Before the Portugueses comes there is no businesses with the humans fleshes.'

It was not just Portuguese that gave us problems. Jon Paul Nevin, at nineteen our youngest member, was a tough, wiry, resourceful little soldier with an impenetrable Scots accent. And he seemed to have no comprehension that his thick Glasgow patois is not easily understood outside Scotland. 'He's frae Pairth, same as me,' explained Jenny Campbell, 'but they moved tae Glasgae.' He would use arcane British Army terms in talking to Marcelo, and then look sadly at the Brazilian lieutenant as if he were stupid or not listening when he failed to understand. Pittsburgher Eric Niemi said of Jon Paul, 'I can get Portuguese better.'

The classic differences between English and American were no problem, but once I said, 'We're approaching Humaitá. I wonder if we can bunker here?' Bill Holmes: 'What's all this about bunking her?' I told him it only meant refuelling ships.

Humaitá was the first place of any consequence that we came to after Pôrto Velho. Named after the site of the Brazilian naval victory over the Paraguayans in the Triple Alliance War of 1865–70, it had grown bigger than its Paraguayan counterpart, where we stopped for a while during the 1999 expedition. In 1952 Peter Grieve described it as 'A single ghostly row of houses standing pallid in the moonlight on the top of a low cliff'. At first we thought it might still consist just of the port offices, a covered market, the municipal library and a substantial white church – all visible from the river – plus a fine pink and white merchant's residence dated 1908; but it now extends far inland and is linked to Pôrto Velho by a metalled road.

We had a good buffet supper at a *churrascaria* there, but at the next big town – Manicoré – we experienced a unique problem: though it was a quite big town, it seemed to have no functioning restaurants. Some of us eventually found good fare at an open-air grill, where Richard discovered that tasty little fish the pacu. There was no Internet café either, but a very helpful Spanish priest, Fr José Antonio, lent us the use of his equipment. Founded in 1798, Manicoré was a scruffy place and in no way geared for tourism.

That evening I managed to find a restaurant and Geoff Hoskins, Marcelo, Geraldo, Yoli and Patricio joined me for a supper of roast meats, chicken, fish and salad in a quieter corner of the plaza. Conversation turned to the situation in Bolivia, where our patron, President Hugo Banzer Suárez, had resigned owing to his illness with cancer. What would happen about the coca farmers' rebellion? How would our friends in Guanay fare under a new regime? The new president, Jorge Quiroga – thirty-seven and married to an American – was said to be a mountaineer, eager to climb Everest. 'That bodes well for expeditions,' commented Geoff. 'If the President doesn't fall off,' said Yoli, who was now tucking into her favourite ice cream. Perhaps it did but I wondered what our Austrian opposition would be up to.

Yoli and Patricio were talking in Spanish, and I heard the name 'Barbie'. My ears pricked up. 'Yes,' said Patricio, 'I often saw Klaus Barbie taking his coffee in the Confitería La Paz, but I didn't realize who he was – he seemed an inoffensive old man.' I was to learn more of this friend of Hans Ertl who drank little and – for good observation! – always sat with his back to the wall facing the door. He was described as slightly built, and usually sported a Tyrolean hat. Before his extradition by the French in 1983, the 'Butcher of Lyons' – known locally as Señor Altmann – had been a familiar figure in La Paz and, because of his influential connections, was both feared and respected. It emerged that he was much involved in the trade in quinine, a product for which the Great Paititi region was famous. 'Could this be a link between Ertl, Barbie, and Paititi?' I asked Yoli. 'It's possible' she said, 'but I guess we'll only discover that in Bolivia.'

Because Rondônia and this part of Amazonas have few foreign visitors, we were faced with another, more serious, hindrance – the inability to change money. This was experienced first of all at Guajará-Mirim, and the problem persisted until we reached Santarém. At Itacoatiara we had to resort to sending an urgent request to the British Embassy in Brasilia, where the staff had a whip-round to enable the naval attaché, Captain Stephen Timms, to bring $4,000 worth of reals out to us at Parintins. Despite arrangements made beforehand and assurances given in the UK and the USA, no traveller's cheques were accepted until Santarém (and those not by a bank), and even the ubiquitously coveted American dollar bills were spurned. I mentioned to several bank managers, mayors and heads of chambers of commerce that it was ironic that they were bidding for tourists – and sometimes had much to offer – but at the same time were perpetuating a severe inconvenience for them. Only the previous November I had been told by the staff at the very grand Brazilian stand at the World Travel Market that money-changing along the Amazon was '*não problema*'. How wrong they were.

Even those few banks that would change dollar notes made the process so long drawn out and Byzantine in its complexity that tourists would wilt. Some of us drew numbered tickets and stood in line for up to two hours only to find that it had been the wrong queue, or that there was a punitive commission charge – $20 on any transaction, however small.

Graham Catchpole had a money order for $200 drawn on his HSBC branch in Taunton, but the HSBC branch in Pôrto Velho wouldn't recognize it. 'I got money with my Mastercard more easily in Mongolia than in Brazil,' said Eric Niemi – 'and that wasn't just in Ulan Bator, but in Mörön in Mongolia's Wild West.'

Automated teller machines spat cards back at us. Inside banks we waited three, sometimes four, hours to complete an exchange. Everyone had his own dire tale of frustration or defeat. We were not angry that there were no ATMs, but that they were there and didn't work; not that there were no banks or that they were shut, but that they were open and unwilling to part with any money.

Richard said, 'Only a few miles from Pôrto Velho eighty years ago Colonel Fawcett was being hacked to death by club-wielding Indians, and now we're getting uptight because the holes in the wall don't work.' 'True,' I replied, 'but why do they have a programme for promoting tourism in the Amazonas if there's no efficient infrastructure?'

'John, which do you think is the most difficult, bureaucracy-bound country to work in – Bolivia or Brazil?' Yoli asked. 'At the moment it's Brazil.' 'In Bolivia you expect things not to work,' Richard said. 'But it's a surprise when a flourishing, potentially First World country, once touted as the next Great Power, can't cash money quickly for tourists.' 'It's only true in the deep interior – Rondônia, Acre, Amazonas,' Yoli said. 'On the coastal strip and in the central highlands things will be *perfecto*.' 'Yes, but we're not going there,' I added. 'Let's hope things are better in Borba.'

Things were better in Borba. It was the neatest, cleanest, most imposing town on the Madeira. But its banks still offered no money. We had stopped briefly at Novo Aripuanã, where the clean Rio Aripuanã joins the sudsy Madeira, but had not expected banks. It had been down the Rio Aripuanã that former US President Theodore Roosevelt had come in 1904 with his Brazilian host, Coronel Cândido Mariano da Silva Rondon – who renamed the Rio de Dúvida (River of Doubt), an Aripuanã feeder, the Rio Roosevelt in his honour. Borba had a beautiful, multi-towered church in white and Cambridge blue, with a not so beautiful but staggeringly larger-than-life wooden statue of Santo Antônio gazing upriver. And when we were there the third annual meeting of municipal managers of towns on the Madeira was being held and delegates were spilling out of an air-conditioned hall all wearing identical white T-shirts with a map of the river on their chests. It looked a bustling place.

It had come a long way since João de Sampaio had set up a Jesuit mission there in 1728. Only 100 miles from the Madeira's confluence with the Amazon, Borba – once Araretama, or City of Light, our Brazilian anthropologist, Eurípedes, told us – is the oldest settlement on the Madeira. It is modern enough now. Its bars and nightclubs entertained the younger set, while Jim Masters, having sailed 70 miles in what proved to be the longest day of the whole journey at twelve and three-quarter hours, enjoyed a couple of beers on the upper foredeck of *Capitão Azevedo* with Richard. 'We got fried,' he said, 'and basted on both sides.'

'We had a lot of dolphins following us,' he went on. Nothing soothed this frazzled mariner more than the sighting of dolphins. They abound in the Amazon and its tributaries and, having lungs and a blowhole in the top of their head, they surface frequently and gracefully. We found them in good numbers, particularly wherever two arms of the river met. Mario Alberto Cozzuol, the Argentinian palaeontologist who had put Richard up for a few days in Pôrto Velho, told us that there were two types of freshwater dolphin in Amazonia: the pink (*boto*, or *Inia geoffrensis*) and the grey (*tucuxi*, or *Sotalia fluviatilis*). They were easily differentiated. The pink has a pronounced beak and a seemingly broken back and is convincingly pink, while the grey looks facially more like the familiar marine dolphins, though much smaller, and has a prominent dorsal fin. However often we saw some, they always aroused interest – and the pink always excited more delight than the grey. (The psychology of colours is interesting.) Neither sort came very close to our boats: there were no hand feedings or strokings of heads.

There is a kind of dolphin (*Inia boliviensis*) above the Madeira–Mamoré rapids, but none are found today within the chain of cataracts, though Mario has discovered a supposed ancestor of both types of dolphin 120 feet below ground there, in the diggings left by gold prospectors. There have certainly been freshwater dolphins in the Amazon for a very long time, he explained. The pink dolphin is related to ones found in the Yangtse and the Ganges, so its ancestors must have become used to fresh water before the split-up of Gondwanaland separated South America from Africa–Europe–Asia–Australia–Antarctica. The grey is not solely a freshwater fanatic but is fairly well habituated to coastal salt.

The freshwater dolphins are less sociable, both with humans and among themselves, than the marine variety. The two Amazonian species live harmoniously together, however: the pink, almost blind, detect and stun fish and crabs along the bottom by sonic means. The grey hunt the faster fish along the surface. Fortunately the people of the river rarely kill them. The only time we became angry with them was when we tried to photograph them: their surfacings were usually swifter than our camera fingers, and I used six films before managing to catch a pink one leaping upward in the early-morning light. It really was a huge creature – far larger than its grey cousin.

Like all the Avons and the Zaire (now the Congo again) many of the world's rivers are named simply after the local word for river. The indigenous people along its banks knew the Madeira as Caiari – the Wooden River – because of all the timber that washes down its Bolivian and Brazilian feeders. Francisco de Orellana, the first European to navigate his way down the Amazon, in 1542, was perhaps too beset by problems of survival to come up with anything more original, and called it the Rio Grande as he passed its broad mouth. The Portuguese, when they found it, sensibly adopted the local name and called it the Madeira, 'Wooded', as they had also called the Atlantic island they had discovered in 1419. It was already called the Madeira when the first European to sail up the Amazon, Pedro de Teixeira, passed it in 1637.

Ten years later two intrepid Portuguese were sent by King João IV to look for precious metals and extend the Portuguese empire – Portugal having just become independent again after eighty years under Spanish rule. Antonio Raposo Tavares, a *bandeirante* from São Paulo, and (interestingly, in view of the name of our support ship) Antonio Pereira de Azevedo set off on an amazing journey which took them to Corumbá, on the Paraguay river in Brazil, up into the Andes to Potosí, and down the Bolivian Rio Grande and the Madeira to Belém do Pará. It took them three years, and they were the first outsiders to encounter the rapids on the Mamoré–Madeira.

The Jesuits reached the lower stretches of the Madeira in 1669, and thereafter settled many missions on its banks to spread the gospel – and to thwart the Protestant Dutch, who attempted a settlement in 1687. But the power of the slave-owners in Brazil was always too great, and the Jesuits were never able to establish there enclosed communities of Indians such as those – the Reducciónes – whose impressive stone ruins today grace eastern Bolivia, southern Paraguay and the Misiones province of Argentina.

Francisco de Melo Pacheta is described as 'a legitimate *bandeirante*'. He entered the Madeira in 1723, met the missionary João de Sampaio, who had now lived there ten years and was to survive at least another five, and reached the rapids at Santo Antônio on 22 June. His account is the first full one we have of how the cataracts were passed. He forced a way up the Santo Antônio falls and the next set, known to him as Iaguerites. Thereafter, for several days, his men had to push and pull their *galeotas* with ropes round the bigger rapids and falls, 'not having an excess of people for this great work and with such persecution by the bites of piums, each bite drawing blood'. It took them forty-five days to travel the 250 miles to the confluence of the Mamoré and the Guaporé.

More Portuguese expeditions up the Madeira followed: by Luis Fagundes Machado in 1749, to reach the mines of Mato Grosso; by Francisco José de Lacerda e Almeida in 1781, to mark the limits of Portuguese dominion after the Treaty of Ildefonso with Spain in 1777; and the scientific expedition of Alexandre Rodriguez Ferreira in 1788. All these grappled with the cataracts with reasonable success.

Trade up and down the Madeira did not reach significant proportions until the value of Brazilian and Bolivian wild rubber became apparent in the mid and late nineteenth century. The river's easy navigability by ocean-going vessels all the way up to the Santo Antônio falls – some 1,600 miles from the Atlantic – made it a vital outlet for rubber: vital as much for the *seringueiro* who marked out his trees on its banks and those of its tributaries as for the *patrão* who ran him and for the merchants in Manaus and Belém who handled the commodity on its way to the markets of the northern world.

In fact the Madeira runs into the Amazon downstream of Manaus's site on the Negro, so it was natural that another entrepôt should spring up nearer the confluence. This was Itacoatiara.

An older Portuguese settlement called Serpa, near some bas-relief inscriptions on the left bank of the Amazon, had in 1874 been elevated to the rank of a city and given the name Itacoatiara – 'Painted Stones'. (I had a lot of problems with this place-name. I practised it most of the way down the Madeira, and had it reasonably well by the time we got there.) Although an Amazon river port, Itacoatiara was the logical end of the Madeira section of our journey.

'There are only two places between Pôrto Velho and Belém that have Internet,' observed Sam Allen subsequently: 'Santarém and Itacoatiara.' Now a city of 70,000 souls, with, on its main-street dual carriageway, the longest avenue of trees that I have ever trudged along, Itacoatiara also had six banks, none of which was prepared to give us any money. It does not appear in any of the four guidebooks we used, but is now bidding for visitors, and the local tourist-authority people gave us a good look round their city and its hinterland. (Only one road leads out of it – to Manaus.) We saw examples of the spectacular royal water lily (*Victoria amazonica*), whose flowers trap beetles and release them coated in pollen to inseminate others. We saw wild rubber trees scored with the many parallel cuts made by past *seringueiros*. We saw everything from the pottery in an ancient Arawak Indian settlement site to the vast modern 'Hermasa' soya-bean storage plant, to which barges bring the produce of farmers from as far away as Pôrto Velho to be collected in shiploads of 5,000 tons at a time by ocean-going bulk carriers. Itacoatiara is coming along nicely.

It had been here that H. M. Tomlinson – stretching his legs with the ship's doctor after a long confinement on the *Capella* – had taken his 'first walk in equatorial woods'. His first impression of the Amazon from the high ground on which the Panorama restaurant now stands was of 'an immensity of water, a plain of burnished silver'. This immensity now awaited us.

14

Developments on the Amazon

> The fact of the Amazons being a limited stream, having its origin in narrow
> rivulets, its beginning and its ending, has never entered the heads of most of
> the people who have passed their whole lives on its banks.
>
> Henry Walter Bates, *The Naturalist on the River Amazons*, 1863

THERE IS SOMETHING surreal about the Amazon. As we were carried
along on it we knew it was a river, yet, from as early as the first Iberians
to encounter it, writers repeatedly call it a sea. It is undeniably a river: it
rises somewhere, is fed by tributaries, and flows between banks, wherever they are. But its very vastness baffles. For the first time in my experience it was impossible, without some reference to charts, to have a sense
of where one was.

It offers a paradise to statisticians. Sooner or later we are bound to trot
out the familiar facts and figures – not quite the world's longest river (Old
Father Nile wins by 138 miles), but overwhelmingly the greatest in terms
of its outflow: one-fifth of the world's fresh water is continuously
pouring out of it into the Atlantic. Two of its tributaries, little known
outside Brazil, each bring into the Amazon more water than the world's
next claimant to the outflow crown, the Congo. Richard and I once
stood at Banana and marvelled at the massive Zaire (as it then was), which
we had run down with an earlier scientific expedition in 1975; we little
knew then that the Madeira and the Negro were pushing it into fourth
place. It takes the Thames a year to disgorge one day's worth of Amazon.

I say that we were carried along on the Amazon, not that we were
carried down it. In the course of a mile it drops only a quarter of an inch
– hardly enough slope to empty a bath. The Congo starts as the Lualaba,
but the Amazon has half a dozen names in its early days in Peru, and is
the Solimões until near the point where we joined it, at Itacoatiara.

Its catchment area is 2½ million square miles – almost the size of

Australia – and it draws water from eight other countries besides Brazil. Almost all of it is less than 650 feet above sea level, and in the wet season it becomes an inland ocean. The seasonal variation itself of course varies: 12 feet at Belém, rising to 35 feet at Óbidos. Our Madeira could lift 40 feet, and its parallel neighbour, the Purus, a monumental 50 to 60 feet. Even at Iquitos in Peru the seasonal difference is 20 feet. Where else can vegetarian fish graze off leaves in the high rainforest canopy during the annual flood?

Before statistic fatigue sets in, may we just say that wedged like a lollipop in the mouth of the Amazon there is an island, Marajó, which is itself the size of Switzerland or Denmark and is composed of aeons of river sediment now over a mile deep? And as I settled on my sleeping-bag on the deck of my office in the vessel's tiny shop I consoled myself with the thought that there is an Amazonian fish, the pirarucú, which can be twice my size.

In Itacoatiara we had managed somehow to change $1,000 and had photographed some of the fine plasterwork on the houses of nineteenth-century rubber entrepreneurs. Marigold, Patricio, Graham and Peter had taken a day trip by bus to nearby Manaus and had seen the amazing opera house, with its 3 tiers, 700 stalls and circle seats, and 90 five-seater boxes. Everything in its construction – marble, ceramic tiles, statues, chandeliers, crystal – had come from Europe, except the wood, which came from the Brazilian province of Bahía. But even then the mahogany had been sent to Europe to be worked. Marigold was pleased to note that Patrick Shelley, founder of Dorset Opera, for which she sings, was booked to conduct Verdi's *Macbeth* there in November. Completed in 1896, the opera house evidently flourishes still.

After two days it was time for us to leave Itacoatiara and head east. As *KM3* was about to cast off from *Capitão Azevedo*, I made a siren call on the dreaded loudhailer and noticed Richard wincing.

'What's the matter?' I asked.

'It's just that I remember being in air raids in Sheffield in 1940.'

Maybe I'll just do a 'whoop, whoop' next time.

'All aboard?' I shouted.

Yoli looked anxiously up and down the lower deck. 'Where's Geraldo?'

'He's out shopping,' said Paul. 'He had to pick up some bread rolls.'

'He's late,' I roared, in assumed rage. 'Yet again! Remind me, Paul, I must buy a tapir-hide whip at the next town.'

Eventually *Capitão Azevedo* cast off and edged out into the Amazon's fast stream.

We were soon aware of a new problem. A box-like silhouette on the eastern horizon grew larger as it came slowly upriver. It was the *Yardimci*, a giant container ship registered in Istanbul – our first reminder that the Amazon is navigable by ocean-going vessels for 2,300 miles. Smaller craft can ply as far as the Pongo de Maseriche rapids in the Peruvian foothills, 2,600 miles from the Atlantic.

After a long day's 50-mile slog, the support ship came to a settlement on the right bank. High on the 'What was the name of that place, Richard?' list must come Urucurituba – a trim, tidy township: no roads, no cars, just a long wooden walkway overhanging the river along its well-tended grass foreshore.

Graham, Michelle and Jenny soon got to work in the clinic, and it was not long before *KM3* came roaring up. A strange thing then happened. Instead of the reed boat manoeuvring neatly in alongside *Capitão Azevedo*, skipper Pat Troy swung sharply into the shore 100 yards upstream and rammed a sandy bank. Was this to be read as some sort of statement? Were the crew unhappy with the day's level of support? Not enough jam in the lunchtime sandwiches? No, it was a miscalculation of the strength of the current, which had not carried Pat downriver as far as he thought it would.

Some of the crew leaped ashore to find a telephone. The Brazilians have English-speaking international operators on a certain number, and most of us found them a very efficient way of keeping in touch with wives and girlfriends. But Jon Paul Nevin soon returned disconsolately to the jetty: he had given his instructions in thickest Scots, and the young *operadora* could make no sense of it. All along the river he kept trying to phone home, and four times out of five he failed.

'Why don't you put on an English accent?' James Culshaw asked him. 'I cannae.'

'I'll phone for you, if you like.'

But he was too proud to have a Sassenach do it for him.

In the evening, Marigold and Marcelo gave a harp-and-guitar recital in the town bandstand by the church. It was a magical, heartening occasion. Crowds of schoolchildren stood about with their mothers, some of the crew sat on stone benches, and all were bombed by moths and night beetles.

The next day was the hundredth for those of us who had been on the expedition from the start. Graham had now taken out 1,017 teeth, so he was averaging 10.17 per day. Would his right wrist stand up to it all? Most of us were beginning to look a bit war-scarred and travel-stained. Patricio Crooker's lengthening black beard gave him a piratical look, and Pat Troy's legs were sunburnt to a walnut colour and knotted like the legs of a Jacobean dining-table.

It was also the seventy-first birthday of our field treasurer, Geoffrey Hoskins, and cards and presents showered on this popular member of our team. His hair, which he had determined not to have cut during the four months he would be away in South America, was now a profusion of sandy curls. A slightly raffish old charmer, he must have set the dovecotes a-fluttering in Happy Valley when he was a subaltern in the King's African Rifles. So slim is he still that it was impossible to tell whether he was in his hammock or not. Now he kept us all amused with his sibilant, infectious laugh. He was often with the younger set, flirted outrageously, and enjoyed visiting nightspots ashore, when his prowess on the dance floor was the subject of much envy by the older members of the team.

Blustery weather was coming in from the distant sea as our fleet moored up by a lone farmhouse. While his wife was away in Parintins, Senhor Nezinho's only company was his cattle, sheep, pigs and dogs. He had dense forest round his little farmstead, no neighbours, no light at night, nothing visible across the enormous river. His only distraction: passing barges and cargo ships.

One of our wildlife parties had combed the fetid swamps in the surrounding jungle, and I questioned Nezinho about anacondas, with Geraldo interpreting.

'Yes, I saw one once,' he said. 'It was 2 metres thick.'

'I must tell you one thing,' Geraldo interposed: 'the country people here all lie.'

'So do they in England,' I said.

Wherever we went I had asked about snakes. Celso, the chief at faraway Quilapituni, had warned us of their ubiquity at 'Paititi', and Ertl's book had been full of serpent stories. I was disappointed not to see more, though we did have our encounters. Juan Blanco had killed a large, multicoloured one with the butt of his rifle on the Mapiri trail. Surveyor John Gorski had dispatched a highly venomous coral snake with his machete at the Rio Tulani, and quite a few snakes of other kinds had found their way into our stewpot there. And I had come upon a bush-master killed by one of the Indians on my way down.

When the expedition had become waterborne at Guanay there was a chance of seeing anaconda. I have to confess that this prospect excited me considerably. I have always been an ophiophilist, and was as keen to find a big anaconda as Richard was to discover an old steam locomotive. There was to be some gratification for me later.

The morning reconnaissance behind Nezinho's farm revealed no anaconda but was rewarded with a rich bird haul. There are 1,708 entries in the checklist of Brazilian birds in the *Birder's Diary* for March 2001 – parrots, parakeets, macaws galore, but also tanagers (23 different varieties), tinamous (20), spinetails (33), and outlandish birds that most non-twitchers have never heard of – chacalacas, guans, yellowlegs, topazes, noddies, jaegers, anis, potoos, sabrewings, jacobins, miners, violet-ears, woodnymphs, sapphires, goldenthroats, brilliants, starthroats, visorbearers, trogons, motmots, jacamars, nunlets, piculets and that's not even taken us halfway through the list. Caroline Ralph, our ornithologist, had a hard time identifying what we saw, but a few minutes in the hinterland behind Nezinho's shack produced a toco toucan, a channel-billed toucan, a laughing falcon and four hoatzin, as well as treesful of red and green macaws.

Drew Craig, now navigating on *Capitão Azevedo*, had promised us another 50-mile day, so it was with some surprise that at noon we saw buildings and television masts on the horizon. Could this be Parintins already? By early afternoon we were tied up behind the city in a creek crowded with similar ferry boats and loud with the noise of saws and sledgehammers. Drew returned to his calculations with a scowl.

At an evening dinner in Parintins, in the Restaurant Aos Amigos in the Avenida Nações Unidas, we met the new British naval attaché in Brasilia, Captain Stephen Timms, who was to join us as a *KM3* crew member for the passage to Santarém. It must have made a change from trying to sell Type-42 destroyers to the Brazilians.

Parintins is well known – at least in Brazil – for mounting an annual festival second only to Rio's. The Boi-Bumbá happens every late June, and runs for three days. It is not only a celebration of the city's Indian heritage, but also a competition between two factions. Just as almost everyone in Sheffield supports either the Wednesday or United football team, so in Parintins the citizens are devotees of either the black bull with the blue star blaze or the white bull with the red heart blaze – the *Boi-Caprichoso* or the *Boi-Garantido*. Founded by Lindolfo Monteverde in 1913, the two competing teams spend months preparing giant papier-mâché figures on floats, gaudy larger-than-life tableaux, and dazzlingly audacious costumes. It costs $4 million each time.

The white bull was acclaimed the winner in June 2001, and the *Kota Mama* crews were shown round its series of vast aircraft hangars in the city suburbs, chock-full with a phantasmagoria of Amazon goddesses, evil spirits, Virgin Marys, pink dolphins leaping, *tigres* prowling, red and green macaws with wings that flap, and even a giant Manaus opera house. The floats and tableaux in the hangars of the black bull – the loser that year – looked appropriately forlorn and down-at-heel.

Forty thousand people come in by boat or plane to take part in the festival (Parintins is unapproachable by road), and the majority sleep in hammocks on board their hired boats. In 1988 the city built a vast *bumbódromo* to house the six-hour-long spectacle, whose theme is the victory of a mixed-race slave and his attractive wife, Catirina, over a rapacious landowner whose prize bull the slave had killed so that his pregnant wife could enjoy its cooked tongue.

'"Grouse shooting begins," it says in my diary.'

'Yes, it's the Glorious Twelfth,' I said to Richard, who was making up his log at a table on the upper deck. 'Will you give one of your talks after the briefing?'

Richard, whom I regarded as the ship's historian, from time to time gave us a few minutes on some relevant theme. Two nights before, his subject had been 'Why half of South America speaks Spanish and the other half Portuguese' – all about the 1494 Treaty of Tordesillas, when the two Iberian nations had divided the western oceans along a line of longitude which was to give Pedro Álvares Cabral's subsequent discovery of Brazil to Portugal and all the remainder west of the line to Spain, and the Treaty of Ildefonso of 1777, which tried to draw up some internal frontiers when both powers had spread inland and met.

After the briefing on 12 August he talked about the first Europeans on the Amazon. A Spanish captain, Vicente Yáñez Pinzón – one of the three Pinzón brothers who had sailed with Columbus's first fleet in 1492 – had led his own voyage of discovery seven years later and had struck further south than Columbus. Still over 100 miles off the land, he noticed that the sea had become a murky brown. Letting down barrels, he found that he was in fresh water. He was in the mouth of the Amazon, and he called it Santa Maria de la Mar Dulce (St Mary of the Freshwater Sea). That was in January 1500.

The first European to trace the actual course of the river was Francisco de Orellana, and he did it from west to east. A Spanish expedition coming over the Andes from Quito in Ecuador in 1541, led by Gonzalo Pizarro and in search of gold and cinnamon, with a vast army of pressed Indians carrying its gear, had reached the junction of the Coca and Napo rivers when it ran out of food. Orellana, Pizarro's second in command, under-took to go downstream to forage. But he found he could not beat back against the current, and he and his fifty-seven men were forced to voyage all 1,875 miles to the Atlantic. They suffered tremendous hunger, and at one point resorted to stewing their own shoes and leather belts. When their brigantine broke up under them they built another. Constant attacks were made on them by Indians, and at the confluence of the Trombetas and the Amazon they were attacked by a force including light-skinned women archers with long tresses. Orellana remembered reading about the female Scythian warriors of old, and, according to his chronicler, the friar Gaspar de Carvajal, he called them Amazons. It took him eight months to reach open sea, and somehow he then clawed his way back to the Caribbean with rigging made from grasses and cloth blankets for sails. He returned to the river of the Amazons in 1546, and died there.

Our privations were nugatory by comparison. At this point on the river sudden storms often drenched us. Purple clouds would build up, and rain would cascade down in sheets. Katabatic winds would blow the rain fiercely one way and then moments later the other. On the support boat we rushed to roll down the bright-blue plastic sheeting on each deck, but the downpour often caught us unprepared and left our kit sodden. Jim reported that *KM3*'s starboard outrigger was soaking up water and sinking lower. The crew were having to bail.

We left Amazonas and entered Pará province, where we tied up along-side a busy river-front road in the centre of a town called Juruti. Hills had been rare so far, and any that there were from now on had towns built on them clear of the seasonal flood levels. Here a road led steeply inland up the hill to a church. The last long inclined approach I remem-bered was at Novo Aripuanã on the Madeira, where an impressive flight of steps from a floating quay led up to the town, reminiscent of the ones at Odessa down which a pram came famously bouncing in the film *Battleship Potemkin*. At Juruti we made many ascents of this hill to visit the Internet café, buy food, and get stamps at the *correio*.

Ironically, just as the reed boat was beginning to show signs of wear the weather worsened. The Amazon was whipped by an easterly gale into 5-foot waves. Transferring crews in the Avon became difficult. Jon Paul Nevin fell in the river – without his life-jacket, to my annoyance – but we pulled him out. *KM3* began to have problems. The outboard engine – now crucial, as we were sailing into what seemed to be a permanent head wind – was beginning to sink below the waterline. The transom on which it was hung had somehow to be fixed into the tightly bound reeds of the central hull. After weeks of hard use, the socket in the side of the hull had become waterlogged and was widening, and the transom was beginning to fall out.

Richard said that this reminded him of his injured right arm, which, twenty-five years previously, had been struck by a rock in a volcanic eruption. The three bones constituting the elbow had been shattered, and a titanium prosthesis was later inserted into two of them. After some months of use, one spike of the prosthesis, fixed in the shaft of his humerus, began to gouge its way out of the bone from the inside, and the whole prosthesis had to be removed. He could, in fact, manage well enough without it; but *KM3* was different: it could not proceed under the present weather conditions with no motive power. We would have to work on this at Óbidos, 47 miles away. Meanwhile we crept along the banks of the river, where the strain on the engine was less and the waves were not quite so forbidding.

There came a time, however, when we had to brave the open water. We were hugging the southern bank, but Óbidos, where we wanted to shelter and carry out some repair work, was on the northern bank. The expedition was at a very significant point on the Amazon's course. Here the river – all of it – is confined to a single mile-wide channel. A thousand miles upstream of Óbidos it is seven times as wide. A little way downstream, at Santarém, still 800 miles from the sea, it is as far from one bank to the other as Paris is from London. And at Óbidos the Amazon is also at its deepest as well as its narrowest: some 250 feet, its bottom lower than sea level.

Drew Craig, who had read geology at Imperial College, London, explained it to us one evening.

'I expect you'll find it hard to believe that the Amazon once flowed in exactly the opposite direction and ran out into the Pacific . . . '

He told us how the high ground in the eastern half of South America – the Guyana shield in the north and the Brazilian shield to the south – was once a continuous range, and the Amazon then rose in hills more or less where we now were, near Óbidos, and ran westward through today's Ecuador.

'When was that, Drew?' came a voice from the ring of chairs.

'About when Gondwanaland began to split up and South America began to drift away from Africa–India–Australia–Antarctica. Say about 125 million years ago.'

'Gone where land?'

'You must have noticed how well the bulge of South America fits into Africa's Gulf of Guinea. Well, it was all one land mass once. As South America moved westward it pushed against the sub-oceanic shelf – the Nazca plate and the Pacific plate – and this caused the Andes to be formed. The pressure pushed them upwards.'

'Whenabouts did that happen?' said the voice.

'Toward the end of the Tertiary period.'

'Hey, come on, Drew! When?'

'About 25 million years back. And that meant that the Amazon's outlet to the ocean was blocked off. A giant lake was formed, but eventually it broke through near where we are now and flowed eastward through the Óbidos gap.'

'Wow!' said the voice.

It was in the Óbidos gap that *KM3* had her closest call since Ribeirão. With a strong force-5 wind on the nose, we edged her out towards the middle. Grappling with the problems of the loosening transom were helmsmen Barry Igoe, Jon Paul Nevin, Patricio Crooker, Marcelo Mendes and our latest recruit, Captain Stephen Timms RN. The wind gusted fiercely, and *KM3*'s three jaguar heads were dipping into the river, their shaggy beards (caused by the *totora* fraying) frequently awash. *Capitão Azevedo*, with *Southern Gailes* lashed alongside, tried to man-oeuvre ahead to provide shelter, but the reed boat found it impossible to stay in her lee. And this stratagem was not pleasant for the support ship: beam on to the wind she wallowed horribly, and at one point a Worcestershire-sauce bottle was hurled horizontally off the galley table and splattered all over the floor.

The two boats were still trying to synchronize their movements when a worse threat appeared. Storming upriver with the wind behind her came *Bertolini XXXVI*, a powerful *empurrador* pushing two barges, one of them with twenty lorries and trailers.

'This is going to be one hell of a motorway pile-up,' said Graham.

'Quick, get Captain José to give them a siren blast,' I shouted to Yoli.

KM3 had very little steerage way, but she managed to slip crabwise a fraction to starboard. *Capitão Azevedo* inched a little to port, and with hair-raising precision *Bertolini XXXVI* and her barges came neatly between the two.

KM3 was now shipping a lot of water and *Capitão Azevedo* attempted to take her in tow, but the rope could not be firmly enough secured. Slowly, however, our battered reed boat, the Avon butting at her stern, neared Óbidos and got into more settled water.

It had been such a nerve-jangling hour that both boats made a total cock-up of mooring. *Capitão Azevedo* went badly aground in a muddy creek, nobody having noticed that some cows were grazing nearby and the water came only halfway up their chests. *KM3* seemed unable to get into the creek and made several bosh shots at it. I became exasperated, and after a while loudhailed them, 'Take down that red ensign!'

But Jim Masters and the crew were doing their best in the strong wind and Barry, Eric Niemi, Jon Paul and Drew were soon up to their thighs in the mud trying to make some sort of jury rig for the transom so that we could get on to Santarém.

Óbidos was well worth exploring. It occupied a strategic position, and there were two Portuguese forts on hilltops which could command some of the mile-wide gap with their cannon and keep out Dutch, English, French and Irish interlopers. As early as 1610 Sir Thomas Roe had reached the entrance to the Rio Tapajós. His English crews had then rowed their ships' boats a further 100 miles upstream – most probably through the Óbidos gap. They met only Indians: the Portuguese did not establish themselves at Belém do Pará until five years afterwards.

Roe left twenty men behind – establishing the first trading station on the Amazon – and a few of them subsequently returned in a Dutch ship with, it was believed, gold and tobacco.

The next Englishman through the Óbidos gap was William White, in a 300-ton pinnace in 1620, but the Portuguese soon began to flex their muscles and to send punitive expeditions to slaughter intruders like these. No doubt Fort Pauxis in Óbidos, to which many of us climbed, was a key part of their defences. Its cannon still point menacingly towards the southern shore, with pyramidal heaps of round shot nearby.

While the trimaran's crew worked on their battered craft Yoli,

Geoffrey and I went in search of money-changers, but as usual no one wanted US dollars let alone traveller's cheques.

Visiting Fort Pauxis, we gazed out across the narrows as the sun was dipping on the western horizon. A huge oil tanker was ploughing upstream.

'I've heard that a German submarine came right up the river before World War Two,' said Yoli.

'Probably bringing Klaus Barbie and Ertl on a recce,' I laughed.

KM3 sailed the following morning at 5.30 a.m., and made rather uncertain progress out of the creek. The engine was now in a new position, on the starboard side of the central hull, but the craft seemed incapable of being steered. Was the motor too high out of the water? After spinning round several times, Jim decided to detach the water-logged starboard outrigger and let *Capitão Azevedo* take it alongside. A few moments later they hauled up the engine and begin a mid-river repair. Mercifully, it was a calm morning on the Amazon.

Steve Timms then restored the outboard to its old position. As the support ship drifted with the current, I watched all this in some confusion and called Jim on the radio. Would *KM3* continue as a twin-hulled boat?

We were still around 600 miles from Belém and the Atlantic, and I knew the river would get rougher. The prevailing east wind continued to blow strongly on to our bows, even pushing local sailing-craft up river against the current.

'That's how ancient traders went home,' commented Richard as we watched a couple of gaff-sailed canoes slipping past along the bank. However, we knew these conditions lasted only from August to November. Outside that period it could be a real battle to reach Manaus with only sails, as my old friend Tristan Jones had found when he had taken his 38-foot yawl up in 1972.

Of course it would have been much easier to sail downriver at that time of year, but Jim and I had been forced to make our passage when the wind was against us by the need to cross the cataracts in Bolivia and on the Mamoré at high water.

'I suppose the ancient traders would have done the journey at a slower pace,' said Ernie, who had emerged from the overheated galley for a breath of fresh air. Then 'Jim's having some fun out there,' the old soldier grinned.

KM3 was now battering her way through the short waves, spray flying over the jaguar figureheads. 'We're making 6 miles per hour,' reported Pat Troy. 'She's going a damned sight better as a catamaran.'

We had learned a useful lesson, and I wondered if Jim would want to take his discarded outrigger back or whether we should simply tow it along with the support vessel until we neared Belém, then lash it back in place and sail in as a trimaran. It was quite incredible how that bundle of reeds was standing up to the punishment.

Just then the support ship's tin boat returned with Sam and his team from a medical assignment, and Patricio on *KM3* inadvertently let loose the Avon, which was seen drifting away ahead of us. 'At such moments', said Caroline Ralph, 'one must view the expedition through latticed fingers.'

As all our vessels slid silently towards an enormously wide horizon, I was reminded of paintings of First World War tommies shepherding their wounded comrades across Flanders fields back to the trenches. I hoped we would somehow make it to Santarém.

Some 300,000 people now live in this important staging-post between Belém and Manaus – over 100 times more than when Henry Walter Bates established himself there in 1851 to begin three and a half years of entomologizing along the Tapajós. Founded by Jesuits in 1661, Santarém too has a fort that used to keep the peace on the river – a job now done by the Capitania dos Portos, which sent out a patrol boat to meet us and escort us in to the Marinho do Brasil jetties. Marcelo Mendes was now back among his naval colleagues.

Santarém is so called because, albeit still 520 miles from Belém and the Atlantic, it is at the limit of the Amazon's tidal effect, just as is the city of Santarém on the Tagus in metropolitan Portugal. Our skippers would from now on have not only wind and current to consider, but also the tide.

As we drew nearer the waterfront, we left the *café au lait* of the Amazon and entered the greeny-blue Tapajós. This tributary, by no means the Amazon's greatest, is 17 miles wide at this confluence. So Santarém seems to be on the shore of an inland sea.

It was close to here that in 1934 Henry Ford tried to match the astonishing productivity of the British rubber plantations in Malaya on 2½ million acres he called Fordlandia. But the *seringueiros* would not co-operate, parasites attacked the trees, and Ford lost $30 million before pulling out.

Paul Overton and big Bill Holmes had left us at Parintins to prepare the ground at Santarém, and they had met with an amazing welcome from the Serique brothers, Gil and Flavio. Of Moroccan descent, their father had come in from French Guiana. Flavio had been a tour guide in Manaus, but after the removal of a brain tumour he was now partly paralysed and almost immobile. All this did not stop him from running Cultura Inglesa, an English-language school in Santarém. An extrovert and great Anglophile, Flavio had issued his staff and friends with 'SANTARÉM SPEAKS ENGLISH' T-shirts, had housed Bill and Paul for several days, and had assisted them in their hunt for our next support ship. The *Capitão Azevedo*, based in Pôrto Velho, had undertaken to look after us only to Santarém. Now we must hire another, and it was here that Bill's legal expertise and Flavio's local know-how came into play.

The Serique brothers had also organized a party of local dignitaries to welcome the *Capitão Azevedo* and come on-board. Yoli, Marcelo, Geraldo, Richard and I were kept busy greeting our many local sponsors and friends, chief among whom were Hugh Beveridge and his wife, Eliza, old friends of the brothers. Even before the expedition began, Hugh was doing his utmost to assist us. More recently a considerable boost to morale had occurred when, while still on the Madeira, we had heard that Hugh had arranged a grand reception for us all at Santarém's Hotel Tropical (now renamed Hotel Amazon Park) and had booked accommodation there for those of us who wanted a good rest and a clean-up. Ex-Irish Guards, Hugh is in the oil business in Brazil, and his company, BS & B, kindly sponsored our life-jackets.

Flavio was himself assisted up a companionway and settled at a table. His boyish smile broke out at the sight of the first of many tins of Skol and Kaiser beer, and he held court with great good humour until the last guest had departed.

His efforts had enabled us to secure a bigger support boat for the final run to Belém. The stronger winds and steeper waves called for a longer, wider three-decker, and we took the *Viageiro IV* – which everyone immediately found it simpler to call the *Viagra*. It could carry 186 passengers – 136 more than *Capitão Azevedo* – and sported eight *eles* and *elas*. We were sad to say goodbye to Capitão José and Gorete, and the crewmen Jorge and Gallo – all soon to head back up the interminable Madeira. We now had a crew of ten or a dozen whom we never came to know quite so well – except for Giselle, in the *cozinha*. We were much encouraged to see another fat cook: she enjoyed her own food, and obviously flourished, and so might we, at one remove. '*O Senhor e Meu Pastor, Nada Me Faltara*' – 'The Lord is My Shepherd, I Shall Lack Nothing' – was the promising inscription over the galley. Ernie got on well with her from the outset.

'I have always been a bit of a late developer,' Richard told me. 'It was not until we reached Santarém that I discovered one of Brazil's alcoholic specialities, the *caipurinha*. It's a splendid aperitif on a cane base. There's a variant called a *caipurosco*, which I think is vodka-based. But I'm not quite sure of all this, because I'd had four of one before I tried two of the other.'

Santarém was an oasis, and we enjoyed three full days there – between Thursday 16 August and Monday 20 August. The fort was hard to find, but there is an attractive cathedral – Nossa Senhora da Conceição, built by the German Jesuit João Felipe Betendorf – standing up blue and white behind the trees in the Praça do Bandeira. Patricio Crooker exulted about the wonderful pictures he had shot in the fish market earlier. Our younger set went 20 miles south-west to Alter do Chão, a superb bank of white sand on the Tapajós, where Santarém takes its weekend break.

The highlight of Hugh Beveridge's party at the Hotel Tropical was a pair of incredibly be-feathered *garotas*. The energetic dancing of these two erotic beauties had all the men's eyes popping out. Later, when they returned to socialize with us dressed in jeans and T-shirts, we hardly recognized them. It's amazing what a few feathers will do for the female body.

Next day Yoli, Marigold, Graham, Richard and I took a break of a different kind. On Sunday 19 August, Hugh and Eliza Beveridge hired a fast launch, the *Reflexo*, to take us downriver to Monte Alegre and the site of some rock-wall paintings, the work of early man.

It used to be thought that, during the last ice age, over 12,000 years ago, the spread of the polar cap lowered sea levels everywhere, and when it began slowly to retreat people from Asia were able to migrate over a land bridge across what is now the Bering Strait and into North America. Subsequent moves southward took these incomers to Central and South America – even to its very tip and to Tierra del Fuego. They were small groups of nomadic hunter-gatherers, and have become known as the Clovis people, after their flint spear- and arrow-heads found near Clovis,

New Mexico. There were thought to have been two further migrations from Siberia – to the North Pacific coastal regions and eastward to the lands of today's Inuit. And that was how *Homo sapiens* came to South America.

These traditional ideas were challenged in the 1990s. The Amazon river lands which were thought to have been bypassed by the Clovis invaders were shown to have been occupied by a physiologically different population, some of them established in caves at Monte Alegre, near Santarém, and foraging in the forest for plants and animals. They were the first artists in the western hemisphere – the Pedra Pintada caves at Monte Alegre bear witness to this. Other finds in South America began to indicate human occupation before the time when Clovis people had even arrived in North America.

It was once thought that, of the earliest South Americans, the most sophisticated settled in the Andes and were superior to whoever might have been living in the flat, flooded lands to the east. This was contested by Erland Nordenskjöld in the 1930s and by Donald Lathrap in the 1960s. Both these Swedes found evidence of sedentary, structured communities to the east of the Andes which cultivated plants that were found to have only later been grown on the coast of Peru. It was from the river line between Santarém and Manaus, they said, that populations moved upriver to the highland regions: the Incas, it was postulated, came from the Amazon.

The *Reflexo* bombed down 90 miles of Amazon for three hours, and by 10.30 a.m. we had turned off and were puttering up a quiet arm of the main river. Fishermen's shacks were dotted all around, but the staggering feature was the appearance of a considerable cluster of flat-topped hills on the northern bank. Up the sides of one of these hills sprawled the red-roofed stucco houses of a rather Italianate town, Monte Alegre, home to 40,000.

A smiling *Brasileiro* of Middle Eastern origin met us at the quayside. Local schoolmaster Nelsí Neif Sadeck is a recognized guide to the Pedro Pintada region. We climbed into the back of a small truck and drove up through the town and into the hills, the Serra da Lua. The shock after over a month sailing through the flat *várzea* was almost palpable.

'Look at those fields and fences and farms,' said Richard, holding his baseball hat on with a free hand. 'This is more like some ranch in northern Argentina!'

We drew near a large mesa called Erere, crowned with vertical-sided sandstone cliffs. The Toyota bounced over rocky stream beds until it came as close as it could to the base of one of these cliffs on the Serra da Lua. There followed a punishing scramble up a 45° slope in the noonday heat, rewarded at the top by the sight of a remarkable series of painted walls: geometrical figures, stickmen, whorls, ghostly handprints – red and yellow mostly, and dating from about 9,200 BC: the oldest examples of art in the Americas.

It was near here in 1983 that Dr Anna C. Roosevelt – curator of archaeology at Chicago's Field Museum, professor of anthropology at the University of Illinois, Chicago, and great-granddaughter of Theodore, the former US president who had himself charted 950 miles of hitherto unknown Amazonian rivers before running out into the Madeira – made her important discoveries in the Caverna da Pedra Pintada. It had been Nelsí Neif Sadeck, Monte Alegre's secretary of culture, who had first taken her to the caverna.

'I could see right away that it was a good bet,' Dr Roosevelt said. 'It looked very liveable [in] – light, airy and dry.'

They dug through layers of deposit in which were signs of occasional human occupation, and then reached a sterile level. 'Well, that's it,' she thought. 'Where else can we look in this area? But we dug a bit more and suddenly something flicked up into my face. It was a spear-point flake. Then the soil turned black.'

This must have been a marvellous moment for someone who could understand the significance of such a *trouvaille*. There was a layer of soil filled with charcoal from human campfires and detritus from an early society that nobody knew about. It could all be dated: bones of fish, birds and rats and burned seeds. Later she found the rest of the spear-point.

Anna Roosevelt – a woman with 'a stern site manner' – now challenged the prevailing view of how South America was first settled and how the first settlers lived. The Palaeo-Indians of Amazonia were not the direct descendants of North American plains hunters, she said, but a contemporary people with their own ways of foraging for fruit and fish, and of painting rock and shaping stone. She believes they were present in this region as long as 11,200 years ago and maintained a robust society which reached its apogee from the tenth to the sixteenth century AD; she therefore maintains that early human development was not constrained by a humid, tropical environment, but could evolve in that as well as in any other.

These views have themselves been challenged by a fellow American archaeologist, Dr Betty J. Meggers, a research associate at the Smithsonian Institution's National Museum of Natural History in Washington DC. She believes that what Dr Roosevelt has found is merely evidence of the repeated reoccupations of a site by people who hunted, gathered and cultivated on a nomadic basis and not the epicentre of a settled, complex society.

The two women had clashed earlier. Dr Meggers and her archaeologist husband, Clifford Evans, began an ambitious research project to survey the mouth of the Amazon in 1948. On the island of Marajó they found mounds which were the work of a 'large, solitary . . . society'. Dr Roosevelt went later to the same site and argued that it was 'one of the outstanding indigenous cultural achievements of the New World'.

Since then the two have been ding-donging away, and not much quarter has been given by either side. 'Anna's a good researcher,' said Dr Gordon Willey, a professor emeritus of archaeology at Harvard, 'and very passionate about being right.' But some think she may be over-interpreting her evidence. How good has been her dating of pottery? She has certainly revealed an early human presence in the Amazon, but should it cause us to revise our view of New World archaeology?

Roosevelt feels that Dr Meggers has regarded the Amazon basin as her own intellectual property and tried to bar pro-Roosevelt archaeologists from working there. Dr Meggers dismisses these insinuations, and says of her rival, 'She's gotten nastier and nastier. She likes to be a sensationalist. She seems to feel she's untouchable, being a Roosevelt.' 'I'm temperamental, outspoken and tough,' says Dr Roosevelt, 'but most of my colleagues like me and think I do interesting work. You have to be persistent. Twenty people can't run a dig. Only I have a global view of what the project is, and I raised the money for it and believe I should be responsible for how it's spent. [You] have to be stern.'

Pottery fragments, claimed to be 7,500 years old – the oldest known in the Americas – and Roosevelt's jagged, triangular spear-point, so unlike the streamlined, fluted equivalents of the Clovis people, are clear indications that there was a different, independent, stream of development in the Amazonian rainforest.

We moved on round the sandstone mesa and climbed this time to a cave known as Ita Tupa Oka, which means God's Stone House in Tupi. From its mouth there was a glorious view over the distant Amazon and its parallel lakes. Nelsí assured us that the cave's flat floor was once the seabed, and the interior certainly looked as if it had been eroded by wave action.

'They all came here,' he said – 'Dr Roosevelt, Henry Walter Bates, Alfred Russel Wallace, Francisco de Orellana, even Pinzón.' We were not so sure about the last one: it's still a long way to the Atlantic.

15

The Anaconda Moment

Explorer extraordinaire is oor JBS,
Huntin' fur sponsors fur SES.
Anacondas and caimen shack wi' fear
When John's juttin' jaw comes anywhere near!

Dick the author sits and writes
Awe aboot the exped's plights.
We're awfy sure he'll mack us proud;
Either way he'll bring a crowd!

Jenny Campbell, Burns Night organizer

OUR DEPARTURE FROM Santarém was somewhat chequered. Jim had decided that the starboard outrigger should remain detached. So Pat Troy took *KM3* off at 7 a.m. as a sort of catamaran – two hulls tied together closely by cordage, and an outboard engine between them. *Viagra* now had to tow both the sick outrigger and *Southern Gailes* alongside, which her captain, José Caetano, was quite happy to do.

Unfortunately it was not done well. After refuelling, *Viagra* set off, and immediately the outrigger came adrift at its forward end. Everything in it was suddenly awash. Bits of wood, useful as transoms, rope, fender tyres – all went into the river. Jim was in anguish. However, most things were recovered. We turned the outrigger's head towards *Viagra*'s bows and hauled it up higher in the water. Its jaguar figurehead was taken inboard and placed, rather incongruously, on *Viagra*'s stern-post.

KM3 had now gone so far ahead that Pat was out of radio contact for three or four hours. At the evening briefing he gave a typically brisk report on the day's activities. 'It was all right. We made progress.' But it had been unsettling for him to be on the wrong side of one of the

Amazon's enormous inter-riparian islands and totally unable to hear me (though we could hear him and so did not share his anxiety).

In the late afternoon *Viagra* was moored to some trees by a large swamp, and soon the fleet was reunited. We now had the use of an oven, and Ernie and Giselle baked chicken in ginger and pineapple. It was a magical evening: all around were islets and semi-submerged trees, stilt houses, moored launches and roosting egrets flying in great white clouds from tree to tree as if they could not make up their minds which to settle on.

In the morning the sun revealed a water wonderland – one of the most attractive places visited in this phase. Richard said it reminded him of the Stockholm archipelago.

'Look, white chalet-like buildings, boats tied up to little jetties, mosquitoes . . . '

'Yes, but the trees don't look all that coniferous,' said Bill Holmes. 'And what about this early-morning heat and humidity? It's hardly Scandinavian.'

'I know, I know. But there's that sense of water, islands, water beyond – for ever.'

One of Richard's serendipitous discoveries when we were all wandering around *Viageiro IV* on day one, seeing what it had in store for us, was a small office on the lower deck, forward of the crew's cabins and directly below the *comando*, the captain's bridge. It was designated as the *escritorio*, and the ship's papers and other valuables were kept in a safe there. Richard reckoned that not only did it sound like a writing-room, but it was sufficiently far from other centres of activity to be private and peaceful and it had a sort of shelf on which a laptop could be perched. He could write up his log here, and we could both perhaps produce preliminary drafts of a chapter or two of this book. He spent hours there, sometimes staring out of the open door at the passing river for inspiration, occasionally enlivened by social visits.

'Hi, Richard,' said Bill Holmes. 'Just thought I'd stop by to see how things were shaping. In this place you should be writing a *roman fleuve*, not a travel book.'

There was a sudden clanking noise. The chains from the ship's wheel, which ultimately cause the rudder to swing, passed down through the *escritorio* in metal tubes. There was a flurry of activity in the *comando* above. We were in some narrows between the Ilha do Curuá and Barreiras Grandes, and the wind had become boisterous.

'*Viagra*, this is *Kota Mama*,' said Jim. 'Can you come to windward of us to give some protection from these gusts? Over.'

Yoli translated this into Spanish and Geraldo put it into Portuguese. Capitão Caetano said, 'No, I can't do that in this channel. And, besides, there's another vessel coming up aft.' This news was relayed to Jim.

True enough, the *Frotamanaus* of Belém was bearing down on us fast.

'There is a reed boat ahead of you,' the first mate said over the radio to the container ship. 'Please alter your course. Please alter course. *Cambio*.'

A moment's silence, then a crackle of Portuguese, which Geraldo and Yoli rendered as roughly 'I cannot change course or slow down for a big straw bale with a lot of mad English on it. *Cambio*.'

It was like the Security Council of the United Nations on a bad day – three languages, the bell ringing constantly in the engine-room, and much gesticulating and Latin American attitudinizing. In the end *Frotamanaus* creamed past us with sea-room enough.

We turned off the main river and ran up to Monte Alegre, where some of us had been the previous Sunday. The priority now was not prehistoric rock art but the need to get the outboard engine of *Viagra*'s tin boat repaired or replaced. Richard went on to the quayside with a fistful of postcards and took a taxi to the *correio*, which was up the hill in the higher part of town. Near the top the taxi ran out of petrol, so the driver turned round and coasted back down to the quayside petrol station. He put in 1 litre and asked Richard for 2 reals. He then drove him back up to the post office, waited a few moments, returned to the bottom, and charged Richard 5 reals (about $2.30).

Towards dusk *Viagra* motored down towards the Amazon and moored up near *KM3* at the Boca de Monte Alegre. It was almost dark when an extraordinary invasion occurred: black beetles flew on board in their trillions – far too many to avoid or swat. Some dashed themselves on the ship's lights and died, but otherwise they bombarded the galley, where a very good meat-and-potato pie was being served, followed by fruit salad. The trick was to convey the food to the mouth without ingesting the Coleoptera. Richard's *escritorio* was full of beetles and mosquitoes for days.

Richard told me he was going to take a couple of dead beetles home, together with a rubber-tree seed, for use at talks. I told him I hoped he would get them to Britain safely, and was reminded of poor Alfred Russel Wallace, who, after four years' work in the Amazon basin, set off home on board the brig *Helen* in July 1852. Three weeks out in the Atlantic the ship caught fire, and his entire collection was lost except for one parrot and a tin box with his priceless fish drawings. Henry Walter Bates, the friend Wallace had met when both were young men in Leicester, fared rather better. Bates remained on the upper Amazon, above the Rio Negro, for four and a half years more, and discovered over 7,000 insect species around his simple cottage base. He returned to the coast in 1859. Pará was now a rubber boom town, four times the size that he had first known it and very expensive. He returned home to write *The Naturalist on the River Amazons*, published by John Murray of Albemarle Street in 1863. It made him famous. His South American collection numbered 14,712 species of animals, 8,000 of them new to science.

We were not collecting but observing. At Monte Alegre a pleasant moment had been enjoyed as some of us watched a large iguana swimming across the river towards us. It seemed not to notice *Viagra* and butted her amidships.

A *paraná* is not a fearsome fish but a narrow channel of water, and we now proceeded down the lengthy Paraná de Monte Alegre with the Ilha do Gurupatuba on our starboard hand, sausage-like red pods hanging from the kapok trees on its banks.

After some time we emerged into the main river again. It was 5 miles wide here, and as we scanned to east and west the line of trees on the far bank perceptibly thinned out and the lower parts of their trunks disappeared from view at the extremities. The earth's curvature could not have been better exemplified.

The expedition continued to have the sort of problems that all long-drawn-out ventures do towards their end. People's tempers get frayed; a sense of the sameness of everything saps some of the early enthusiasm; equipment begins to wear out. Though Paul Overton had been in Monte Alegre all the previous day trying to resolve the problem, the outboard engine of *Viagra*'s tin boat was still on the blink. What we really lacked was a good engine-fitter. Jon Paul, Drew and Barry tried hard, but we missed Ben Cartwright, the mechanical wizard on *Kota Mama* 2, or perhaps the fifteen-year-old American boy, domiciled in Paraguay, who in 1999 had coaxed into life an outboard that had defeated even Ben.

A cheering thought to counter this was that the Mariner 15 outboard supplied to us by one of the SES's longest-standing supporters, E. P. Barrus, which was pushing *KM3* along with no signs of any hiccup, was the same engine that had driven *KM2* the lengths of the Paraguay and Paraná rivers in 1999.

Although a much larger boat than the *Capitão Azevedo*, the *Viagra* seemed more crowded. We had sixteen hammocks slung side by side. The metal folding tables and chairs were noisy and uncomfortable. But the thumping of the ship's generator was far worse, and it was incessant. The crew seemed to be in their hammocks all the time. The duck-boarded floors of the *eles* and *elas* were always inches deep in water or worse. Even the cockroaches seemed bigger.

There were some mutterings about our strategy. We were well up to time, but instead of proceeding steadily in a series of short days and maybe having eventually to rush to Belém, why not go hard now and sail for longer each day, just in case? 'Let's kick ass,' said Eric Niemi, in a voice that could be heard on all three decks. As the British Embassy was organizing a reception in Belém on 6 September and air flights were booked for the team on 7 and 8 September, we could not afford to be late. So I decided to get as close to the Atlantic port as possible before having a recreational pause.

By far the worst deterioration in *KM3* was to be seen in its starboard outrigger. We had tried in vain to fit it back on to the other two hulls, but the damage it had sustained was too great: it had never recovered from being twisted internally in the spill at Ribeirão. Now it was water-logged. Jim radioed me. 'We'll have to leave the damaged hull,' he said with a tinge of sadness. 'She's sinking lower all the time and slowing us down.' I agreed. It was 22 August and we had just passed a red-painted navigation light on Amazon's northern bank, the Fuente Ponta Peregrino. What to do with an enormous baguette of sodden reed? It was of no use to anyone, but to let it loose would be to create a hazard for small craft, and it was too wet to burn. We took it close in to the shore, then Jim and Pat jumped into the river and, wading up to their thighs, pulled it to the tree-fringed-bank, where Jim secured it to the trunk of a cecropia. Local people or passing fishermen would have the yellow cordage off it in no time, and its biodegradable remains would quickly rot.

It was sad to see these two stalwarts abandoning a hull they had nursed all the way from Guanay (in Jim's case) and Pôrto Velho (in Pat's). Francisco de Orellana had had to abandon his broken brigantine on his way down the Amazon in 1542. He had carried on – and so would we, in much greater certainty of safe arrival.

★

Since leaving Santarém with just two hulls, Jim had operated a new system of watches on *KM3*. In the old regime all the crew members remained on board all day, some of them not doing very much. It was then that the physical-fitness fanatics got to work on their triceps, biceps, quads, pectorals and the like. Helming for an hour broke that routine, but there was still plenty of time to sleep in the shade of a canopy. The two skippers, Jim and Pat, had a harder time of it, however, because they had to remain alert all day.

With only two hulls, fewer hands could be accommodated on board and so Jim introduced the more efficient scheme of having two watches of five men, each watch with a guest from the HQ group. One watch would be on *KM3* from departure at first light until 1030 a.m., then the other watch of five plus one would man the boat until the end of the day – usually in mid-afternoon. Each six would have more to do, but would have half the day to relax on the support vessel. A certain healthy rivalry between 'A' watch and 'B' watch was soon evident. Each would scrutinize the other's comings alongside of *Viagra* with great interest, and there was unbridled glee when the arriving helmsman managed to ram her. Pat Troy's increasingly inventive explanations of how 'B' watch had contrived a spectacular tie-up were much enjoyed.

The reduction of *KM3* from three hulls to two might have been expected to spark a few doubts about her chances of reaching Belém. The indications were not good: the two A-masts were no longer neatly in line but at a distinct angle to one another; a couple of areas of rot became noticeable and the smell of decaying *totora* became more and more nauseating; and she was slowly but unmistakably settling in water.

Despite all this, everyone had huge confidence in her ability to complete the voyage. Although the wind remained adverse and the waves grew steadily choppier, a relaxed air prevailed on Jim's watch: when any crew member nodded off at the helm, spilled a drop or two of fuel or committed any other such peccadillo, Jim pretended in the manner of a soccer referee to draw out a yellow or red card from his pocket. His hand had only to move towards his trousers to trigger general hilarity and loud cries for the name of the supposed offender to be revealed. There was evident bonhomie on the reed boat and the Avon until the very end.

The Avon inflatable had a 25 h.p. Suzuki outboard engine, and was now employed as a permanent pusher against *KM3*'s stern. The reed boat's 15 h.p. Mariner was thus handsomely augmented, and a speed of 6 to 8 m.p.h. was possible in almost any conditions. The helmsmen of the Avon and the catamaran were generally changed every hour. Others kept watch for driftwood, water hyacinth, fisherman's nets and passing vessels.

'Are you going back by São Paulo?' asked one crew member.

'I think we all are,' said another.

'Who's going to come on to Rio afterwards?' asked Drew.

There were still two and a half weeks to go, but expeditions always experience this early talk of the return home. It's no reflection on the expedition itself, which will on the whole be much enjoyed up to the last day, but members will always fantasize about their first meal back home and relish the rosy prospect of their first home drinks.

'We've a lot of packing up of kit to do,' said Ernie, injecting a more sober note. And already he and Jim were drawing up lists of what to put in the various mule-boxes and considering how we might get bulkier items back to England in a container. Some of our days in Belém would be occupied in the tedious but necessary business of winding the expedition down.

Red-roofed Prainha, which we reached three days after leaving Santarém, had a Mediterranean look, and we moored to its jetty. It is a fishing town, and its speciality the acarí. A man rowed up with hundreds of them in the bottom of his shallop – shiny, black, leathery fish, like pairs of new sandals.

Heading east again, we entered a *paraná* lined in this instance on both sides by stilt houses linked by high boardwalks. The houses' occupants enjoyed the experience of solid ground underfoot for only a few months in the low-water season, and only for a few yards inland of the *paraná*, for in place of a back garden there was the vast *igapó* – mile upon mile of standing water from which protrude tall trees, small trees, scrub, ferns and grasses. Millions of acres of *igapó* flank all the Amazonian tributaries, and cover an even greater area in the high-water season.

It was still a surprise, in the evening, to see hills on the northern bank – this time small conical ones. We came to Praia Verde, and *Viagra* ran its nose on to a perfect sandy beach where naked boys were frolicking. Uncle Graham Catchpole earned much kudos later by picking them up and tossing them back into the river like Scottish cabers.

As I came down *Viagra*'s gangplank on to the beach, intent on an afternoon foray into the hills, Richard said, 'You're obviously setting out on the final search for the lost Colonel Fawcett. Can I come with you?' It's true that I was fully accoutred in Australian bush hat, old army jungle green, full belt kit, compass, water-bottle, machete, trekking-pole and jungle boots. Yoli followed me in her neatly pressed trousers, khaki shirt and stout size-4 boots. Incongruously, Geoffrey Hoskins joined us a few moments later wearing only a pair of disintegrating green shorts.

As a guide led us up a path into a bit of rainforest, I broke out into a mild sweat. It was a muggy afternoon. Richard saw a bat. I poked a termite's nest and photographed a bromeliad in a tree. Another tree – the sucuba – produced a potable milk of some medicinal use, said the guide. The most interesting find was a trail of ants, each carrying a yellow flower to its nest. 'We saw . . . the Sauba ants,' wrote H. M. Tomlinson on the outskirts of Itacoatiara in 1911, 'sometimes called the parasol ants, in endless processions, each ant holding a piece of leaf, the size of a six-penny bit, over its tiny body.' It was all gently mesmeric, but by no means prime-time wildlife television, and after 1½ miles Richard was looking a touch underwhelmed. And I have to confess that the area was a bit light on jaguar, tapir and anaconda.

'Never again am I going out on one of Miss Blashford-Snell's guided nature rambles,' said Richard, rather uncharitably.

He changed his tune minutes later, when we found a very large wasp on the edge of the track, pulling a dead tarantula three of four times its own size. It had presumably just stung it, and was hauling it home to its larder. Richard scooped up hunter and hunted in his blue J. P. Knight baseball hat, and I took several useful sponsorship shots while the wasp, with manic determination, continued to drag its victim over and round the hat.

That evening *Viagra* suffered the first of a number of successive embarrassments. A picturesque display of lightning came slowly from the east and brought torrential rain, during which the support ship's engines were fired up to keep her off the bank. Violent revving precluded sleep. The crew ran about hyperactively. In the morning we were in the same place but aground.

After fifteen minutes we eased off into the river and motored to Almeirim, where we stopped for food and fuel. The town was in *festa*, and the *Titanic* film theme was being blasted from amplifiers in the *praça*.

Later in the afternoon, as *Viagra* purred along the narrow Paraná dos Arraiolos, a frightful warning whistle sounded from the engine-room. Suddenly we were just drifting. I tried to find out the score from Capitão Caetano, but he was too preoccupied. There was a lot of high-pitched shouting below. The engineer rushed about frantically for an hour and then – apparently defeated by the problem – fell asleep in his hammock. Last night's incessant revving seemed to have taken its toll. Eventually a mechanic was brought from Almeirim in a tin boat and a repair was effected, which the captain tried vainly to get me to pay for. Since the tide had now gone out *Viagra* was aground again, and this time we had to wait several hours before we could refloat.

As we inched away tentatively along the *paraná*, with the Ilha do Comandai on our starboard hand, disconcerting news came to us over the ship's radio from another vessel, a fuel carrier, warning others that it had been attacked twice by pirates in the Boa Fé channel. This was still a little way off towards the next day's destination, Gurupá.

'You must take this seriously,' pleaded Geraldo, fearing the intrepid British might not.

Clearly it was not the sort of news that one could afford to ignore. At the risk of incurring ridicule from the more sceptical crew members, I knew we had to devise some contingency measures.

'Have we any guns on board?' asked Marcelo, who, as our Brazilian Navy liaison officer, was understandably concerned.

'No,' I replied, 'but we do have the parachute flares given to us by General Hurtado in Bolivia.'

'I doubt if anyone will see those in time to come to help us,' he said.

'I don't intend to use them as distress rockets,' I explained. 'Fired horizontally they have a range of over 100 yards, and should scare the pants off a pirate. We'll use them like a bazooka.' We had done something similar when attacked on the Blue Nile in 1968, and it proved pretty effective. A ball of fire rushing at one can be far more frightening than an invisible bullet.

That night I ordered a two-man watch to be kept – one from our team, one from the *Viagra* crew – to look out for the approach of unlit vessels. If the watchmen saw such a vessel they were to wake me, and if I deemed it necessary they were to give three long blasts on a whistle to alert everyone. On hearing this the ship's lights would be doused, Marcelo would call the Brazilian Navy and the police on the satellite phone, and Yoli, Jon Paul and I would go up to the *comando* with a loud-hailer and our improvised weapons. Other designated pairs were to move to bows, stern, port and starboard sides, armed likewise with para-flares.

What about the rest? It was with a mixture of concern and amusement that the remainder learned that they were to lie down around the dining-table under the direction of Ernie and Bruce. It was obvious that they would be much more secure if they congregated there, but I expected the usual murmurs of dissent. At various places on *Viagra* I had 'IN THE EVENT OF HOSTILITY – READ THIS NOW' notices posted up explaining all these arrangements.

'I'm not lying under any galley table,' said one.

'I doubt if I could physically get under it,' said Bill Holmes.

'You don't have to get *under* it,' said Yoli – 'just somewhere near it.'

'It's the safest place in the ship: the cockroaches know a thing or two.'

'The last time I took refuge under a kitchen table was in our cellar during the Sheffield blitz,' added Richard.

Any expedition member who smiled superciliously on reading these notices was to be given pause for thought when news broke on 6 December 2001 of the murder by pirates in the Amazon of the legendary New Zealand yachtsman Sir Peter Blake. At 10.15 p.m. four hooded men armed with pistols boarded his schooner *Seamaster* at Fundeadouro, near Macapá in the Amazon mouth. He shot and seriously injured one of the gang before being shot twice in the back. Two other members of his crew were injured. The Auckland-born fifty-three-year-old, had been knighted by the Queen for services to yachting in 1995, had won the America's Cup twice with Team New Zealand, and had crossed the Southern Ocean and rounded Cape Horn five times.

For a reason never fully understood, we celebrated Burns Night on Friday 24 August. Can it be true that Rabbie's birthday is honoured on a different night in the southern hemisphere? Surely 25 January is a worldwide dig-out-the-kilt night for expatriate Scots as well as those at home? And anyway we were only just over 1° below the Equator. However, complete Burns suppers had been provided in tins by Stahly Quality Foods of Fife, and thus we had the essential items for a traditional menu.

At all events, nurse Jenny Campbell, our most Scottish of Scots, and Drew Craig, who ran her close, got busy. After the soup, two chieftains o' the pudding race were borne in and were followed by pineapple, toasts to the lassies and the lads, and woefully under-rehearsed sketches. One of our Brazilian crew who tasted the haggis enquired, 'Where did you catch this?' *Viagra* had anchored in midstream, and a high wind blew our heads clear by morning.

Eddie Stobart truck-drivers who pass each other in different directions on a British motorway can't stop and exchange news of Carlisle, but the Amazon is not like that. When we met the *Cidade de Terezina II* – owned, like *Viageiro IV*, by Navegação Sousa – the two boats circled round one another and came alongside, drifting with the current. Giselle, our chubby cook, leaped over the bulwarks and affectionately greeted one of the other crew. Some transactions occurred. Money changed hands. There was laughter. Then we heard our crew explain that they were carrying a party of *inglês* and *inglêsas*.

After a 61-mile day, *Viagra* and, later, *KM3* tied up at Gurupá on the south bank of mainstream Amazon. This has always been a place of strategic importance, and it was with no surprise that we found its fort on a high bluff overlooking the broad river, though perhaps not capable of covering it with its cannon shot. Forte Santo Antônio de Gurupá had been built in 1623, seven years after the Portuguese established themselves at Belém do Pará, and marked the defeat of the Dutch from Nassau and the British from other forts.

Gurupá, a substantial town, is off the tourist circuit. The guidebooks go blank between Santarém and Belém, with the exception of a solitary mention of Parintins and its annual June Boi-Bumbá festival. Yet it has this ancient fort and also a magnificent but crumbling edifice with a classical portico whose tympanum bears the letters PMG (Prefeitura Municipal de Gurupá?).

A weather pattern was forming now: each evening, behind cloud, a fireworks display of lightning worthy of the Millennium or the Queen's Golden Jubilee was followed by thunder, then a rushing wind and finally a colossal deluge. One of these hit us at Gurupá.

Next day it had all cleared, and we proceeded to a stilt village in a picturesque *paraná*, São Francisco de Ituquara. This time Sam, Michelle, Jenny and Graham set to work at their daily ministrations in a series of dingy, interconnected wooden rooms whose rear windows looked out over the watery *igapó*.

That evening I was at last able to say, 'We've seen an anaconda.'

'What?' said Richard incredulously. 'I was talking to a man who's lived here fifty years, and he hasn't seen one yet. Another man had once been bitten by a *surucucu* and had to be taken to Belém for anti-venom, but they don't see anaconda.'

'Well, we have,' said Yoli. 'But it's dead.'

'It's 4 to 5 metres long,' Geraldo said.

'Surely that qualifies for the Bronx Zoo $50,000 prize,' said Richard.

'Alas, it has to be over 30 feet to win that,' I explained, 'and, as Geraldo said, this one's only 4 to 5 metres.'

Simon, an elderly member of the crew of a raft of logs on the Beni river in Bolivia, had first told us of the prevalence of the dreaded green anaconda (*Eunectes murinus*) there. A few weeks before we met him he had seen one of these huge snakes in the water while lashing the logs together. Apparently they often live under the logs, because fish congregate there. When Simon approached this one it reared up, striking him repeatedly.

'It was about 16 feet long,' he said, 'and seemed determined to eat me.'

In the end they had to borrow a shotgun from a villager and kill it.

A Bolivian hunter had earlier told me of a 28-foot anaconda that had taken his dog as they walked along a fallen tree in a swamp: the snake had attacked the man, but the faithful dog had defended him to the end. We had also met a fisherman who had had his leg seized by a 14-foot specimen. The anaconda immediately coiled itself round him and began, in time-honoured fashion, to squeeze him to death. He felt his ribs cracking, screamed for help, and was saved by his colleagues, whose machetes hacked the snake from him.

Herpetologists believe it is rare for these massive creatures to exceed 30 feet, although in Brazil we obtained copies of a photograph that appeared to show one of 36 feet caught in the Mato Grosso after it had eaten a man. The price of $50,000 that has been on offer by the Wildlife Conservation Society at the Bronx Zoo since about 1910 is for anyone able to produce a live specimen of 30 feet or more. The problems of catching an anaconda of such a size, if indeed one exists, and transporting it to New York make it unlikely that the prize will ever be claimed. The largest one we saw was some 15 feet (about the size of the largest that Henry Walter Bates ever saw), but I was shown the skin of another that was very large, and the police officer at a Madeira river port who had shot it while it was eating a dog swore that it was over 21 feet long.

At up to 500 lb, anacondas are the world's heaviest snakes. Jesús Rivas, a Venezuelan biologist, has found that adult females tend to be five times heftier than their male partners – an imbalance exceptional in the animal kingdom. With its eyes and nostrils conveniently placed on top of a flat head, the anaconda is a lethal submarine, coming on land only to sunbathe or to eat prey.

We had now left the mainstream Amazon (having failed to see the confluence of the massive Xingu, a tributary entering on the southern side), and entered a series of narrow *furos* which separate the Amazon's vast gobstopper, the Ilha de Marajó from the mainland – the Furo Ituquara, Furo de Limão and Furo do Talapuru, and finally the Estreito de Boiuçu, where other recent acts of piracy had taken place. Tomlinson in the *Capella* had come this way – he called Boiuçu 'Buyassa'.

Marcelo had called the Brazilian Navy for support and, as we left the narrows of the Estreito de Boiuçu and entered the gigantic Rio Pará, Bill Holmes, who was on radio watch, called out, 'There's a large boat coming up fast astern.'

Grabbing my binoculars and loudhailer I dived out of the office cabin thinking, 'Not pirates, I hope.' Bill was right: now only half a mile away, a sleek grey vessel was emerging at speed from the early-morning mist. On its foredeck was a black pom-pom cannon.

'It's a gunboat,' I cried. Then, seeing the lettering on her bow, 'P13, the *Pariti* – she's a Brazilian Navy patrol boat.'

'Thank God,' said Yoli, rising from her computer to inform our gallant captain, whose eyes were still looking dead ahead.

'There's a gunboat coming up astern,' I told Jim over the radio.

'Seen,' he replied. 'Ask them not to swamp us with their wash.'

Five minutes later *Pariti* was almost alongside and we dipped our respective flags to each other. 'Good morning, *Kota Mama*,' said a voice in good English. 'Please, I wish to speak with the commanding officer.' I introduced myself, and the Brazilian naval officer replied, 'Admiral Kleber sends you his compliments, Colonel. We hear from Lieutenant Mendes about the pirates, and find part of your boat beached upriver. We wonder if you are in some trouble.'

I explained why we had abandoned the damaged hull, and the officer said, 'OK, Colonel, no problem – that is good. We will go ahead of you and look for pirates now. Good luck for the rest of your voyage. See you in Belém.'

With that, *Pariti* sounded her siren in salute and, rapidly gathering speed, headed into the rising sun. It was a fine and reassuring sight.

16

A Bumpy Finish

Founded in 1616 by Portuguese colonizers, Sta. Maria de Belém do Grão Pará,
as it was known, Belém became a true historic monument of the colonization
in the Amazon region. For its geographical position, Belém with its 1,600,000
inhabitants, started to be called 'The Gateway to the Exuberant Amazonia'. . .

Belém-Pará: Ver o Peso, tourist handout

A LATTICE-FINGERED view of the expedition seemed to be more and
more appropriate in these final days.

'Accidents always happen and things go wrong towards the end,' said
Jim.

It is evident that we half expected something to go wrong with *KM3*,
which had after all come all the way from Guanay in Bolivia. But, ironically, it was the support ship, *Viageiro IV*, that provided the embarrassments. First we left Curralinho, on the Pará's northern shore, without
Southern Gailes, the balsa raft. Luckily Marigold had spotted her, still tied
to the town jetty. Then, once we'd attached her to *Viagra*, the boat started
forward before the raft was fully clear of the jetty and the raft's front
section was shorn off. The nose section was taken on board *Viagra*'s lower
deck, and Jim pronounced the damage repairable.

I was now getting twitchy about *Southern Gailes*, and shortly afterwards, as she was being towed behind *Viagra*, I noticed that some men
offering fish for sale had attached themselves to the balsa.

'Oi!' I shouted angrily, whereupon they smiled and waved at me. I had
not discovered that 'Oi!' is a commonly used friendly greeting in Brazil.

It was at our next port of call that we saw the Amazon's biggest fish –
not in the river but in São Sebastião do Boa Vista's municipal pond.
Richard was walking into town for his customary ice cream from a recommended *sorvetaria* when he saw a park-keeper throwing bits of fish
into a large concrete tank. The resultant explosions were ferocious as

several vast fish fought for scraps. There were eight enormous pirarucú under the weeds, all of them a good 6 feet long and deep-bellied, with attractive red stripes on their dorsal fins. This bony-tongued fish is carnivorous, a predator, and capable of breathing air. Despite its bulk, it has been known to leap clear of the water and snatch small birds off low-hanging branches. Richard thought it was worth sending a man off for 2 reals worth of fish bait to repeat the show.

The pirarucú, also known as the arapaima (*Arapaima gigas*) is the world's second largest freshwater fish and can weigh in at up to 550 lb. (The largest is the European catfish *Siluris glanis* – one 15-foot monster hauled from the Dneiper river in Russia was 720 lb). But the pirarucú has been overfished – its scabrous tongue is used by Indians as a grater – and specimens caught today are likely to be a mere 220 lb.

At 3.30 p.m. on 1 September we were crossing the Pará at a point where it resembles an inland sea something like the Sea of Japan. We were trying to pass between the Ilha do Urubucuá and the Ilha do Capim. I noticed half a ship protruding at an angle from the river a couple of hundred yards away. A quick glance at the chart alerted me to the danger. 'Sandbank dead ahead!' I yelled to the helmsman, who, not understanding a word of English, just smiled back at me. 'What the devil's Portuguese for sandbank?' I cried in frustration, but neither Yoli nor Geraldo was to be seen. 'Stop. Reverse,' I gesticulated at Capitão Caetano, who had come up to see what the trouble was about. Peering at the approaching channel he shrugged, 'No problem, Colonel. Plenty water.' Then the good ship *Viagra* shuddered to a halt. '*Banco de areia*' ('Sandbank') grunted her captain.

'Do you want a tow?' teased Jim over the radio.

The ship's engine revved to a high-pitched whine, the crew ran about shouting, the chief engineer came up from below like Quasimodo, deafened by bells, and the cheerful songs of Roberto Villar continued to throb *fortissimo* from the on-board music system.

We were clearly hard aground, and soon settled at a slight angle. Several thoughts crossed my mind: How much did the river dry out here? Perhaps *Viagra* did not have a flat bottom. Would *KM3* get alongside us before the tide ebbed and it became too shallow for her? Moments later there was a lurch and the angle of list increased to 15°. The wind got up, there was a flurry of rain, and waves started breaking over the sandbank.

Marcelo had informed the *marinho* at Belém that we were aground, and it was not long before flashing blue lights were seen coming up from the east. Although it looked like a police car, it was in fact a Brazilian Navy launch.

Moving aft from my office area I saw Ernie leaning against a bulkhead. He was preparing the evening meal.

'How are you managing in the galley at 15°?' I asked him.

'With difficulty,' he said. 'No, actually it's OK. I'm half pissed, so things seem to adjust themselves.'

In the event he roasted six chickens and cooked rice with a salad. It was not as hard to eat as it must have been to cook, but nevertheless some platefuls slid across the gimbal-less galley table and were lost.

In the gathering dusk there was a chastening moment. A local man paddled up to us in his dugout canoe. Two children sat with him. They waved in friendly greeting and then jumped into the water, which came up to the thigh of the six-year-old.

By 6.30 p.m. the waterline at *Viagra*'s bow showed we were in just 2 feet. But the turn of the tide had been found to occur at 7.15, so we had not long to go.

'What do we do now?' asked Geoff Hoskins, who had been struggling to count the cash in the treasurer's box, as the list increased.

'Will your box float?' I asked; then added, 'Let's have a drink. There's nothing else we can do – except pray!' So as the tilt reached 20° we leaned on the rail clutching our tumblers of J&B and watched the sun sinking into the Amazon.

It was time for the post-prandial evening briefing. Was it my memories of the film *Titanic* that subconsciously caused me to have the briefing at the stern? When I began in military fashion with the word 'Situation' it was received with laughter. 'Delicately poised,' said a voice. 'Sounds more and more like Captain Mainwaring,' said another. But as the briefing progressed there were more lurches – comforting ones this time – and the ship slowly righted herself.

KM3, drawing only a few inches anyway, had slipped from the mother ship at 8 p.m. and sought a mooring on the Ilha do Urubucuá. At 10 p.m. *Viagra* followed. It was good to be afloat again. Richard remembered how he had been with John Wilsey in his Sandhurst colleague's converted Watson lifeboat in the Normandy port of Diélette on an ebb tide, and how the keel had bounced on the harbour floor and they had not fixed both the wooden legs on in time. The boat had canted over and smashed one of the legs against the granite harbour wall. Happily

Viagra was now cruising through the darkness with the Brazilian Navy launch still attentively standing by.

A confused night followed. There seemed to be a problem over exactly where on the shores of the Ilha do Urubucuá we should moor. The whole Furo do Capim channel is shown on the charts as being subject to drying out, and I was not clear why Capitão Caetano thought it would be better to go close inshore. We had suffered damage by going aground – the water tank on the top deck had slopped over and, worse than that, many litres of diesel in the hold had spilled.

Then at 2 a.m. there was great commotion everywhere. *Viagra* moved forward, revved, reversed. Bells rang. Chiefie slammed his engine telegraph handle from DEVAGAR to MEIA FORÇA to TODA FORÇA and back again to DEVAGAR. The computer on which Richard was still working in the *escritorio* began to dance on the table. The wind started to get up. So did some expedition members. Marigold and Geoffrey were wandering around in their life-jackets asking, I think jestingly, where the attached whistle was.

Then came a flurry of shouts in Portuguese and I felt myself sliding off my foam sleeping-mat. 'Oh Lord, he's done it again,' I thought.

'He cannae be moving yet again,' said Jenny from her hammock.

The first mate, in a white T-shirt, ran ashore carrying a long line.

'Are they trying to bring the stern round?' asked Geoffrey.

'No. I think they're trying to stop *Viagra* from keeling right over,' Marigold replied. Beaching the bow of these large riverboats at night was common practice, but clearly our captain had not appreciated the much increased tidal range as we neared the ocean.

By 6 a.m. *KM3* had detached herself and moved 150 yards up the beach. *Viagra* lay, listing ominously, at an angle of 45° to the shoreline. Her crew and half our team were in the water trying to prop up the stricken vessel with logs they found along the island's jungle fringe. The bows were resting on a beach of compressed mud – virtually stone – and, more crucially, the stern was also firmly wedged. And the tide was still falling.

The port bow was now shored up and more logs were being pushed under the keel to stop the back breaking. *Viageiro IV*, a *barco motor* built in 1985, was now the boat at risk and no longer the support ship to *KM3*, the subject of our three months' navigational experiments. Jim, Pat, Jon Paul, Drew, Barry, Bill and Graham were all hock-deep in the sludgy water carrying beams and hauling ropes. Geoffrey found he could not open the *ele* door, and when Richard tried to secure the *escritorio* the key would not turn in the lock: *Viagra* was twisting in her agony, and was so warped that the doors had jammed.

A ship grounded fore and aft but not centrally is very unstable. The tide would go on ebbing until 7.45 a.m. Would the boat roll over? There was a nervous edge to our banter. Long warps were now strung out from *Viagra*'s starboard side to the trunks of trees at the forest's edge. Piums, the unpleasant native flies, were homing in on us. But luckily it was now becoming light and the rain had eased.

It was all a bit surreal: Drew was thigh deep in water, shoving beams under the ship's keel; Ernie, unconcerned, was preparing breakfast in the *cozinha*; Caroline Ralph was debating with herself whether to stay with her credit cards or go ashore. In the event she did both: strapping on her bumbag, she climbed gingerly down the ship's side and sought safety on land. 'I think we should be told whether it is the captain's plan to go aground every night or not,' she said.

At 8.15 a.m. on 2 September *Viagra* assumed an upright position and rose from the river bed on a rising tide. The Marinho do Brasil launch had left fifteen minutes earlier. Our somewhat bruised fleet moved off on the final leg to Belém.

After crossing a broad tributary of the Pará, we chose to sneak through a final *paraná* to our last overnight stop, Barcarena. Youths jumping from a high jetty bombed the already battered *Southern Gailes*, climbed on to her, and had to be bawled out by Geraldo. Otherwise it was an uneventful visit to a quiet town – a restful Monday after a stressful Sunday.

We ate ashore, and made good friends with some local teachers. Our custom of playing soccer at every port of call had fallen into abeyance. I thought at first that this might have been because at Itacoatiara our team had said goodbye to Craig Cocks, an HSBC man who had once had a trial for Millwall. But on reflection it was because almost every place we had recently visited had been too waterlogged. Endless square miles of *igapó* stretched behind the houses where up-country there would have been a soccer pitch. I suppose we could have offered to take them on at water polo.

Early explorers of the Amazon were accustomed to seeing virtually naked Indians, painted, be-feathered and clad only in beads or a small apron. If any of us harboured any illusions that we might witness the same thing in 2001 they were to be disappointed: all along the busy Madeira–Amazon river line Indians appeared, like other Brazilians, in western attire. Only in remote reservations in the interior might one today find Indians as H. M. Tomlinson and the crew of the *Capella* saw them in the Madeira settlements.

But the appearance of young Brazilian women now seemed in some way to echo the undress order of the past. Street wear for young girls in Barcarena is minimal, which is sensible in the heat and humidity of Pará province. They wear either a microskirt, like a tea-towel with its ends sewn together and not much over a foot deep, or a pair of denim shorts cut below the umbilicus and giving the appearance of having been sprayed on. A bra top is very often enough above the waist, or a top with a brief panel in front and boot-lace ties across the back. Lipstick and nail varnish – but sadly no feathers these days – complete the ensemble.

As we rounded the northernmost corner of the Ilha das Onças next morning, we caught our first exciting glimpse of the high-rise buildings of Belém on the far shore. In no way did it look like its namesake, Bethlehem, in Israel.

The passage across to the city was a sporting one, and a final test of our mettle. Both watches, Jim's and Pat's, had had rough runs in these last few days. Crossing the Pará in a force-5 wind, Pat's crew had seen waves coming over the now headless prow of *KM3* and flooding the decks. The cool-box for Patricio's cameras and film and the plastic water-container were swept aft and nearly lost.

Now Jim was butting against an incoming tide, and the freshening wind from the nearby Atlantic caused his array of flags to snap like ring-master's whips. They made a brave show. The Brazilian standard flew highest, then came Bolivia's and Great Britain's. The Stars and Stripes flew for Eric Niemi and Bill Holmes, the Colombian flag for Yoli, the Sri Lankan for Peter Kannangara, and of course there was the Jersey flag that has always brought me luck. The flag of St George was there too, and J. P. Knight's blue house flag and Air BP's banners. On the sterns of *KM3* and *Southern Gailes* the red ensign flapped proudly.

We were in busy shipping lanes again. *Ivan Susanin* of Murmansk, carrying bauxite away to Russia, nearly rammed *KM3* astern. Soon we came into the shelter of a maritime knacker's yard where old barges and their pushers lay rusting. Our bow line snaked ashore, and was caught and tied. The long journey was over. We had reached Belém – albeit at one of its less savoury suburbs. Now came the hectic preparations for our formal arrival in the city centre next day.

Ernie had all spare hands packing stores, and Peter Kannangara sat at his computer passing our final report to the Affno web site. Since reaching the Amazon his PC had refused to function without the aid of a large domestic table-fan which blasted it with cool air. Congratulatory e-mails started coming in from around the world – many from people we'd never met who had followed our progress on the web site.

Yoli handed me a fax. 'Who do you know who lives at a Balmoral Castle?' she asked. 'It's signed by Elizabeth R.' This personal message from Her Majesty Queen Elizabeth II was read out to the team that evening, and clearly moved even the foreigners among us.

At our final briefing Jim said, 'I must admit that at Pôrto Velho I had thought this phase was going to be a doddle – a trip for old ladies. I couldn't have been more wrong. It was not easy or boring: something different seemed to happen every day.'

'Be very careful when you go ashore,' warned Marcelo. 'The "water rats" are especially active here. You should go in groups of three.' Thankfully no one was mugged, and on the morning of 6 September, as coxless fours from the Belém Rowing Club came scudding past, TAM and Varig planes dropped low on their approach to Belém Airport. We were now in another world.

We had brought a traditional balsa raft and a reed boat – battered, stinking and only two-thirds of its original size – to their destination. We had proved not that the same had been done in past centuries, but that it could have been done.

A reception had been laid on for us at the *Flutuante*, the floating quay on Belém's river front, which bobs up and down on the tide close to a magnificent new development, the Estacão do Docas. The original port development at Belém had been the achievement of Percival Farquhar, the Pennsylvanian Quaker who had finally managed to build the Madeira–Mamoré railway between 1907 and 1912. Three giant warehouses, with lofty mobile cranes running on rails in front of them, had for years dominated the Belém skyline. By the end of the twentieth century maritime trade had become much reduced and was now carried on in a separate port district. The authorities in Belém had recently converted the three redundant warehouses to an ultra-modern, glass-fronted, interconnected shopping-mall with restaurants and arts-and-craft boutiques. Inside the food hall, the old overhead pulleys slung from rails in the roof had been adapted to convey music-makers up and down the hall in a suspended tray.

It was to the *Flutuante* that our fleet was to come on the morning of

6 September. A characteristically boisterous wind filled *KM3*'s sails and sped her upriver to the quay, but turning into it to berth up was difficult, and while the waiting crowds held their breath she slowly clawed her way in on her motor.

Hugh and Eliza Beveridge were there, and Admiral Kleber and Captain Stephen Timms, the British naval attaché. The British consul came and the HSBC regional chief, the DHL manager, BP's boss and many others. Flavio Serique had organized a band from Cultura Inglesa wearing nineteenth-century British military uniforms to play us in, and a colourful troupe of dancers gyrated on the quayside. It was a great welcome.

A Brazilian naval band then took over. There were speeches. Caterers arrived. We received our guests on the upper deck of *Viageiro IV*. There were more speeches, and Her Majesty's letter was read out. Then we presented our reed flagship to the Brazilian Navy. The senior officer present looked a little perplexed, but accepted her with good grace.

'There cannot be many expeditions that have increased the size of the local navy,' remarked Bill Holmes as he sipped a welcome glass of Californian Chardonnay – the first decent white wine we had tasted in eighteen weeks.

17

New York, New York

This was the bloodiest day on American soil since our Civil War, a modern Antietam [in which 10,000 Confederate troops died in 1862] played out in real time, on fast forward, and not with soldiers but with secretaries, security guards, lawyers, bankers, janitors.

Nancy Gibbs, *Time*, special 11 September 2001 issue

THIS CHAPTER HAS nothing to do with reed boats, ancient peoples, rivers, rapids, coca, rubber, *KM3*, *Capitão Azevedo* or *Viageiro IV*. It is the story of how nine members of the expedition took ten days to get back from Belém to Britain.

Varig flew them effortlessly to São Paulo, where they knew they had to wait overnight. This stopover – inconvenient, resented by some, but not uncomfortable – was spent in a hotel found for them by the efficient tourist-information desk at the airport. 'This is not São Paulo,' a girl said. 'This is another city called Guarulhos, which is the name of this airport. You don't need to go into São Paulo unless you want to. It's a 35 reals taxi ride.' So they stayed in Guarulhos, and flew from there to New York the next evening.

Even transit passengers arriving at John F. Kennedy Airport have to pass through US Immigration and customs. This they did, swiftly and unhindered, and they were able to join their flight to London Heathrow, AA142, in good time for an 8.30 departure on the morning of Tuesday 11 September.

The Boeing 777 was fairly empty as the cabin crew moved about closing overhead-bin lids. It was already 8.40. 'Sorry about the delay,' said the captain. 'We've had a slight technical problem at this time, and as soon as I've signed the clearance log we'll be off. Keep your seat belts fastened and I'll come back to you when I know something more.'

As the cabin crew came round with newspapers, Jim Masters idly looked out the plane window and a saw a factory chimney pouring out black smoke. Was it a power station? 'Look at that, Sam. I'm surprised that New York allows such pollution.' 'That's not a factory chimney. It's the World Trade Center. One of the towers is on fire.'

'This is the captain again. I have to tell you that there's been a terrible accident. A plane has crashed into one of the World Trade Center towers.' Cellphones and pocket radios came out. The news soon filtered through that a Boeing 767 had been hijacked.

It was the archaeologist who saw what happened next. Bruce Mann, glancing out of his window, distantly witnessed the most shattering impact in the history of the twenty-first century so far – he saw the second hijacked Boeing 767 from Logan International Airport in Boston hurtle into the side of the second World Trade Center tower and a rolling ball of ignited aviation fuel emerge from an adjacent side. This was not prehistory, but the most horrible manifestation of a war between the United States and her faceless, fiendishly well-organized, obsessively driven enemies. Prehistory, with its funerary urns in the plains of the Beni, awaited Bruce the following year, but for now it was the brutal present, history after Fukuyama's End of History. The Japanese historian had declared that the collapse of world Communism and the triumph of capitalism marked the closing of an era, after which there would be little to get excited about. The events of 11 September seemed set fair to overturn this judgement.

Everyone sat dumbfounded. At 9.40 all passengers were told to leave the plane and gather in the baggage-reclaim area. Every aircraft in JFK, incoming and outgoing, received the same order. It led to chaos as thwarted passengers milled five deep round virtually empty luggage carousels. 'There's a hundred containers out there,' an airport worker told Richard. No information came down to the overcrowded hall. People waited with surprising forbearance as an over-reactive official closed all the loos. On a TV screen, the CNN news channel showed the two towers billowing smoke. Americans and non-Americans stared in disbelief.

Moments later there was a sudden gasp of horror as one of the towers collapsed, agonizingly slowly imploding on itself in clouds of concrete, steel and glass. It dropped vertically in the same time that Carl Lewis had taken to pound down the 100-metres track to win at Sydney, and forced billows of dark-grey dust and smoke along the grid of neighbouring streets and avenues.

It was not long before the second tower fell and a New York landmark, familiar since the early 1970s, was gone.

Bill Holmes, gathering information, told the others that the situation was worse than they had so far thought. A total of four aircraft had been hijacked – two from Boston and one each from Newark and Washington. Our party was still waiting for its baggage to appear when news came that the Pentagon had been hit by one of the planes. Another was still in the air.

With bags retrieved, our group of eight (one had left for Manhattan immediately on arrival from São Paulo at 6 a.m.) stood outside on the airport concourse. An F-16 fighter plane speared across the sky. It seemed a very long time since they had been on the broad, brown Madeira watching pink dolphins lazily surfacing for gulps of air.

Slowly came the realization that a great many lives had been lost. Fifty thousand people normally work in the twin towers and the surrounding areas, but at 8.45 not all would have reached their offices and it was to be hoped that many others would have had time to escape. Some 266, including the hijackers, were in the crashed planes – the fourth had now come down in southern Pennsylvania. All flights had been cancelled *sine die*, but it seemed churlish to feel bad about the predicament the *Kota Mama* group was now in. America was under attack, and soon after was on a war footing.

A courtesy bus took the party to the JFK Airport Holiday Inn – a matchbox on end amid trim lawns, with a busy freeway behind. Bill Holmes told a policeman that there were two doctors in the group, and presently Sam Allen and Michelle Phillips were whisked away to Manhattan in an NYPD patrol car. They went to Chelsea Piers and into a large hangar-like building with eighty stations, each with a surgeon, a physician, a nurse and an orderly. Drip sets hung above them. White gowns bustled about. But the awful truth soon dawned – there were no patients. A few construction workers came in with inhalation problems, and some policemen with grit in their eyes and a fibrillating heart or two, but all those office workers in the 110 storeys of the two towers had either run for it or were as dead as the occupants of the two Boeings that had thundered into them.

Our two doctors moved from the St Vincent's Hospital area south towards the mountain of rubble that had been the twin towers. A fine dust lay thickly everywhere. Smoke spiralled upward, and Sam especially remembered the papers blowing about the streets – the contents of countless filing-cabinets, the secrets of unnumbered litigants, the contracts made by scores of businessmen.

Sam and Michelle stayed overnight. Their workload increased in the morning, but the expected rush never came. Pitifully few bodies were prised out of the tangled ruins.

Barry Igoe had the closest call. He had left JFK Airport as soon as he had cleared customs, shortly after 6 a.m., and had taken a cab into Manhattan for a day or two's sightseeing in the Big Apple. He had headed south straight away, hoping, in all innocence, to visit the World Trade Center and take the lift to the top for the fabulous view: Battery Park, Ellis Island, the Statue of Liberty, distant Staten Island and New Jersey. Feeling peckish, he stopped at a deli and went in for a sandwich. Fifteen minutes later he resumed his walk only to hear a low-flying aircraft which, though unseen behind the high-rise buildings, Barry heard immolating itself in the side of tower number one. His hunger had saved him.

Lunching a few days later in the Brooklyn Diner on Third Avenue, Faanya Rose, president of the Explorers Club, told Richard, 'Your American Airlines plane was due to take off from JFK at 0835. The four hijacked planes – two American and two United – took off from neighbouring airports at 0800 or so. The hijackers might have targeted yours too. You are survivors, all of you.'

'Yes, but we hoped to be survivors of the Beni, the Mamoré, the Madeira and the Amazon.'

The dollars were haemorrhaging away at the Holiday Inn, despite the blind eye that some waiters turned on a few members of our group when bills were to be presented after the buffet breakfast. When they finally checked out, Ernie had to dig deep into his treasury. No matter, they were booked on to a Thursday flight and were all off to JFK. Flight numbers and times had been confirmed by the tireless Melissa Dice in Motcombe and by Jim in New York.

At the airport an air of unreality prevailed. The outside precincts were all open, but a long queue tailed from the harassed girl at the information desk and a smiling black heavyweight stood four-square at the entrance to the check-in hall and barred all prospective fliers. A Saudi national with a false pilot's licence and dressed in a Delta Air Lines pilot's uniform had earlier been stopped and taken into custody. He had carried an airline ticket dated 11 September. The Federal Aviation Administration had blocked all flights once again.

All public payphones in the airport were down. Hotels, gorged on the increasing backlog of frustrated passengers, were now full, and would-be travellers were sleeping in lobbies and car parks. Borrowing an official telephone, the group with difficulty found three rooms in the nearby JFK Inn. This expedition remnant was now slipping downmarket, for the JFK Inn was cramped and uncongenial. But frantic, stranded travellers will pay good dollars for almost any sort of bed, and our team was happy to be under a roof when, after days of unbroken sunshine, rain was now seen to be pelting down from leaden skies.

At 11.30 p.m. guests were roused from the beginnings of sleep by a repeated beating on bedroom doors. When opened, these revealed NYPD officers shouting, 'Everybody out and down into the parking lot!' The entire hotel was emptied and its heterogeneous occupants were herded out into the rain until the problem, whose cause was never revealed and remains undiscovered, was solved and all were allowed back to their rooms.

America was jumpy. Bomb scares in New York were legion. All leads were being followed up – including, no doubt, numerous hoaxes. Jim and Paul, out on the street using a satellite phone to talk to Melissa, were seen by a zealous citizen and questioned. Shortly after, a posse of police arrived to investigate the report and take copies of their passports.

Our group slowly found friends who offered beds or floor space. Some stayed with Barbara and David Price, whose charming English-country-house apartment lies in New York's smart Upper East Side between the Madison coffee house and a sex shop called Come Again. Barbara had been with me in Panama and Nepal, and had played a leading part in Operation Drake in the 1970s. Bill Holmes and Bruce Mann were with Duke Savage, lawyer husband of Ann, my co-author in Operation Raleigh days, who was away at this time in her Scottish home. Sam Allen stayed with Armenian relatives.

It was still a jittery time. When would flights be resumed out of JFK? Could we take a train to Montreal or Toronto and fly from there? Do ships still leave from the East Side quays? Would an American Airlines early-morning departure be hit a second time? What would we do if there were some Arab passengers waiting with us in that last airport limbo?

In the event the whole party of eight arrived safely at London Heathrow late on Wednesday 19 September. 'I felt like doing a Pope John Paul,' said Richard, 'but it seemed a bit naff to kiss the carpet in a Terminal Three walkway.'

18

Aftermath

It'll show some of the cynical, fainthearted sods on this earth that nothing is impossible, that if you put your bloody mind to something you should keep at the bastard until you win.

Tristan Jones, *The Incredible Voyage*, 1977

THE INTERNATIONAL OFFICE of the Association of Universities in Belém had asked Yoli, Marcelo and me to give a presentation on *Kota Mama* at the Goeldi Museum in Belém on 10 September, so I was not with Ernie and the other eight members who had left to fly home via New York on the 9th. However, at dawn on the 11th Yoli and I boarded a Varig flight to São Paulo. She would go on to Santa Cruz to discuss the next *Kota Mama* project with Alan Raven and others, then on to La Paz to brief the prefect and our Bolivian supporters on the results of this year's expedition. I was going home via New York.

Our plane was late, and as we reached the arrival gate Yoli ran for her connecting flight to Bolivia. At the American Airlines check-in I found the staff in some distress, and quickly learned of the terrorist attacks. I spent the rest of the day in the Diners Club lounge bemused by TV replays of the awful atrocity. I wondered what had happened to the nine of our team that had been flying into New York with American Airlines that very morning. As the full extent of the hijackings became known, I didn't imagine the American Airlines staff would have much time for one traveller who was perfectly safe at São Paulo. However, with commendable efficiency and helpfulness they diverted me on to a British Airways flight direct to London.

Yoli knew nothing of the events in America until she reached Santa Cruz. One of her calls there was at the offices of *El Deber*, a major newspaper that wished to do an article on our expedition. While researching into Hans Ertl's past we had heard of neo-Nazi paramilitary groups from

Bolivia and Brazil carrying out training exercises in the Mato Grosso in the 1970s. It was said that they had been discovered and attacked by both Brazilian and Bolivian armed forces, and largely wiped out. *El Deber* was thought to have published an account of this. Indeed, friends in Santa Cruz remembered reading it. So, when the interview was over, Yoli remarked to the woman reporter, 'I'm interested in the story of a battle between the military and some neo-Nazi groups in the seventies. Is it possible to get any information about this from your archives?' The friendly journalist seemed eager to help and thought it would be no problem. She went off to seek the material. Some fifteen minutes later she returned. 'There is nothing here,' she said coldly, and left. Noting the sudden change of tone, Yoli decided not to press the enquiry.

Next day, back at the hotel in La Paz, Yoli collected her locked grip from the secure left-luggage store. It felt a little light, and she soon found out why. The bag had been expertly slit open along a seam. Some clothes and jewellery had been taken but, strangely, so had her files containing research information for the *Kota Mama* project. These would hardly be of much value to a casual thief. Whoever had taken them must have obtained the key to the only door in the windowless store, which is right beside the reception desk. The hotel manager could offer no explanation. The police were called; a former staff member was suspected; a full report was promised. Six months later, in spite of numerous phone calls, faxes and e-mails, there was no response from the hotel management. 'How peculiar!' we thought.

Back in Britain, immersed in the usual host of post-expedition tasks, I was delighted to have a call from my old friend Jim Allen, whose theories that Bolivia was a possible site of the legendary lost city of Atlantis we had helped to investigate during the *Kota Mama* expedition in 1998. We talked of Ertl's involvement with Hitler's quest for Atlantis, which was believed by some Nazis to have been the original home of the Aryan race. I told Jim of our work at Cerro Paititi, and this led on to our discussing other archaeological sites where the *Ahnenerbe* had sought evidence of German links with superior early civilizations. 'The Nazis are supposed to have occupied an ancient city in eastern Peru,' remarked Jim – 'on the Amazon headwaters, near the Brazilian border. It's called Akakor.' 'Akakor, Akakor,' I blurted out – 'I know that name', and I remembered the little old man in the trilby hat at Mapiri.

It took only a few visits to the Internet to unearth an outline account of this place. Before 10,000 BC, it is alleged, a great city had been founded in the mountains between Brazil and Peru. It was said to be surrounded by no fewer than twenty-six other stone-built cities, of which one of the largest was Paititi. It had disappeared following a catastrophe – probably an earthquake.

In AD 570 a thousand white-skinned, bearded foreigners named Goths had reached Akakor in forty ships. Always fascinated by history, I recalled having read about the Ostrogoths at school. This tribe of fierce warriors of Germanic origin had invaded and occupied Italy, but had eventually been defeated by the Roman general Narses in AD 553. The tribe then disappeared, although certain words of their language are believed to be found in the south of France and Spain.

According to Karl Brugger, a German journalist who wrote a book called *The Chronicle of Akakor*, these Ostrogoths were capable sailors and some reached South America and Akakor. Brugger did a great deal of research into the legend. He thought it possible that Hitler and his henchman Heinrich Himmler, intrigued by the story, had sent a U-boat to reconnoitre the lower reaches of the Amazon as early as 1938, and in 1941, after contact had been made with an Indian who knew the location of Akakor, they had sent soldiers to occupy it. More troops, it was said, followed right up to 1945, and the Brazilian government considered it likely that Germany was planning to invade. Was Akakor part of this plan? Was this just another fanciful legend, or might there be a grain of truth in it? Unfortunately we can't ask Brugger. He was shot dead under mysterious circumstances in Manaus some while ago.

Still seeking Ertl's real purpose in going to Cerro Paititi, I came across yet another strange account. A day or so before the Second World War ended, two German submarines sailed from the Baltic. The U-530 and U-977 slipped past Allied ships and out into the Atlantic. In July and August 1945 they surrendered in Argentina. Who and what they carried, and where they had been long after the war in Europe ended, has never been fully revealed, in spite of various accounts by their crews.

Interestingly, in 1991 the *New York Times* reported that Hitler's deputy, Martin Bormann, had directed an operation to ship concentration-camp booty to Argentina by submarine. Nazi records are said to show that 550,000 ounces of gold, 3,500 ounces of platinum and 4,638 carats of diamonds were dispatched, as well as many works of art and a huge quantity of currency notes. But when U-530 and U-977 surrendered they were empty.

Bormann himself was originally believed to have been killed while trying to escape from Berlin through the Russian lines with a tank, and a skeleton found in Berlin in 1972 was firmly identified as his from anthropometric analysis of the jawbones and teeth. Nevertheless, rumours of his survival persist. Since 1945, claims to have sighted him have come from a dozen countries, and several reports linked the notorious Nazi to South America. In Peru, a master forger named Don Federico Schwend had appeared. A pal of Klaus Barbie, Schwend had worked on a project to undermine Britain's economy in the Second World War by flooding the UK with forged British banknotes. When arrested for currency offences he had a framed photo of Bormann on his desk, and he told the Peruvian police, 'Bormann is alive. I have met him frequently.' Indeed, there was a story that in south-eastern Paraguay Bormann had set up an estate called Waldner 555, not so very far from the original colony of Nueva Germánia created by Elisabeth Nietzsche and others in 1886. We had met a number of former German soldiers and their sons in Paraguay during earlier *Kota Mama* expeditions.

If all this were true, did Bormann get to South America by U-boat? If so, who exactly was aboard those two submarines that surrendered in Argentina? There was even an extraordinary suggestion that the Führer himself, the location of whose remains has long been disputed, might have been a passenger! Fifty-six years after the collapse of the Third Reich, all this would have seemed very far-fetched and rather irrelevant had it not been for the strange event surrounding our investigation of an ancient site in the Andean foothills.

South America is a land of many mysteries, and our expedition seemed to have unearthed more than it had solved. However, we had located and investigated Ertl's 'Paititi' and many other important archaeological sites. The medical team's work had been greatly appreciated, and Graham Catchpole's tally of extractions had reached 1,125. Hopefully our wildlife studies may do something to encourage conservation, and the community tasks carried out by the engineers will be of lasting benefit to Guanay. Most importantly, the links established between children across the Atlantic should help foster understanding and friendship in this war-torn world.

Finally, the arrival of *Kota Mama 3* and *Southern Gailes* in Belém had shown that the ancient people of central South America could have reached the ocean by this route, although at this stage it cannot be proved that they did. However, the axe-heads discovered along our route indicated the probability of early trade, either in finished tools or in raw materials.

It had been a very long haul, and much of the journey on the Beni, Madeira and Amazon had, as Jim had forecast at our pre-departure briefing in Dorset, been monotonous and boring for the reed-boat crew. Of course there had been differences of opinion, and once or twice tempers had flared. However, compared with most of the large expeditions I had led, these incidents had been relatively minor. The administrative and logistic battle had been every bit as difficult as the archaeology, community aid and navigation – and at times more so – but by and large we had remained a well motivated, effective and cheerful team. The public are always fascinated by the interplay of human relationships, and some feel that these are the most titillating part of an otherwise successful venture. However, it is my firm policy never to discuss this subject. I have seen enough anguish and hurt caused by criticism of people's behaviour when read at a later date in a different environment by families and friends.

On the whole the weather had been kind, and, with the exception of a few sinister folk, we had been welcomed by the local people all along our route and had been encouraged by the governments to continue with our work in South America.

Back at expedition base in late 2001, Melissa and Yoli were firing off e-mails to arrange an operation for little Ronalda, the girl with the cleft palate we had seen on the Madeira. Since his return, Jim Masters had worked tirelessly to raise the money for an operation to be carried out in Brazil. We all felt the importance of fulfilling our promise to try to help the poorer people of the river, who had been so kind to us.

By early February 2002 some £4,000 had been collected for Ronalda's operation, and Richard Drax, the presenter from BBC South TV who had been with us from Guanay to Rurrenabaque, took out the funds. Safely back in Dorset, a week later Richard told me his story.

'Having flown in to São Paulo, I took a local flight to Portõ Velho,' he said as I poured him a Scotch. 'Then it was five hours by bus to Humaitá.' I remembered the sprawling little town on the banks of the Rio Madeira from when we had tied up there in July. 'From there,' continued Richard, 'I travelled with an interpreter downstream in pouring rain for seven hours in a small motor boat, and after a trudge along a muddy jungle trail we found a dugout canoe which we paddled to Ronalda's home'. At the door of the thatched wooden hut, Rosie, Ronalda's mother, greeted Richard. 'You are a day early,' she smiled, her dark eyes twinkling with pleasure. Although only twenty-five, she already had six children and was carrying a seventh. Word of the amazing good fortune that had come about when she stepped aboard our support vessel *Capitão Azevedo* six months before had been passed to her by the Brazilian charity Sobrapar, which is supported by the US-based international body Smile Train, which Melissa had contacted via the Internet.

'I spotted Ronalda immediately,' said Richard. 'She was standing behind her mother, one hand placed protectively over her deformed mouth. Her beautiful eyes were fixed on me.'

A small open boat with a motor was ready for the return trip, and Richard found himself sitting with Rosie, Ronalda and two other children in the flimsy craft as it threaded its way through the black jungle night. 'My only thought was which child I'd try to rescue if we capsized,' he said. Eight long hours later, three of them in darkness, the lights of Humaitá welcomed them.

After a night's rest the little party boarded a bus for Campinas, some way inland of São Paulo. The journey took three days, but a guardian angel awaited them. Nilva Fornasare works for Dr Cassio Raposo do Amaral, the surgeon at the Craniofacial Plastic Surgery Hospital, and this wonderfully kind lady took over. The hospital had been set up by Dr Cassio in 1979, and treats, cares for and rehabilitates patients with facial deformities. Sadly there are many in the Amazon region. After an initial examination, little Ronalda had a special treat: Richard took them all to the zoo and provided copious ice creams.

Then came the first of several operations. Richard filmed the little form disappearing into the operating theatre on a trolley, and watched as gowned surgeons and assistants surrounded her. Seconds before she slipped into unconsciousness, Ronalda's brown eyes settled on Dr Cassio's wife, Vera. A psychologist, she'd spent hours preparing the child for this moment. The eyes were peaceful and trusting.

Two hours later Dr Cassio had closed one cleft lip. Two weeks later he would tackle the other, and then the cleft palate.

'What happened when the little girl woke up?' I asked.

'Ronalda was clearly in pain and very distressed,' said Richard. 'But Rosie comforted her, and the next morning she'd recovered and was soon playing with her mum and Vera.'

As Richard left, Rosie gripped his hand, tears rolling down her cheeks. They were tears of gratitude. 'I am so thankful that now my daughter will look like me,' she said. So a life had been transformed, thanks to her chance meeting with a group of crazy explorers riding a bale of straw to the sea.

The funds raised were more than enough for Ronalda's treatment, and so we decided also to help a Bolivian child at Mapiri whom Sam Allen had seen at the start of the expedition. She is suffering from suspected Burkitt's lymphoma, a form of cancer in children, and as luck would have it Patricio Crooker's uncle is the director of the children's hospital in La Paz and thus can help.

Another breakthrough came at the SES Grand Reunion of past expeditioners in February 2002. Viscount Shane Gough, who had been on Operation Drake, generously offered to donate £20,000 to start a trust fund which would allow us to give further medical assistance to needy South American children.

However, although there were successes, we had problems too. For reasons beyond our understanding, the expedition stores that Ernie had so lovingly packed up at Belém were still there in early 2002, held up by Brazilian customs, who demanded £8,000 in duty. 'The customs are a law unto themselves in Brazil,' said an old business pal of mine. Our balsa raft, *Southern Gailes*, was there too, and as it was destined to go on display at a new golf course being built by the sponsor near Glasgow we had to get it back. For six months faxes, phone calls and e-mails flashed across the Atlantic. The British Embassy did all it could to help, and so did our good friend Hugh Beveridge. In the end it was Hugh's colleagues in Brazil who unblocked the logjam and, once a 'fine' for late submission of some documents by the shipping agent had been paid, our stores were dispatched. 'Don't ask me to run the logistics for another expedition in Brazil,' groaned Ernie – 'it's a nightmare.' We all agreed that the bureaucracy was enough to wear down even the most seasoned explorer.

There was sad news from Santarém, where our stalwart supporter Flavio Serique had died suddenly. Although seriously disabled, Flavio had long championed Anglo-Brazilian relations with his Cultura Inglesa organization. His good cheer and helpfulness will never be forgotten.

Shirley Critchley was lecturing almost nightly to raise funds for a school project in Mapiri that we plan to tackle on the next *Kota Mama* expedition. In preparation for this, maps and aerial photographs of mountains and inhospitable terrain were spread across the SES conference-room table. The coffee cups piled up and the lights burned late as once again we got ready to tackle a formidable jungle quest. There were charts too of the Southern Atlantic, which a planning team was already working on the possibility of crossing from west to east by traditional craft.

Aftermath

I was reminded of a quotation by Will Henry of the *Chicago Tribune*. It appeared above the office door of US Army engineer Colonel Hans Rathe in the Panama Canal Zone when we were struggling across the infamous Darién Gap with Range Rovers in 1972. It read, 'Only he who attempts the ridiculous can achieve the impossible.'

Epilogue

In January 2002 I was preparing an address for the memorial service of our great supporter General Sir John Mogg. A cold had gone to my throat, and to my horror I lost my voice. 'If you're to deliver this speech in two days, you mustn't talk until then,' advised my doctor son-in-law, Will Cave, dosing me with some powerful medicine. So when a reporter from the *Sunday Telegraph* called I was loath to speak to him; but he insisted it was an important matter and wouldn't take long. However, it was neither a short nor a pleasant conversation. To my amazement, he came out with an extraordinary string of criticisms of the *Kota Mama 3* expedition by a couple of people whose names meant nothing to me. A Dr Alexei Vranich had attacked us for claiming to have found the legendary city of Paititi and said that our team had been ill-prepared for its task. He also claimed we had been told by the Bolivian Minister of Culture that everything there had been discovered before. None of this was true. Vranich – thought to be an American anthropologist – said he had spoken to a number of expedition members, and there were also claims that we had used petrol and dynamite to clear the rainforest, the reporter told me.

A Mr Faldin was quoted as having written a fifty-page report deeply critical of the expedition: he said our 'discoveries were worthless and from an archaeological perspective the expedition was a fraud'. Apparently Faldin was speaking as an official Bolivian spokesman. As we had not yet published any statement on our work, this was an ill-founded criticism.

I denied everything, pointing out that dynamite had been used only to clear boulders at the river crossing 10 miles from the archaeological site, not in the rainforest. And the idea of carrying petrol up into the mountains to set fire to the vegetation was preposterous. As a conservationist, I found this particular comment most offensive. I suggested that the reporter speak to our senior archaeologist, Bruce Mann, which he did not. Nor did he contact any of the journalists who had been with us.

The following Sunday an article attacking us appeared, with further comments added by a respected British archaeologist, Dr Elizabeth Currie. At once several of our team wrote to the editor, and a week later the *Sunday Telegraph* printed a five-column statement by me refuting the allegations under a bold headline 'Blashers' Worthwhile Adventure'.

By now I had discovered that Mr Faldin was in fact the Bolivian archaeologist we had known as Juan Domingo. From La Paz, Javier Escalante, the director of UNAR faxed me as follows:

> The National Unit of Archaeology (UNAR) under my direction, has received with surprise and annoyance the comments of the publication made by the British News Paper.
>
> At that respect I must say that neither the Inv. Juan Faldin nor UNAR have authorised any publication or criticism related to the project KOTA MAMA. The expedition was co-ordinated and supported by our institution and they accomplished all the terms of the agreement subscribed.
>
> In relation to the report from Inv. Juan Faldin I must say that his report only had scientific-technical contents, at no point is there mentioned any accusation or are described any misleading actions of any of the members of Kota Mama expedition and the report never mentioned damages to the patrimony of the archaeology or ecology of the region. On the contrary UNAR is very pleased with the work carried out by the Kota Mama project.
>
> We do hope you will return with our projects and continue with your plans programmed to research in our country.

So much for the tale of the fifty-page critical report!

Bruce Mann contacted Elizabeth Currie, who explained that a free-lance journalist in America who said she was working for the *Mail on Sunday*, had asked her to comment on our use of dynamite and petrol to clear archaeological sites. Later it transpired that the *Mail* had decided not to use the story but the *Sunday Telegraph* had. When the truth was put to her, Dr Currie told Bruce she supported us and wished us well.

Several newspapers and the BBC contacted me following the initial *Sunday Telegraph* article, but lost interest on hearing our side of the story. However, the *Jersey Evening Post*, whose reporter had been with us, came to our defence and had a field day. Alasdair Crosby did not mince his words about Juan Domingo Faldin's shortcomings in the jungle and ended with 'Now, suddenly, a cock-and-bull story attributed to Faldin is drawn to the attention of the British press. The story, the Colonel believes, is getting curiouser and curiouser.' Indeed it was, and if anything I was more puzzled than annoyed, for quite clearly someone was going to a great deal of trouble to discredit us. Why?

Yoli called from Bogotá. 'Do you think the British newspapers are confusing Sigfried Trippolt's claim to have found Paititi with our expedition?' she asked. 'After all, he dashed up there as soon as we left and issued a press statement to that effect.' However the key seemed to be Juan Domingo. Was all this, as Alasdair Crosby wrote, 'Faldín's revenge for the jungle torture'? Somehow I thought not. In spite of all our caution, there were many in Bolivia who desperately wanted us to prove that Paititi was there. There was even a poster produced in Guanay claiming the area to be 'The Home of Paititi'. Economic pressure was quick to outrun scientific proof. Some newspapers in Britain proclaimed a discovery, though admitting that I was 'cautious' about the claim. Those who e-mailed us in the field were told straight, 'We cannot claim to have located the legendary city, although it is a fascinating site.'

So great was the pressure that I began to think there might be something at the 'Paititi' site that we had missed. On return to Britain I therefore consulted the author Tony Morrison, who with more than forty years experience of Bolivia, is a leading expert. Having listened to the description of our work at the site and noted the date on the rock, Tony explained that the Incas or those before them had used gold for decoration. They found the richest gold veins on the eastern slopes of the Andes. The Spaniards, Tony said, had seized all the obvious gold from temples and shrines and had then set out to locate the mines. The site on the Rio Tulani that we had investigated, with its waterfalls and cascades, was probably a rich deposit in a natural pot known simply as an '*olla de oro*'. 'Hans Ertl knew what he had discovered,' said Tony, 'and, being a good mountaineer, could easily have reached the pots in the cascades.' 'Whether Ertl made any money from this may never be known,' he said. 'However,' he added, 'anyone familiar with the history of Inca mining will think you were after a pot of gold, and they'll follow you everywhere. I reckon you have a problem . . . Take care.'

Perhaps, I thought, it was gold that had made Ertl try to raise funds to return to the site. Like Trippolt, he had claimed to have discovered Paititi, yet no archaeologist had accompanied him and, although he had spent eight months there, several of his workers had claimed that he found nothing. Did he really recover golden artefacts, as he claimed? If so, what happened to them? Building such a substantial house and planting crops indicated that he, or someone, intended to return. Could it have been the person he radioed at nights speaking only in German? Who had financed all this? There had to be a good reason for this skilful and intelligent man to have spent so much time, money and muscle on the project. Or was he like an earlier talented explorer, Colonel Percy Fawcett, simply obsessed with an idea?

Back in Bolivia in May 2002 I sought answers. At the offices of UNAR, Yoli and I met with the director, Javier Escalante, the administrator, Freddy Acre, and Juan Domingo Faldin. Yoli produced the *Sunday Telegraph* article, and Faldin – looking very uneasy – categorically denied having made the statements attributed to him. Javier Escalante confirmed his support for *Kota Mama* and reiterated that Faldin's report was purely technical and contained no criticism. Speaking to Yoli, Faldin confessed that Dr Vranich, who he said had worked in Bolivia and was believed to be an acquaintance of Trippolt, had called him several times, pressing him to criticize us. Faldin had simply referred him to his technical report and refused to make further comments. But if Faldin had not made the statements in the *Sunday Telegraph*, who had – and why? Later Yoli called UNAR asking for Faldin. 'He has gone on three days' leave,' she was told. Later it became 'He is away sick,' and finally 'He's disappeared.' Furthermore Vranich continued to make ill-founded attacks on the *Kota Mama* expedition in the press. It was getting even more strange.

Next we visited the hotel, to discover why it had not responded to our repeated enquiries about the theft of the expedition files from Yoli's luggage. The manager sat behind his desk, his fingers trembling nervously as he kept apologizing while giving no good reason why the hotel had failed to reply to numerous e-mails and faxes. Lamely he promised to look into it.

As we walked out on to the street, Yoli reached for her mobile phone. 'You had it in the hotel,' I said. She rushed back to the desk where we had been sitting. The phone had gone, and no one would admit to having it. 'Of course all the numbers I've been calling are recorded on it,' she said. 'Perhaps someone wants them.' Then she added, 'By the way, I forgot to tell you that when I returned to Bogotá in October my apartment was burgled. A few small things were taken, but the main item lost was my laptop containing the expedition reports. Luckily I had back-up files, but now I wonder if someone was after that information.'

More pieces of the jigsaw emerged. We heard that a number of Nazis who had fled to Bolivia had congregated at a town in the Yungas named Chulumani, where the graveyard is full of German names. Ertl's travels in the region had certainly taken him there. It also emerged that a large farm we had seen in the distance when looking eastward from 'Paititi' had been German-owned from about 1950 to 1980. After the death of Che Guevara, the ill-fated Monika Ertl's terrorist group had moved to Teoponte in the Yungas, where it was said they had been wiped out by the Bolivian Army. Monika had escaped to murder the Bolivian consul in Hamburg, and was herself killed later in La Paz. However Teoponte was believed to be Trippolt's home. Could there be a link with Hans Ertl?

In Santa Cruz we learned more of Hans Ertl's latter days. Half a century after he had made his name by documenting the Nazi leaders and their military machine, this expert photographer was living alone in the rambling hacienda he named La Dolorida. Now his only interests were his cows and wildlife. He allowed the farm to become overgrown, and it was soon a nature reserve. Ertl's wife had returned to Germany with ill health, but she regularly sent him money – and, it was said, young women to look after him. Though rarely venturing off his property, Ertl did not object to visitors. 'Did he have much money?' I asked a woman who had been there. 'He claimed that he had much jewellery in the attic, and even offered to let me take some,' she said – adding, 'However, he warned me to be careful of the snakes that he kept with it, so I declined.' Indeed Ertl was fascinated by snakes, and made a study of treating snakebite, even advocating the consumption of one's own urine as a cure.

It was a warm, humid morning when Alan Raven drove Yoli and me out to meet Heinrich Lutz, a German who had known Ertl. Lutz's 10-foot wall was topped with razor wire, and two Dobermans raced to meet us when the heavy hardwood door swung open to admit us to the garden. Heinrich Lutz preferred to speak in German, and a friend with a string of languages at her fingertips was on hand to interpret. 'I will only speak to the Colonel if he guarantees to write exactly what I say,' he had told Alan. I was happy to agree. He turned out to be a tall, upright man without a hair on his head. Wearing dark khaki shirt and trousers, he moved easily, his eyes darting about as he strode over to shake my hand. 'You are a colonel in the British Army?' I nodded. 'It is through you that we lost the war,' he laughed – or I think he did.

He answered my questions on Ertl without hesitation. 'He had fantasies,' he said when I brought up the subject of Paititi. Taking occasional pinches of snuff, Herr Lutz talked of Monika and other members of Ertl's family, of Ertl's filming, and of how he had photographed Hitler and Mussolini in Rome. He pointed out that, although loyal to the party, Ertl had eventually broken up with his business partner because he did not wish to be overly involved in political photography. Lutz was a mine of information on the Second World War. Discussing Ertl's relationship with Field Marshal Rommel, he produced first Ertl's own book on the war and then a signed copy of David Irving's biography of Rommel. More books and albums were fetched. Autographed photos of Nazi leaders, German military heroes and pictures of post-war reunions covered the pages. As Lutz was in his early sixties, I assumed his lookalike in the photos was his father.

'When did Ertl go to Tibet?' I asked. 'He was there with Heinrich Harrer. He knew the Dalai Lama as a child,' Lutz replied. Knowing that Harrer, the well-known author of *Seven Years in Tibet*, had been there from 1944 to 1951, I queried the date. 'He was there during the war,' said Herr Lutz and, sensing my surprise, added 'I do not know how he got there.' 'When did Ertl come to Bolivia?' I asked. 'First he came to Colombia and then Bolivia,' was the answer. Again I pressed for a date. 'Ertl was here during the Third Reich,' said Lutz, then added – 'at least that is the rumour.' The significance of this remark was not lost on us.

As we drove away, Yoli remarked, 'Do you think Ertl could have come by submarine?' I had no idea, but nothing in this extraordinary matter would have surprised me.

Knowing the good we were trying to do for their country and its people, our Bolivian friends were dismayed by the unwarranted criticism of our efforts. However, one influential person offered a possible explanation. 'A great deal of money is made from the sale of artefacts smuggled out of our country. The last thing those involved want is a foreign scientific expedition with government backing in their area,' he said. 'It may also be they believe you have found Nazi gold or treasure at the Paititi site, or you might find it. Perhaps Ertl hid something there – or they think he did.' Were the strange story of Hans Ertl, the appearance in a bookshop of a man with a swastika armband, the thefts of the expedition files and computerized reports, the disappearance of Yoli's phone and the attacks in the press just coincidental, or had we inadvertently stumbled into an eagle's nest? 'It gets more like *Indiana Jones and the Holy Grail* every day,' said Anne Gilby when I returned to Dorset.

The three *Kota Mama* expeditions had made many discoveries but lacked the time to investigate them fully. Thus in July 2002 the Scientific Exploration Society launched a fourth project which carried out excavations and surveys at the sites located previously. Impressive Inca fortresses near Santa Cruz were mapped and further north the ruins Mike

How's recce party had located at San Lorenzo turned out to be an extensive town, probably of Spanish construction, possibly built on top of an earlier Inca settlement. This too was surveyed, but incredibly we could find no record of its existence in Bolivia. Why it was built and why it was abandoned remains a mystery. I doubt it was Paititi, but the stone buildings, drainage systems, roads, massive tombs and a large well-built plaza, indicated a place of importance. 'Not a lost city,' said Bruce Mann who was with us again, 'perhaps a forgotten town.'

Shirley Critchley, Jim Masters and others had raised $5,000 to help equip clinics and buy books for the Mapiri School. The Children's Hospital in La Paz got $1,100 and we were able to assist our friends at Quilapituni too.

In September 2002 Eddy Loaiza's boats took us down the Rio Beni to excavate the cemetery to which the Muchanes Indians had led Bruce the previous year. Sure enough funerary urns dating from between AD 800 and 1200 were tumbling out of the eroded bank and Maria Mason, American osteo-archaeologist who had been with us earlier, found bead and shell necklaces around the neck of a female skeleton. Further down-river another burial site produced a skull of a man who had died 1,000 years before. Our dentist Paul Liddiard found that he had healthy teeth – 'No sugar cane in those days,' he commented. But the leg bones indicated a height of around six feet, far taller than the Indians of today. 'Have we found the race of giants the people talk of ?' wondered Yolima.

Two young archaeologists from La Paz came with us for a few weeks, but in spite of receiving every courtesy they wrote a scathing and unwarranted report on us. Our Bolivian Army Liaison Officer, a rugged and impressive colonel named Hugo Cornejo and our friend José Luis both of whom accompanied us, easily refuted these accusations but we wondered what had caused the youngsters to bite the hand that fed them. However we discovered they had been working with Dr Alexei Vranich, the American who had so often attacked us in the press. 'Would you like to meet him?' asked Yolima. 'You bet,' I replied and we came together in the UNAR Director's office. The Bolivians discreetly left us alone. Vranich was younger than I'd imagined. Slightly built with short brown hair and Eastern European features, he seemed ill at ease as we questioned him. 'I attacked you because you were friends of General Banzer,' he said. 'Banzer did bad things and I hated him.' 'That's ridiculous,' I protested, 'General Banzer was simply our Patron because he was President of Bolivia. This does not mean we agreed with his politics.' 'I could not speak to you openly for fear of being imprisoned, so used the press,' explained Vranich. 'Why did you not e-mail us in Britain from America?' demanded Yoli. Vranich had no answer, but went on to accuse various high officials of the previous Bolivian government of corruption. 'The international press always consult me on Bolivian archaeology,' he said, a touch of arrogance in his voice. Vranich gave a halfhearted apology and we parted. 'He has no official position here', commented an embarrassed UNAR administrator after the meeting.

Back in the mountains near Quilapituni two of our Bolivian helpers were confronted by men with sub-machine guns who ordered them out of the area. It seemed a narcotics farm was thriving on the slopes of Cerro Paititi. 'That's another reason why certain people do not want us in this area', said Yoli. 'I wonder if all these strange people and events are connected.'

If any Nazi sympathizers were at Guanay when we set out for the Amazon in June 2001, the sight of our fleet sailing away with the Union Jack flying and the school band thundering 'Rule, Britannia!' must have stuck in their craws. My dear departed pal Tristan Jones would have admonished them with a few well-chosen Anglo-Saxon expletives.

Dramatis Personae

Allen, Dr Sam, MB, ChB, MRCP, DTM&H, 35: specialist registrar in tropical medicine and infectious diseases at Royal Free Hospital and University College London; from Matlock, Derbyshire – senior medical officer, throughout

Alonso, Gregory, 24: IT technician; from Preston – assistant archaeologist, La Paz to Guanay

Barrow, David ('Bas'), 28: corporal, RE; from St Helens – engineering tasks and *KM3* crew member, La Paz to Pôrto Velho

Baugh, Billy, 33: staff sergeant, RE – *KM3* coxswain, La Paz to Pôrto Velho

Birch, Dale, 24: lance corporal, RE; from Walsall – engineering tasks and *KM3* crew member, La Paz to Pôrto Velho

Blashford-Snell, John, OBE, DSc(Hon), DEng(hc), FRSGS, 64: colonel, RE (retd); chairman, Scientific Exploration Society – expedition leader, writer and photographer, throughout

Brown, Dr Joanna, MBBS, BSc, FRCS, MRCCP, 31: GP in Bath – medical officer, La Paz to Pôrto Velho

Buitrago, José Luis: driver and interpreter – La Paz to Emanay

Campbell, Jennifer, RGN, 28: corporal, QARANC; nurse at Musgrave Park Hospital, Belfast; from Perth, Scotland – nurse, Pôrto Velho to Belém

Catari, Máximo C.: Bolivian Aymara – builder of *KM3* at Huatajata and repairer at Pôrto Velho

Catchpole, Graham, BDS, 56: dentist; from Taunton – dental surgeon and video cameraman, throughout

Cawkwell, Paul, 32: sergeant, RE – engineering tasks and *KM3* crew member, La Paz to Pôrto Velho

Churcher, Craig, 33: HSBC; from Bromley, Kent – archaeological section, La Paz to Guanay

Cipagauta, Yolima: lecturer in economics at Colombian Military

University; SES representative for Latin America – PA to expedition leader and chief liaison officer, throughout

Cocks, Craig, 24: HSBC marine-insurance broker; from Kent – *KM3* assistant quartermaster, Pôrto Velho to Itacoatiara

Corrêa de Cavalheiro, Nilto, 35: missionary with JOCUM – liaison with Madeira river communities, Pôrto Velho to Humaitá

Craig, Andrew ('Drew'), MSc, DIC, BSc(Hons), MIMM: lieutenant (TA), RE; full-time reservist and geologist; from Aberdeen – reconnaissance 2000; *KM3* crew member and navigator, throughout

Critchley, Shirley, 68: retired teacher; from Dorset – community-aid coordinator, La Paz to Pôrto Velho

Crooker, Patricio Muñoz, 26: freelance photojournalist writing for Air BP and *Escape/La Razón*; from La Paz – *KM3* crew member, Guanay to Belém

Crosby, Alasdair, 48: journalist; from Jersey – archaeological section, public-relations officer, scribe and reporter, La Paz to Guanay

Culshaw, James, 21: student at Nottingham University; from Jersey – interpreter, video cameraman and *KM3* crew member, La Paz to Santarém

D'Arenberg, Prince Leopold: Prince of the Holy Roman Empire; Belgian; from Geneva – reconnaissance 2000; reconnaissance leader, La Paz to Guanay

Dias Da Cunha, Dra Eurípedes, 62: professor of anthropology, Brasilia – anthropologist, Pôrto Velho to Itacoatiara

Dix, Elizabeth, BA, 23: from Jersey – assistant archaeologist, La Paz to Pôrto Velho

Dolman, Jon, 30: corporal, RE; from Devon – engineering tasks, La Paz to Guanay

Domingo Faldin, Juan, 50: Bolivian archaeologist – La Paz to Guanay

Drax, Richard: BBC TV presenter; from Blandford – Guanay to Rurrenabaque

Durey, Ernest, MBE, 71: lieutenant-colonel, RE (retd) – quartermaster, throughout

Foley, Hon Alexandra, 41: public-relations consultant; secretary of Explorers Club (British chapter); from London – sponsorship officer, Pôrto Velho

Friedman, Karen, 33: postwoman; from Hereford – animal transport team, La Paz to Guanay

Galvão, Roberto, 35: education officer; from Pôrto Velho – community liaison, Pôrto Velho to Humaitá

Gargan, Ray, 28: corporal, RE; from Southampton – engineering tasks and *KM3* crew member, La Paz to Pôrto Velho

Dramatis Personae

Gledhill, Katie, BSc, BVetMed, MRCVS: captain, RAVC; from Warwickshire – veterinary surgeon, La Paz to Guanay

Gorski, John, 22: lance corporal, RE, topographic surveyor; from Whitchurch, Shropshire – surveyor, La Paz to Guanay

Halford, Craig, BSc, 33: warrant officer, RE; military clerk of works, Gibraltar; from Wales – engineering section leader, La Paz to Guanay

Hamilton, Vanessa: lance corporal, RAVC; army dog handler, Northern Ireland – animal transport team, La Paz to Guanay

Hay, Eric, 32: lance corporal, RE; from North Shields – engineering tasks and Avon safety boat, La Paz to Pôrto Velho.

Henry, Steven, 27: mail-room worker; from Nottingham – assistant archaeologist and assistant quartermaster, La Paz to Pôrto Velho

Holmes, William, J., BA, MA, JD, LLM, FRGS, 47: environmental lawyer/academic (visiting fellow at Centre for Socio-Legal Studies, Wolfson College, Oxford); major, USAF (retd); from Oklahoma – information officer and assistant quartermaster, throughout

Holt, Andrew, BSc, DipM, 41: captain, RE (retd) – photographer, La Paz to Rurrenabaque and Pôrto Velho to Humaitá

Hortop, Paul: warrant officer, Intelligence Corps; from Shrewsbury – camp commandant, Waricunca; naturalist and video cameraman, La Paz to Guanay

Hoskins, Geoffrey, FCA, 71: retired accountant; from Micheldever, Hampshire – field treasurer, throughout

How, Michael, 31: captain, RE (retd); from Bracknell, Berkshire – reconnaissance team, La Paz to Pôrto Velho

Igoe, Barry, 31: architectural technician; from Westmeath, central Ireland – engineering tasks and *KM3* crew member, throughout

Jauregui, Teddy: from La Paz – Bolivian liaison officer, La Paz to Guanay

John, Dr Tania, BM, DTM&H, 31: GP in Bath – medical officer, reconnaissance 2000

Kannangara, Peter, 39: civil engineer and e-business integrator for Affno; Sri Lankan; from Crawley, Sussex – IT and communications, throughout

Leavold, Nathan, 22: lance corporal, RE; from Isle of Wight – engineering tasks and *KM3* crew member, La Paz to Pôrto Velho

Loaiza, Eddy: boat owner from Guanay – Guanay to Esperanza

Lulham, Michael, 45: HSBC manager; from Helensburgh – assistant archaeologist, La Paz to Guanay

Lydiatt, Graham, BA, MA, 26: senior travel consultant, Airline Network Plc; from Preston – assistant logistics officer, La Paz to Guanay

Mann, Bruce, MA, FSA (Scot.), 24: Aberdeenshire Council Archaeology

Service; from Aberdeen – senior archaeologist and Avon safety boat, throughout

Mason, Brittain, 16: veterinary-science student; from the USA – reconnaissance 2000

Mason, Maria, 49: osteologist, from the USA – reconnaissance 2000

Masters, Gerald, 65: specialist restorer of old churches; company chairman; from Ilchester, Somerset – reconnaissance 2000; Avon safety boat, La Paz to Pôrto Velho

Masters, Jim, MBE, 73: captain, RE (retd); experienced white-water expert, from Kingsdon, Somerset – reconnaissance 2000; fleet commander, throughout

Mendes, Marcelo, 30: captain, Brazilian Navy; from Belém – liaison officer in Brazil, Pôrto Velho to Belém

Nevin, Jon Paul, 19: lance corporal, RE; from Edinburgh – engineering tasks and *KM3* crew member, Pôrto Velho to Belém

Niemi, Eric, BA, MA, 55: teacher at Woodland Hills Schools, Pittsburgh, Pennsylvania; from Pittsburgh – reconnaissance 2000; biologist and Avon safety boat, Pôrto Velho to Belém

Overton, Paul, 55: PT instructor, RN (retd); freelance tour manager; from Bere Regis, Dorset – adjutant, throughout

Parker, Kaye, 23: HSBC; from Leeds – animal transport team, La Paz to Guanay

Pereira, Marcia Leila de Castro, 25: student at University of Brasilia; from Brasilia – assistant anthropologist, Pôrto Velho to Itacoatiara

Phillips, Dr Michelle, BSc, MBBS, FRCA, 32: anaesthetist; from Stockport – medical officer, Guanay to Belém

Pickup, Matthew, 27: lance corporal, RE; from Torquay – engineering tasks and *KM3* crew member, La Paz to Pôrto Velho

Player, Andrew ('Andi'), BSc, 48: teacher at outdoor-education and field study centre in Bournemouth; house converter and motorcycle enthusiast; from Poole, Dorset – assistant quartermaster at Quilapituni; handyman, La Paz to Pôrto Velho

Plaza, Ruden: Bolivian archaeologist – La Paz to Guanay

Prado, Dr Marco Antonio; from Ministry of Health, La Paz – briefly medical officer from Guanay

Ralph, Caroline, BA, LIM, 41: barrister; from Bristol – assistant historian and ornithologist, Pôrto Velho to Belém

Raven, Alan: British businessman living in Bolivia – SES representative, Santa Cruz

Reid, Karle, 28: sapper, RE; from Preston – surveyor, La Paz to Guanay

Reinaldo de Lima, Geraldo, 42: teacher of English in public school in

Manaus and Presbyterian pastor; from Manaus – Brazilian liaison with local people, Pôrto Velho to Belém

Rivera Sundt, Oswaldo, 55: Bolivian archaeologist - expedition archaeological director

Smith, Clive, TD, BSc(Hons), DMS, CEng, MIEE, 38: major, TA; chartered engineer; from Bristol – reconnaissance 2000

Smith, Darren ('Smudge'), 27: corporal, RE; from Aldershot – engineering tasks and *KM3* crew member, La Paz to Pôrto Velho

Smith, Michael, 27: IT and communications officer, La Paz to Guanay

Snailham, Richard, MA, FRGS, 72: tour-group leader, writer and lecturer; from Windsor – writer, Pôrto Velho to Belém

Timms, Stephen, OBE, MSc, MBA, CEng, 50: captain, RN; naval attaché, British Embassy, Brasilia; nuclear submariner; from Bristol – *KM3* crew member, Parintins to Santarém

Torres-Martinez, Francisca: from Guanay – cook, Guanay to Esperanza

Troy, Pat, 69: major, RM (retd); yachtsman; from Jersey – *KM3* skipper, Pôrto Velho to Belém

Turner, Carla, 20: HSBC bank clerk; from Bristol – animal transport team, La Paz to Guanay

Verity-Dick, Marigold, 57: musicologist; from Sherborne, Dorset – sponsorship public relations and expedition harpist, Pôrto Velho to Belém

Wilkinson, Matt, MEng, 28: captain, RE – *KM3* skipper, Guanay to Pôrto Velho

Winkler, Wilma: Bolivian archaeologist; from Santa Cruz

Wood, Ivan, 55: captain, Canadian Air Force; engineer with Rolls-Royce; from Ontario – Avon safety boat, La Paz to Pôrto Velho

Patrons and Supporters

Few great expeditions would even set out without the support of many people, companies and organizations who have the imagination, foresight and generosity to help them. This was especially true for *Kota Mama*. The list that follows shows those who so kindly gave advice, funds and services to make the venture possible. In most cases they did so because of their genuine interest in fostering Anglo-Latin American relations, the spirit of the adventure and the quest for knowledge. The expedition is very grateful to all who helped, for without their backing this enterprise could not have succeeded.

PATRON
The late General Hugo Banzer Suárez, President of Bolivia

HONORARY PRESIDENTS
HE Roger Bone CMG, HM Ambassador to the Republic of Brazil
HE Señor Jaime Quiroga Mattos, Ambassador of the Republic of Bolivia
HE Graham Minter, HM Ambassador to the Republic of Bolivia
Prince Leopold d'Arenberg
Viscount Montgomery of Alamein CMG, OBE
Ing. Julio Sangines Goytia
Alm. Jorge Zabala Ossio
Prefecto German Velasco Cortés
Prefecto Mayor Luis Oscar Zunino
Senador Ruben Poma Rojas
Philip A. McLean CMG
Richard Knight
Dr. Carlos Aguirre
Dr. Jaime Ponce García
Arql. Oswaldo Rivera Sundt

Sr. Lita Kushner López
Ricardo Paz-Soldan
Mrs Elodie C. Sandford

Support was generously provided by

IN THE UNITED KINGDOM

Vijith Kannangara, Affno (Pvt) Ltd; Andrew Ainsworth, Ainsworth; Patrick Cannon and Tim Worrall, Air BP; Anna Nicholas, ANA Communications Ltd; Chris Beale, Ashton Waverley; Robeiro de Silva, Association of Coffee Producing Countries; Alan Morgan, Avon Inflatables Ltd; J. Rinfret, Balcan Engineering Ltd; Gillian Dew, Barts Spices Ltd; Peter Johnson, Blue Chip Data Systems Ltd; Marta Bosacoma and Hernando Velasco, Bolivian Embassy; Hugh Beveridge and Gerry Murphy, BS&B International; David Cunnington, Burton McCall; Morvin Huchinson and Philip McLean CMG, Canning House; David R. Allen, DHL International (UK) Ltd; Karen Griffiths, Diamond Wild Water; Brig. Sebastian Roberts OBE and Lt-Col. Barney Rolfe-Smith, Directorate of Corporate Communication (Army); Robert D. Glen, E. P. Barrus Ltd; Michael Hodgkinson, Freight Agencies Ltd; Gerry Masters, G. Masters & Sons Builders; Paula Foster, Gayne Prospero Ltd; JoAnn W. Hauber, General Ecology Europe Ltd; Margaret Bailey, GlaxoSmithKline; Alan Rind, Hadcliffe Properties Ltd; Neil Coles, Henkel Consumer Adhesives; David Brettell, Henshaw Inflatables Ltd; Alastair Deakin, Hewden Stuart Plc; Michael Lulham, HSBC; Martin McEachran, HSBC Equipment Finance (UK) Ltd; Barry Moss, Dominic Ind and Charles Ledsam, HSBC Insurance Brokers Ltd; Bob Hughes, Isola Werke UK Ltd; Stuart Radlett, J. J. Vickers & Sons Ltd; Richard Knight, J. P. Knight (Paranam) Ltd; Caroline Knox, John Murray (Publishers) Ltd; Mike Rawlings, London Communications plc; Tina Williamson, Motorola Ltd; Shaun Hopkins, Natural Science.Com Ltd; Roger French and Julie Williamson, NERA Satellite Services Ltd; Colin Smith, *Daily Mail*; Elaine Swift, Nikon UK Ltd; Nicholas J. Granger, Norton & Sons Ltd; Andy Whiting, Peak UK Kayaking Company Ltd; Simon Trewin, PFD; T. Hardman, Seven Seas Ltd; Bob Brownsdon, Shakespeare Company (UK) Ltd; Tony Wale, Silva Ltd; John Dubouchet, Simon I. Patino Foundation; Alan Daly, Southern Gailes Ltd; Ken Stahly, Stahly Quality Foods; Richard Whittaker, Suzuki GB plc; John Grindlay, The Eydon Kettle Company Ltd; Suzie Woodward, Tods of Orkney Ltd; Tom Wilson, Tractel UK Ltd; Beryl Bellamy, Varta Batteries Ltd; Philip Church; Caroline Harding; Emma Harris-Curtis; Vaughan Hunter; Vince Martinelli; Tony Morrison; Jaime Ortiz-Patino; Ross Salmon; Elodie Sandford; Anne Savage.

In Bolivia

Alcaldía, Guayaramerín; Alcaldía, Esperanza; Juan C. and Ana Maria Arana, Channel 7 TV; Capn. Armando Ayala Cerruto, commandant of Navy, Guayaramerín; Dra. Hortensia de Bravo, Guayaramerín; Roberto Buitrago, IMBEX Rent Car; Teresa Chavez, tourism office at alcaldía of La Paz; Customs Office, Guayaramerín; Cnl. Angel Conde García, Geographical Military Institute; Dr. Antonio Eguino, Vice-Minister of Culture; Fuerza Naval Boliviana, La Paz; Cnl. Gustavo Gandarillas, Bolivian Army; Arq. Gloria García de Terrazas, Unity of Patrimony; Carlos García Vespa, head of immigration, Guayaramerín; Dr. Juan del Granado Cossio, mayor of La Paz; Hotel Sucre Palace, La Paz; Hotel Italia, Santa Cruz; Genl. Juan Hurtado Rosales, commandant of Bolivian Army; Eduardo (Teddy) Jauregui, interpreter and liaison; Phillip Kittelson, mayor of Caranavi; Hernando Martinez, ENTEL Mobil; Mrs Peter Minter; Ing. Darius Morgan, Crillon Tours; Ricardo Paz-Soldan, DHL; Min. Marcelo Perez Monasterios, Ministry of Presidency; Capn. Carlos A. Raposo de Vasconcellos, Brazilian naval attaché; Alan Raven; Keyner Roca de Roca, tourism office at Guayaramerín; Manglio Roca Melgar, Consul from Bolivia in Brazil; Lic. Luis Saravia, mayor of Guanay; Lic. Alejandro Serrate, General Manager Air BP Bolivia; Arq. Antonio Simoni. C., Hotel Itauba Resort; Arq. German Velasco Cortés, Prefect of La Paz; Jorge Velarde and Ramiro Ostria, Prefectura of Department of La Paz; Tente. José Velasquez, commandant of the Blue Devils; Maria. T. Vidangos, administrator of customs at airport; Arql. Wilma Winkler, UNAR; Dr. Said Zeitum López, University of Bolivian Amazonas, Riberalta.

In Brazil

Steven Alexander, Amazon Tours; Michel Aubreton, Ecotourism Company; Vincent Brown, Honorary British Consul, Manaus; Emerson Castro, executive director, Aquarius Hotel, Pôrto Velho; César Doerner, Rodonave Navegãoes; Capitão Miguel J. C. Maltez, head of Gabinete Militar, Rondônia; Christopher Mayhew, Emam-Belém; Pastor José Joao de Moreira Mesquita, Presbyterian Church of Manaus; Braulia Ribeiro, Jovem con um Misião; Juan Carlos Rocabado, Quick Shipper, Transportes Internacionais; Glauce Roque, DHL Belém; HE Acy Marcos dos Santos, HM Honorary Consul, Belém; Flavio and Gil Serique, Cultura Inglesa; Capitão Jaerte da Silva Bazy, head of Belém Portos; Alan S. Skyrme, HSBC Belém; Capt. Stephen Timms, UK naval attaché in Brasilia.

In Colombia

Dra. Monika Harttman, Consul from Republic of Bolivia

Message from the Prefect of La Paz,
Arq. German Velasco Cortés,
an honorary president of the Kota Mama *expedition*

Greetings!

It was a real opportunity for the Prefectura of the Department of La Paz, to have participated in the *Kota Mama* project since it has shown immediate positive results, such as the identification of the enormous, potential resources of the region of Larecaja Tropical, the tourist potential of that zone, the great capacity of its people to manage the natural environment, and the urgent necessity to create a greater fluvial link of the Rio Beni toward the Atlantic coast, which will give Bolivia a great chance to establish a sound import/export business.

We want to stress the importance that this exploration represents for the Bolivian Prefecture, not only for the integration of the Bolivian-Amazonian territories with the Atlantic Ocean, but also because through the scientific character of Project *Kota Mama* we can reveal cultural and historic secrets hidden for centuries in the Tropical Region of the Department of La Paz, regarding their pre-Columbian culture. It will create new tourist possibilities and will promote the economic, social and cultural development to local, departmental, national and international levels.

I am grateful to Colonel John Blashford-Snell, chairman of the Scientific Exploration Society, who as the leader of the group, and together with other individuals greatly specialized in different fields, gave valuable support to our towns regarding medical and dental assistance, as well as engineering works to avoid any risks to the territories along the fluvial path and, most of all, connecting Bolivia to the rest of the world by means of the NERA satellite communications.

Project *Kota Mama* has been a proud achievement with traditional *totora* boats constructed by Bolivian native-Indians from the shores of Lake Titicaca. I want to take this opportunity to wish you success in the phases 4 and 5 of this project during 2002 and 2003.

Sincerely,

Arq. German Velasco Cortés
Prefect of Department of La Paz

Bibliography

Amélio de Oliveira, Ovídio, *Assim e Rondonia* (Rondônia: Dinamica Editora e Distribuidora, 2000)

Anstee, Margaret Joan, *Gate of the Sun: A Prospect of Bolivia* (London: Longman, 1970)

Bates, Henry Walter, *The Naturalist on the River Amazons* (London: John Murray, 1863)

Bradbury, Alex, *Backcountry Brazil* (Chalfont St Peter: Bradt, 1990)

Brugger, Karl, *The Chronicle of Akakor* (New York: Delacorte Press, 1977)

Chapman, Simon, *The Monster of the Madidi* (London: Aurum Press, 2001)

Childress, David H., *Lost Cities and Ancient Mysteries of South America* (Stelle, Ill.: Adventures Unlimited Press, 1986)

Church, Colonel G. E., *The Route to Bolivia by the Amazon* (London: Waterlow & Sons, 1877)

Collier, Richard, *The River that God Forgot* (London: Collins, 1968)

Davis, Wade, *One River: Explorations and Discoveries in the Amazon Rain Forest* (London: Simon & Schuster, 1997)

Denevan, William, *The Aboriginal Cultural Geography of the Llanos de Mojos of Bolivia* (Berkeley: University of California Press, 1966)

Deyermenjian, Gregory, 'Glimmers of Paititi: Searching for a Lost Incan Refuge', *Mercator's World*, vol. 4, no. 1 (January/February 1999), available online at htttp://www.mercatormag.com/article.php3?=54 (accessed 10 May 2002)

Ertl, Hans, *Paititi: Ein Spähtrupp in die Vergangenheit der Inkas* (Munich: Nymphenburger Verlagshandlung, 1963)

Fawcett, Lieutenant-Colonel P. H., *Exploration Fawcett* (London: Hutchinson, 1953)

Fifer, J. Valerie, *Bolivia: Land, Location and Politics since 1825* (Cambridge: Cambridge University Press, 1972)

Fleming, Peter, *Brazilian Adventure* (London: Jonathan Cape, 1933)

Bibliography

Furneaux, Robin, *The Amazon* (London: Hamish Hamilton, 1969)

Gauld, Charles A., *The Last Titan: Percival Farquhar 1864–1953: American Entrepreneur in Latin America* (Stanford, Cal.: Institute of Hispanic American and Luso-Brazilian Studies, Stanford University, 1964)

Gheerbrant, Alain, *The Amazon: Past, Present and Future* (London: Thames and Hudson, 1988)

Grieve, Peter, *The Wilderness Voyage* (London: Jonathan Cape, 1952)

Hecht, Susanna, and Cockburn, Alexander, *The Fate of the Forest: Developers, Destroyers and Defenders of the Amazon* (London: Penguin, 1990; New York: Harper Perennial, 1990)

Hemming, John, *The Conquest of the Incas* (London: Macmillan, 1970)

——, *Red Gold: The Conquest of the Brazilian Indians* (London: Macmillan, 1978)

——, *Amazon Frontier: The Defeat of the Brazilian Indians* (London: Macmillan, 1987)

Heyerdahl, Thor, *The Ra Expeditions* (London: Allen & Unwin, 1971)

Hoyos, Ladisles de, *Klaus Barbie: The Untold Story* (London: W. H. Allen, 1985)

Jekyll, Grace B., *Two Boys in the South American Jungles, or Railroading on the Madeira–Mamoré* (New York: Dutton, 1929)

Jones, Tristan, *The Incredible Voyage* (Mission, Kan.: Sheed, Andrews & McNeel, 1977)

Kandell, Jonathan, *Passage through El Dorado* (London: Allison & Busby, 1984)

Knapp, Sandra, *Footsteps in the Forest: Alfred Russel Wallace in the Amazon* (London: Natural History Museum, 1999)

Kravigny, Frank W., *The Jungle Route* (New York: Orlin Tremaine Co., 1940)

Kricher, John, C., *A Neotropical Companion* (Princeton: Princeton University Press, 1989)

Machicao Gámez, César Augusto, *Historia de los Pueblos del Norte Paceño* (La Paz, 2000)

Mann, Charles C., 'Earthmovers of the Amazon', *Science*, 4 February 2000

Murphy, Alan, *Bolivia Handbook* (London: Footprint, 2000)

Polentini Wester, Juan Carlos, *El Paí Titi* (Lima: Asociación Librería Editorial Salesiana, 1999)

Pontes Pinto, Emanuel, *Caiari: Lendas, Proto-Historia e Historia* (Rio de Janeiro: Companhia Brasileira de Artes Gráficas, 1986)

Robinson, Alex, and Robinson, Gardênia, *The Amazon* (London: Cadogan Guides, 2001)

Rodrigues Ferreira, Manoel, *A Ferrovia do Diabo: História de Uma Estrada de Ferro na Amazônia* (São Paulo: Melhoramentos: Secretaria de Estado da Cultura, 1981)

Bibliography

Roosevelt, Theodore, *Through the Brazilian Wilderness* (New York: C. Scribner's Sons, 1925)

Salmon, Ross, *My Quest for El Dorado* (London: Hodder & Stoughton, 1979)

Santilli, Marcos, *Madeira–Mamoré* (São Paulo: Memória Discos e Edições/Mundo Cultural Editora, 1988)

Shah, Tahir, *Trail of Feathers: In Search of the Birdmen of Peru* (London: Weidenfeld & Nicolson, 2001)

Snow, Sebastian, *Half a Dozen of the Other* (London: Hodder & Stoughton, 1972)

Spielman, Andrew, and d'Antonio, Michael, *Mosquito: A Natural History of Our Most Persistent and Deadly Foe* (London: Faber & Faber, 2001)

Sterling, Tom, *The Amazon* (New York: Time-Life International, 1973)

Thomson, Hugh, *The White Rock* (London: Weidenfeld & Nicolson, 2001)

Tomlinson, H. M., *The Sea and the Jungle* (London: Duckworth, 1912)

Ure, Sir John, *Trespassers on the Amazon* (London: Constable, 1986)

Velarde Gutierrez, Mario S., *Tipuani: Kori Jahuira* (La Paz, 1989)

Westerman, James S., *The Meaning of Machu Picchu* (Chicago: Westridge Publishing Inc., 1998)

Whiting, Charles, *The Hunt for Martin Bormann: The Truth* (London: Pen & Sword, 1996)

Wilford, John Noble, '[Anna Roosevelt:] Sharp and to the Point in Amazonia', *The New York Times*, C1 23 April 1996

Zeitum López, Dr Said, *Amazonia Boliviana: Primera Parte* (La Paz: Producciones Gráficas Vision, 1991)

Index

230

Index

Index

Index

GlaxoSmithKline, 38
Gledhill, Capt. Katie, 43–5, 50, 69, 74
Goering, Hermann, 12
gold, 51–2, 63, 74, 212
Gondwanaland, 155, 166
Goodyear, Charles, 127
Gorete, 141, 170
Gorski, John, 60, 65, 161
Goths, 204
Gough, Viscount Shane, 208
Grieve, Peter, 137, 151
Guajara-Mirím, 19, 98, 101, 103, 105, 112, 114, 120, 128, 134–5, 152
Guanay, 19–20, 26–8, 32–3, 36–8, 40, 51–5, 73, 75–6, 78–80, 98, 123, 139, 162, 205, 212
Guaporé, river, 156
Guaraní, 8
Guarulhos, 197
Guayaramerín, 19, 97, 99–101, 103, 105, 107, 115, 118–20, 136
Guevara, Che, 14, 214
Guevara, Fr. José, 10
Guinea, Gulf of, 166
Gurupá, 184, 186
Guyana, 9

Haile Selassie, Emperor, 1
Halford, Craig, 41–2, 45–6, 50, 53, 56–7, 61, 63–4, 67–8
Hamilton, Vanessa, 43–4
Harrer, Heinrich, 215
Hay, Eric, 105, 107, 112
Hemming, John, 74
Henry, Steve, 56, 85, 105
Henry, Will, 209
Herndon, Lieut. Richard, 128
Heyerdahl, Dr Thor, 3, 15
Hevea brasiliensis, 127, 134
Himmler, Heinrich, 12, 204
Hitler, Adolf, 11–12, 204–5, 214
Holmes, Bill, xi, 31–3, 36, 77, 79, 84–5, 139, 151, 169–70, 177, 185, 188, 192, 194, 196, 199, 201
Holt, Andrew, 123–5
Hortop, Paul, 44–6, 48–9, 61, 64, 66
Hoskins, Geoffrey, 54, 81, 87, 152, 161, 168, 183, 191–2
hotels: Aquarius, 137; Berlin, 88; Colonial, 92, 122–3; JFK Airport Holiday Inn, 199–200; JFK Inn, 201; Panamericano, 20, 36; Sucre Palace, 5, 6, 34–5; Thalita, 119, 134, 136; Tropical, 170–1; Vila Rica, 137
How, Mike, 38, 48–50, 59, 62, 65, 67, 69, 90–2, 105, 121, 215
HSBC, 32, 43, 57, 101, 153, 193, 196
Huatajata, 2, 16, 55, 117

Huayna Capac, 8
Humaitá, 138, 140, 151, 206–7
Hurtado Rosales, Gen. Juan, 55, 77, 85, 184

Igapó, 182, 186, 193
Igoe, Barry, 50, 56–7, 113, 144, 166–7, 179, 192, 200
Ildefonso, Treaty of, 156, 163
Imperial College, London, 165
Inca, 5–10, 25, 27, 39, 43, 58, 60–1, 64, 67–8, 74–5, 77, 92, 121, 212
Incapampa, 21–3, 25–7, 38–9, 42, 47, 64, 68–70
Incallajta, 8
Incaracay, 8
India, river, 44
India Office, London, 134
Instituto Geografica Militar, 7
Inter-American Development Bank, 20
Internet, 32, 124, 151, 157, 164, 203, 207
Iquitos, 128, 159
Irving, David, 215
'Israel', 125
Israel, muleteer, 65
Itacoatiara, 132, 140, 152, 157–9, 183
Ita Tupa Oka, 174

Jacaré *see* Caymans
jaguar, 45, 69, 133
Jauregui, Teddy, 35, 55
Jersey, 42, 45, 79, 145, 194
Jersey Evening Post, 42, 45, 54, 79, 211–12
Jesuits, 156, 169, 171
JFK Airport Holiday Inn, 199–200
João, 119
João IV, 155
Jochi, 27, 47, 95
JOCUM, 137–8
John F. Kennedy Airport, New York, 197–200
John, Dr Tania, 19, 25, 27
Jones, Tristan, 168, 217
Jorge, 170
José da Silva, Dr Jeronimo, 101
Juárez, Benito, 129
Julio, 90–1
Juruti, 150, 164
Just a Drop, 35

Kaka, river, 28, 78, 83, 85
Kakasaka, 55
Kannangara, Peter, xi, 36, 52, 79, 87, 93, 139, 159, 194–5
Kannangara, Dr Vijith, 32, 36
Keller, Josef and Franz, 129
Kenya, 148
Kew Gardens, 133–4
Kittelson, Philip, 80–1

233

Index

Index

235

Index

The *Kota Mama* expedition was backed by the Scientific Exploration Society. The Society organizes challenging and worthwhile expeditions in remote regions of the world for people of all ages. For further details of these two- to three-week projects, or if you are interested in joining us, please contact:

Expedition Manager
Scientific Exploration Society
Expedition Base
Motcombe
Shaftesbury
Dorset
UK
SP7 9PB

Tel: 01747 854898
Fax: 01747 851351
Base@ses-explore.org
www.ses-explore.org

Illustrated lectures by expedition members may be arranged via the Expedition Manager.